SCHOOL DESEGREGATION

Cross-Cultural Perspectives

SCHOOL DESEGREGATION

Cross-Cultural Perspectives

Edited by

YEHUDA AMIR
Bar-Ilan University

SHLOMO SHARAN
Tel-Aviv University

with the collaboration of
RACHEL BEN-ARI
Bar-Ilan University

LEA LAWRENCE ERLBAUM ASSOCIATES, PUBLISHERS
1984   Hillsdale, New Jersey   London

Lawrence Erlbaum Associates, Inc., Publishers
365 Broadway
Hillsdale, New Jersey 07642

Library of Congress Cataloging in Publication Data
Main entry under title:

School desegregation.

Includes bibliographies and indexes.
1. School integration—Israel. 2. School integration
—Research—Israel. 3. School integration—United
States. 4. Israel—Ethnic relations. I. Amir, Yehuda
II. Sharan, Shlomo   III. Ben-Ari, Rachel.
LC214.3.I7S36 1984   370.19′342   84-10184
ISBN 0-89859-335-2

Printed in the United States of America
10 9 8 7 6 5 4 3 2 1

Contents

Preface

In 1968 the Israel Knesset (Parliament) set into motion a process of school desegregation and ethnic integration of the Jewish population who had come to Israel from countries throughout Europe, Africa, the Americas, and the Middle East. Implementation of the desegregation policy was accompanied by extensive research in Israel by social scientists and educators. In 1978, 10 years after the initiation of the desegregation program, prompted by the accumulation of this data bank on the effects of desegregation, an interuniversity and multidisciplinary seminar was organized whose participants represented most of the institutions of higher learning in Israel and the Ministry of Education and Culture. All the Israeli contributors to this volume were members of this seminar. A grant from the Ford Foundation made it possible to maintain this seminar, which met once every 3 weeks for over 2 years.

The seminar's primary aims were to examine and summarize the theoretical and empirical knowledge available in Israel relevant to ethnic desegregation and integration in the schools, to orient educational policy makers in terms of research results and theoretical topics, and to consider and compare ideas and data generated in Israel with information available in other countries, primarily in the United States. The material presented in this volume reflects the many topics discussed in the seminar, but the chapters were prepared especially for this book after the conclusion of the seminar.

This volume deals exclusively with the desegregation of schools attended by Jewish children in Israel from various ethnic backgrounds. Arab children attend Arab schools. By and large, they do not attend schools with Jewish children. This arrangement reflects the voluntary choice of the two communities. It does not stem from any practice of, or legally sanctioned, segregation. Thus, there is no need or wish for desegregation involving Arab and Jewish children.

The chapters of this book are ordered so that the topics discussed begin with the widest macrosocial level (nation and community) and move on to the various components of the microsocial level (school, staff, classroom, and pupil). Each chapter, too, contains at least three primary components: A review of the re-search literature in general, a review of the research done in Israel, and a comparison of the Israel with U.S. research, with particular emphasis on the conclusions that can be drawn from this work. The editors were particularly gratified that Professors Norman Miller of the University of Southern California and Harold Gerard of UCLA agreed to participate in this volume, thereby enlarg-ing the scope and depth of the cross-cultural comparison of research on school desegregation.

On behalf of all the authors who participated in this volume, we wish to express our appreciation to the Ford Foundation for its assistance since 1978, not only for the conduct of the inter-University seminar, but also for additional help needed to ensure the publication of this volume. Special thanks go to Mr. Edward Meade, Jr., of the Ford Foundation in New York, for his personal attention and help in making this project a reality.

Yehuda Amir
Shlomo Sharan
Rachel Ben-Ari
Editors

ACKNOWLEDGMENT

Publication of this book was supported by the Ford Foundation, New York, and by the Schnitzer Foundation for Research on the Israeli Economy and Society, Bar-Ilan University, Israel.

Introduction

Inadequate educational preparation in school is a decided economic disadvantage in both Israel and the United States as elsewhere. In both countries there is a high correlation between the person's socioeconomic status and the adequacy of his or her educational background. Without good training in the lower grades and in high school, opportunity to go on to higher education is closed off. In our increasingly technified world, access to high level jobs virtually requires preparation at the university level.

Both in Israel and the U.S. membership in certain identifiable subgroups seems to handicap the person in obtaining the requisite educational credentials. Whereas in the United States each of these identifiable subgroups is a relatively small fraction of the population, in Israel the disadvantaged group, Jews with a Middle Eastern or North African background, is slightly larger than the educationally advantaged group, those Jews with a Western background whose roots are in Europe. In his chapter, Adler reveals some startling statistics regarding the educational and job opportunity handicap suffered by non-Western Jews. The data present a striking parallel with the situation in the United States.

Official concern with the problem in the United States antedates such concern in Israel by more than ten years, but it was not until the mid to late sixties that programs to implement educational reforms aimed at reducing group-related educational deficits got underway in both countries. In the U.S. more than ten years had elapsed between the momentous 1954 *Brown* decision and the first intervention attempts. Israelis were aware of their problem even before they achieved statehood but did nothing about it since they were otherwise occupied with a succession of three wars with their Arab neighbors. They also believed that the army served the purposes of desegregation, which it did, but only in part.

It was not until after the Six-Day War in 1967 that official government policy was promulgated to deal with group-related educational handicaps.

In both countries integration, that is, one-nationhood, is a matter of national policy although, in contrast to Israel, statements to that effect rarely occur in the desegregation rhetoric heard in the United States. One is reminded here of the stark portrait of racial separation in the U.S. painted by James Baldwin in *Another Country*. A clear difference between Israel and the U.S. is that Israeli public opinion is overwhelmingly in support of reducing the educational gap— their survival as a nation may ultimately depend on it—whereas in the U.S., a strong pro-segregationist bias still persists. In this regard it is a paradox that in the U.S. a thoroughgoing attempt at desegregation, which is currently losing some of its force, was undertaken in grades K through 12 virtually nationwide, whereas in Israel, with the exception of isolated instances, efforts at desegregation have been limited to the junior high level (grades 7 through 9) only. For one reason or another, the authorities in Israel decided against mandatory bussing. As in the U.S., there is marked residential segregation in Israel and the norm at the elementary level is in clear support of neighborhood schools. There is also the special problem of the religious schools which is discussed at some length in the chapters by Schwartzwald and by Halper, Shokeid, and Weingrad. Another feature of the Israeli situation that distinguishes it from the problem in the U.S. is the apparent lack of discrimination against the disadvantaged group by the essentially middle-class Jews of European origin. In the U.S. the explanation for the disadvantaged position of minorities is laid at the doorstep of anti-racial or anti-ethnic discrimination. That is not to say that such is not the case in the U.S., but the difference between the two contexts as regards discrimination, does argue for the probability of multiple causes. Still another feature that is strikingly different between the two situations is that in the U.S. there are clear differences in physiognomy, in the case of blacks, between the advantaged and disadvantaged groups whereas in Israel no such marked distinguishing features exist. Finally, in Israel the majority of all the citizens immigrated to Israel during the past 60 years. In the U.S., on the other hand, settlement by Europeans antedated the arrival of blacks who were brought in as slave labor.

As we can see, the two situations are vastly different yet the educational gap between the two groups is uncannily the same and in both cases appears to be as refractory to attempts to reduce it. In this book some of the best social science minds in Israel are brought to bear on the problem and throughout the chapters attention is paid to the American problem with its differences and similarities. In the chapter by Eshel and Klein some of the same possible explanations are broached to explain the achievement gap in Israel as have tantilized American desegregation workers. Pinpointing the causes of deficits is an elusive problem that may be mediated by low self-esteem as Bizman and Amir suggest in their chapter on the "contact hypothesis", a chapter which is in itself an important contribution to the contact literature.

This volume provides a detailed, multi-perspective look at the deficit problem in a context different in so many respects from the American one. In so doing, it, along with the American work, gives us a higher vantage point from which we can view the issue. Each chapter is self-contained. Most of the authors were members of the Israel Inter-University Seminar on Ethnic Integration which worked over a two year period to help anticipate and identify problems that might arise from the implementation of school desegregation. Each chapter either looks at a different slice of the problem or takes a different theoretical slant. There is also an excellent chapter by Sharan and Rich on experimental interventions which should be of special interest to Americans who are working along similar lines. This book is the first to examine desegregation from the level of governmental policy-making through the various layers of community and school involvement down to events occurring in the classroom itself. Reading it is a must for anyone interested in inter-ethnic achievement differentials and intervention strategies for reducing them.

Harold B. Gerard
UCLA

List of Contributors

Chaim Adler, Associate Professor, Sociology of Education, School of Education, The Hebrew University of Jerusalem

Benyamin Amir, Chairman, Committee for Secondary Education, Ministry of Education and Culture, Jerusalem

Yehuda Amir, Professor, Social Psychology, Department of Psychology, Bar-Ilan University, Ramat-Gan

Rachel Ben-Ari, Assistant Professor, Social Psychology, Department of Psychology, Bar-Ilan University, Ramat-Gan

Aharon Bizman, Assistant Professor, Social Psychology, Department of Psychology, Bar-Ilan University, Ramat-Gan

Nachum Blass, Department of Research, Ministry of Education and Culture, Jerusalem

Yohanan Eshel, Associate Professor, Psychology, Department of Psychology, Haifa University

Harold B. Gerard, Professor, Social Psychology, Department of Psychology, University of California, Los Angeles

Jeff Halper, Associate Professor, Anthropology, Department of Sociology, Haifa University

Dan Inbar, Associate Professor, Sociology of Education, School of Education, The Hebrew University of Jerusalem

Zev Klein, Associate Professor, Psychology, Department of Psychology, The Hebrew University of Jerusalem

Norman Miller, Professor, Social Psychology, Department of Psychology, University of Southern California, University Park, Los Angeles

Nura Resh, Lecturer, Sociology of Education, School of Education, The Hebrew University of Jerusalem

Yisrael Rich, Associate Professor, Educational Psychology, School of Education, Bar-Ilan University, Ramat-Gan

Joseph Schwarzwald, Associate Professor, Social Psychology, Department of Psychology, Bar-Ilan University, Ramat-Gan

Shlomo Sharan, Associate Professor, Educational Psychology, School of Education, Tel-Aviv University

Moshe Shokeid, Professor, Anthropology, Department of Sociology, Tel-Aviv University

Alex Weingrod, Professor, Anthropology, Department of Behavioral Sciences, Ben-Gurion University, Beersheba

SCHOOL DESEGREGATION

Cross-Cultural Perspectives

1 Why Integration?

Yehuda Amir
Shlomo Sharan
Rachel Ben-Ari

The integration of races or ethnic groups in a given society is, first and foremost, an ideological and political question that each society must decide upon for itself. The decision to desegregate the society and tear down legal and social barriers to integration will be made by elected officials at the government level. However, apart from the moral-political issue of segregation or integration of minority groups, there is the important question of whether desegregation in the schools indeed produces the social effects that its planners claim for it. It is legitimate to ask whether we may anticipate that school desegregation will in fact bring about changes of various kinds—social, psychological, educational—and if so, under what conditions and by what means.

Ethnic integration in schools is generally acknowledged to be a difficult task. If its fruits are negligible or even entirely wanting, then it might be argued that society is ill-advised to pursue this difficult road that, in a democratic society, may be politically appropriate but educationally unproductive. The problem we have formulated in the title of this chapter deals with this portion of ethnic integration; namely, its possible effects on the lives of those involved. We leave aside, in this context at least, the ideological aspects of the problem.

In approaching the question of the effectiveness of desegregation, particularly ethnic desegregation in schools, it is also necessary to ask if, theoretically, similar effects can be achieved *without* it: Is desegregation a sine qua non for achieving certain social and educational goals, or can the same effects be achieved through other means? Thus, for example, it might be claimed that segregated classrooms can yield educational products that are equal or superior to desegregated classrooms, given the appropriate investment in resources, such as teacher training, curricular development, and differentiation in teaching tech-

1

niques. If so, then the goal of improved academic achievement for minority-group children might possibly be achieved more easily without the problems involved in desegregation. Indeed, the question of whether given educational results and goals can be achieved with or without ethnic desegregation in the schools is one of the central problems dealt with in the following pages.

In this chapter, we focus upon the effects of ethnic desegregation in the schools on four broad domains and/or variables that are acknowledged to be of considerable importance in the assessment of the psychosocial outcomes of education. These domains are: nation building or social integration of the body politic as a whole; equal educational opportunity; academic achievement; ethnic attitudes and relationships. Can the goals of these psychoeducational domains best be achieved through ethnic desegregation in the schools, or does society have more effective means for achieving them? Our response to this question considers a variety of theoretical approaches relevant to ethnic desegregation and contact in educational systems.

Israel's experience in the field of ethnic relations differs from that in the United States in several respects. Firstly, the nation's Jewish population is almost equally divided between persons of Western (European, American and South African) origin, the so-called "majority" group, and those whose families came to Israel from the Moslem countries of the Middle East, who constitute the "minority" group. Yet despite their diverse origins, all groups avow their national–ethnic–religious identity with the Jewish people who share a common history. Also, unlike the United States, the ethnic groups in Israel are not easily distinguishable by physical characteristics such as skin color. Therefore, research findings from Israel may shed a different light on various aspects of ethnic integration in the schools than the picture emerging from the literature in the United States. The particular features of social-ethnic conditions in Israel are discussed later in this study.

The following two sections in this chapter discuss several topics that, on the basis of our experience in Israel and in light of the existing literature, we considered relevant to the macro and to the microsocial level. By *macro* we mean the level of the nation and the community, whereas the term *micro* refers to the level of the school, classroom, and pupils. Our discussion of the effects of desegregation at the macrolevel focuses on nation building and on the problem of equal educational opportunity for all subgroups in the society, in the sense of enjoying equal access to public resources. Following this discussion we treat two topics relevant to the microsocial level, namely, academic achievement and ethnic attitudes and relationships in the desegregated classroom. Finally, we consider several potentially negative implications of desegregation that require attention so that their effects can be minimized or prevented.

In the literature originating in the United States, the distinction between the macro and microlevel effects of school desegregation is not prominent, indeed it is hardly mentioned at all. In Israel, however, this distinction appears to be of considerable importance. The implications of this distinction are not merely in identifying the level of analysis or of conceptualizing social and psychological processes. Rather, the macro/micro distinction can actually help assess outcomes of ethnic desegregation in the schools and its social significance for determining national educational policy. National policy in Israel can consider all aspects of desegregation outcomes and not depend exclusively on results emerging at the classroom or school level alone, even though there is frequently no apparent consistency between the results of desegregation on the macro and microsocial levels. Thus, desegregation may contribute to increased tension between members of different ethnic groups due to undesirable short-term consequences of desegregation at the classroom level. It is possible that if the country can achieve macrosocial goals of increased solidarity through the mechanism of ethnic school desegregation, the microlevel outcomes that may be less desirable will continue to occupy us until more acceptable solutions, at the microlevel, are developed, implemented, and evaluated.

SECTION I   MACROSOCIAL VARIABLES

Nation Building: Social Consolidation as a National Factor

The social science literature to date does not emphasize the role of ethnic integration in the schools as an instrument for consolidating the body politic and, hence, for contributing to national solidarity and social cohesiveness. Few writers have identified the nation-building role of integrated schooling. Perhaps the subject of nation building is absent in the research literature of the United States, because this issue is less relevant to ethnic integration in the American school. Yet, for Israel and for other countries with similar demographic or social structure, integration may play precisely this role.

Israel is both a young and a small country. Yet, its Jewish inhabitants come from a large number of ethnic national backgrounds, each with different customs and habits. We are presently living in a period that is seeing the reintegration of Jews from the many countries of their dispersion into a single nation. The scattered groups of the Jewish people who have come to Israel do, however, all identify themselves as members of the Jewish people, so that there is a basic sense of identification with the land and the People of Israel, which accounts for this "ingathering of the exiles," as it is known in traditional Jewish literature. This fundamental historical, national, and religious identification with a common past and future strivings for self-determination are important factors without which the State of Israel would not be conceivable. Ethnic integration, therefore, is a national extension of the desire of all the Jewish subgroups for reconstituting the political unity of the Jewish people and thereby expresses a *positive* social striving that is generally accepted as a national norm in Israel. In other words, there is broad acceptance of the goal of ethnic integration, at least on the level of public proclamations, and no institution or group opposes this policy in principle.

Moreover, policy makers in the realm of social life and education feel a certain urgency about fostering integration precisely because it is currently desired by the various lower status ethnic subgroups as a means of integration into the mainstream of social life in Israel, after having been a minority (often silent, and sometimes persecuted) group in some predominantly Moslem country. This sense of unity of the Jewish people is the basis for Israel's social substructure. However, it could dissipate in the years to come if future generations, removed from their forefathers' historical-religious identification with the strivings of the Jewish people for independence and self-determination, grow up in a society that discriminates against them and does not acknowledge their equality of status in Israeli society. From this point of view, the *lack* of integration could serve as the background for the emergence of disruptive forces in Israeli society.

The integrity of Israel's social life also requires ethnic integration from the point of view of the extraordinary diversity of its small population (Peres, 1976). Because there are so many different groups, each with its own cultural history and patterns, will they accept each other and develop a common way of life, at least to the point where society will not be torn by parochial interests and alienation from the overriding goals of the nation? It appears that the melting pot social philosophy has important relevance for Israel, if it is to engender sufficient integration to create a basis for public support of its national goals.

It may be argued that ethnic desegregation of social institutions is not necessarily the only way to accomplish national integrity. Some countries, Switzerland, for example, have followed a policy of "separate but equal" regarding the relationship among its three constituent ethnic groups. But this approach does not appear to be viable in Israel. Firstly, Israel's many ethnic groups do not enjoy equality in society, so that at present the conditions are not "equal but separate" (Peres, 1976). Moreover, as noted previously, ethnic integration is widely accepted, at least publicly, as a national norm and goal, which, despite group differences rooted in their history of exile in different countries, is an essential part of the common tradition of the Jewish people. Ethnic integration in the national school system serves as a tangible example, and therefore an efficient way of achieving the national goal, of creating a Jewish society that grants all subgroups equal access to public resources.

The potential threat to Israel's social integrity, stemming from a lack of school desegregation, became apparent in several instances of neighborhood demonstrations organized by members of the Middle Eastern ethnic groups. School segregation is clearly viewed by the lower status group as an act of discrimination, a block to equal access to public resources (Pettigrew, 1964). To this extent school desegregation is proof that Israeli society is investing effort in realizing the goal of national unification. For this reason, even though there may be alternative ways to promote the social reconstruction of the Jewish people in Israel (or ways in which any multiethnic society can enhance unity), they do not seem to provide a substitute for ethnic integration in the schools.

This is true at least for those societies where the various ethnic groups wish to be integrated into the mainstream of the national society. They are not likely to feel satisfied by programs to distribute more funds or other material resources to ethnically segregated schools, because they judge segregation itself as a restriction on their goal to be integrated into the national culture. There are classical examples of minority ethnic groups resisting integration into the majority group and wishing to maintain their separateness and identity, such as the Chinese in the United States or in other Western countries. However, when the conditions of segregation are perceived as discriminatory toward any group in a manner unacceptable to it, integration in the schools may be a necessary step for maintaining and promoting social cohesiveness within the society.

One may ask, why choose the schools? What is unique about that institution that it is selected to bear the brunt of this difficult task when the goals are on a national scale, and when other major institutions in the economic and public sector may be equally equipped to carry out such policies? There are, of course, many answers, some of which have already been discussed here. It should be said at once that social integration on a national level will be promoted more effectively if other institutions, in addition to the school, such as the army (which is very central in Israel) or work settings, will also carry out a policy of integration. However, schools are the only public institution that encompasses the entire population of the nation's children, and where the law empowers the government to dictate matters of policy, such as that of ethnic desegregation. Moreover, ethnic integration in schools promises to have a more long-term effect than in other social institutions, because schools influence the youngest members of society. The relevance of the school as the preferred setting for desegregation is evident, too, when considering the fact that children born in Israel to parents from different countries and cultures are more similar to each other and less socially distant from their peers of other ethnic subgroups than are their respective parents (Peres, 1976). The partial closing of the cultural gap among Israeli-born members of the different ethnic subgroups is a facilitating factor that schools can build upon in planning programs for promoting social integration.

Experiencing cross-ethnic relations at an early age and in the school setting may be a critical element in a child's social development, preparing him to live in a multiethnic society and to maintain social attitudes and behavior relatively free of prejudice toward members of other subgroups (Crain & Mahard, 1978; Inbar & Adler, 1977). There are data showing that, under suitable conditions, early exposure to members of other groups reduces the likelihood that children will grow up with negative attitudes toward other groups (St. John, 1975). The dynamics of this development may not be too clear yet. It may be due to greater acceptance of the other group. Or it may be due to the "psychology of inev-itability," which affirms that people simply learn to accept situations if they have no reasonable alternative (Aronson, 1972). Can we expect youth to integrate easily with peers from other ethnic groups at age 18 when they enter the army (in Israel), if they have never mixed with each other before? There is, at least, the hope that a common school experience, assuming that it is carried out under the proper conditions (to be discussed later), can serve to enhance the possibility of improving social solidarity as the children move into adult life.

In sum, the view developed here attributes a dual role to ethnic integration in Israel's schools. The social-integrative dimension is concerned with increasing the cohesiveness of Israel's multiethnic Jewish population. There is also a pre-ventive dimension to integration directed at precluding frustration and a sense of deprivation among members of the lower status groups, which stems from their feeling of being denied equal access to public resources in education. These feelings can lead to the eruption of social discord and unrest. Both factors are crucial considerations in shaping the policy of ethnic integration in Israeli society at large, as well as in the schools.

Equal Educational Opportunity

The previous section led to the conclusion that social integration can contribute to the cohesiveness of a multiethnic society by demonstrating society's interest in providing all groups equal access to resources *and* in accepting all groups on an equal basis in public institutions. Here one must again raise the question of whether there might not be alternative ways of providing equal educational opportunity for all sectors of the population without necessarily placing them physically under the same institutional roof. Would it not be possible, for exam-ple, to equalize the quality of educational "inputs" in ethnically segregated schools, thereby satisfying the desire for equal access to resources or for "quali-ty" education? This approach stems from the "separate but equal" principle.

Theoretically, the "separate but equal" approach might be possible, but evidence shows that in practice it is not likely to be carried out successfully (Minkovitz, Davis, & Bashi, 1977; Orfield, 1978; Razel, 1978). The claim that "education for the poor is poor education" is based upon empirical findings from several studies in the United States and elsewhere. In Israel, for example, an extensive evaluation study of the nation's elementary school system revealed that even a policy of preferential investment in schools for the disadvantaged did no better than to maintain the prevailing gap in educational inputs between schools in lower and middle-class neighborhoods (Minkovitz et al., 1977; Razael, 1978). It seems that schools for the middle class can utilize resources more effectively, thus maintaining the lack of equality in the *delivery* of services despite the formal preference for lower class schools in the *allocation* of re-sources. One reason might be that effective use of resources by middle-class schools may be possible, because better trained personnel are available in middle-class areas than in lower class areas. In some cases, specially trained personnel may not be available at all in lower class schools, such as those in outlying districts. Consequently, in relation to middle-class schools, resources allocated to schools for the disadvantaged cannot be delivered effectively.

The lack of congruence between allocation and utilization of resources highlights once again the need to distinguish between the macro and the micro-level of desegregation processes. Clearly, the utilization of resources *within* the school does not follow automatically from government allocation of funds. Since desegregation occurs primarily in schools located in middle-class communities, and since the latter seem to be more effective then segregated schools in lower-class communities in utilizing allocated resources, it follows that desegregation is a realistically effective alternative to segregation for achieving greater equality of educational opportunity on behalf of minority groups in society. A mechanism has not yet been found to ensure the delivery of quality services in lower class schools even when resources are allocated on the administrative level. Unless such a mechanism is found, lower class and minority groups might interpret the delivery of second-rate services as a manifestation of discrimination that only desegregation can rectify. We conjecture that such mechanisms, administrative or social, are not likely to function in the foreseeable future.

SECTION II MICROSOCIAL VARIABLES

Academic Achievement

Pursuing our argument about equal educational opportunity, the desegregated school should provide a higher level of educational services and stimulation to its lower class pupils than does the segregated school. Consequently, one may expect some positive effect of these improved resources, both material and human, on the achievement level of minority-group pupils in contrast with those in segregated schools (Arzi & Amir, 1977; Crain & Mahard, 1978; Stephan, 1978). This topic is treated in detail in Chapter 7.

The potential influence of peers, raised expectations for investing energy in academic learning, and higher teacher expectations for academic performance can also exert considerable influence on the academic achievement of minority-group children in desegregated classrooms.

The middle-class pupils from the majority group clearly occupy a higher level of social and academic status in the desegregated class (Cohen, 1972; Cohen & Sharan, 1980). This differential in status can provide a positive influence on lower class pupils by serving as a reference group or model in the field of academic achievement, so that the minority group children might be more attracted to learning and motivated toward academic pursuits. Lower class students may strive to raise their status in the classroom through improved academic achievement, in order to be more like their higher status classmates who were not present in their segregated classrooms. Thus, norms for achievement and factors of social-climate characteristic of desegregated classrooms could serve to improve the academic level of some of the lower class children[1] (Gerard, Jackson, & Conolley, 1975; Katz, 1968; Klein & Eshel, 1977; Pettigrew, 1969; St. John, 1975).

Motivation to learn can be improved not only by means of models, but also by the attribution of increased significance to academic learning. Expectancy theory of motivation asserts that motivation to learn is a function of the extent to which we anticipate success in the task, and the extent to which we value that success. The value attributed to academic achievement by lower class students might be enhanced in the desegregated setting, where the peer culture sustains norms more closely identified with achievement (Biener & Gerard, 1978; Epps, 1978; Gottlieb & Tenhouten, 1965; Katz, 1967). In the lower class segregated setting, the peer culture may not support academic achievement norms, even if the teacher conveys high expectations for success and achievement.

The effects of teacher expectations on pupil behavior and achievement, particularly with lower class pupils, have been the subject of much interest in recent years (Brophy & Good, 1974; Insel & Jacobson, 1975; Johnson, Gerard, & Miller, 1975; Katz, 1967; Wilson, 1963). Teachers are more likely to express expectations for higher level achievement in desegregated classrooms in middle-class schools than they are in segregated classrooms in lower class schools. We hypothesize that the presence of middle-class majority-group pupils in the desegregated class influences teachers to raise their level of teaching and their expectations for academic performance. These expectations apply to both middle-class and lower class pupils in the class. This would be true because it is probably quite rare to find teachers who adjust their teaching efforts to the lowest common denominator of ability in the classroom. Rather, teachers are more likely to aim their materials and requirements at some mean level of ability in the class or even at the higher level students. If this is true, then teacher expectations and instructional behavior in the desegregated classroom should also contribute to improving the academic level of the minority-group students.

On the other hand, one could argue that if teachers adjust their level of teaching and expectations to a mean level of ability in the classroom, middle-class pupils may lose out because the overall level of instruction will be lower than in middle-class segregated classrooms. Furthermore, expectancy theory can also support the prediction that under some conditions desegregated classes could lower the achievement of minority-group pupils, because it lowers their expecta-

---

[1]There does not seem to be any basis for the criticism sometimes leveled against desegregation that it results in lowered achievement for the middle-class pupils. This claim is not supported by data available from many studies.

tions for success on academic tasks, and increases their frustration, even while enhancing the importance they attach to succeeding on these tasks (Katz, 1967). Improved academic achievement can be anticipated only when both components—the importance of success and the assessment of chances of success—are perceived positively. Lowered anticipation of success is probably more acute when there is a large achievement gap between members of the two ethnic groups in the classroom (Amir, Sharan, Bizman, Rivner, & Ben–Ari, 1978; Rich, Amir, & Ben–Ari, 1981; Schofield, 1980).

Potentially negative effects of desegregation can also be related to teachers' behavior and attitudes (Biener & Gerard, 1978; Rist, 1970; Rosenthal & Jacobson, 1968; Wellisch, Marcus, MacQueen, & Duck, 1976). Teachers may perceive minority-group pupils as less able than their middle-class or majority-group peers and fall into the trap of making comparisons between pupils based on this perception, thereby decreasing the low-status child's motivation to learn and reinforcing his self-perception as relatively incompetent. Thus, teachers can express to their students two distinct sets of expectations for achievement, each set directed at members of a different ethnic group in the class. These expectations are transmitted to the pupils in various ways, ranging from the most overt to the covert and subtle. Again, this "double standard" of academic expectations may emerge more readily in classes with a relatively large achievement gap between the two ethnic groups.

Ethnic Attitudes and Relationships

One of the prominent goals of ethnic integration in the schools is to foster positive social-emotional attitudes among children from different groups and a willingness to maintain relationships with children from different social settings. The most direct and apparently one of the potentially effective means for coping with the problem of ethnic attitudes and relationships involves the use of direct contact between members of the different groups in any walk of life, including schools. Making the acquaintance of people from other ethnic groups is an important factor, albeit not the only one, in beginning the process of reducing prejudice and stereotyped views of the other group (Allport, 1954; Amir, 1976; Aronson, 1972; Cook, 1963; Festinger & Kelley, 1951; McConahay, 1978; St. John, 1975). See Chapter 8 for a discussion of desegregation and attitudes.

Direct contact between members of different groups provides an opportunity for different social-psychological processes to occur. People previously thought of as different in behavior or beliefs can, upon direct contact, be seen to be more similar to one's own group. Greater similarity in behavior and beliefs is generally associated with less prejudice (Byrne, 1965; Rokeach, 1968). Changes in one group's perception of the other can occur in other fields as well. Members of the higher status group could see that people from the lower status group are less incompetent, less morally objectionable, or less unfriendly than they had previously thought. Contact between members of different ethnic groups can also affect emotional relationships. People of lower social status might find themselves less frustrated and disappointed after contact with higher status people and might see that the latter accept them more readily than they had thought prior to the meeting. Such breaking down of expectations and stereotypes can influence the attitudes and behavior of members of both groups who are partners to a multiethnic encounter. Such changes are possible only under conditions of direct contact between different groups.

Again, it has been demonstrated that although direct contact between different ethnic groups may be a necessary condition for achieving positive changes in ethnic attitudes, it is not sufficient in itself (Amir, 1969; McConahay, 1978). Indeed, ethnic contact *alone,* without control over various conditions of this contact, might have no effect whatsoever on ethnic attitudes, or, even worse, it might produce some negative attitudes than those that previously prevailed (Amir, 1976; Gerard, Jackson, & Conolley, 1975; Kramer, 1950; Schwartz, 1975; Winder, 1952). Clearly, certain aspects of the contact must be planned and controlled to ensure positive effects.

One of the basic factors in planning interethnic settings is that mixed-ethnic classrooms should allow equal status to all participants (Kramer, 1950). If, for example, school authorities and teachers would treat all pupils equally, create conditions for interethnic cooperation, and design the educational experiences of the pupils in order to provide all children with academic and social status in the classroom rather than having the classroom emphasize differences in achievement and friendship patterns, such conditions would promote positive interethnic relationships and attitudes (Becker, 1952; Cohen & Roper, 1972; Cohen & Sharan, 1980; Gerard, et al., 1975; Sharan, 1980; St. John & Lewis, 1973). These conditions would also embody the principles of equal educational opportunity, and pupils would feel free of discrimination. Consequently, minority-group pupils may experience some enhancement of their ethnic and personal self-esteem, as well as their attitudes toward themselves and toward children from other ethnic groups in the class. Under these conditions, the higher status children are also more likely to accept children from the minority group and to alter their view of the latter's incompetence. The result would therefore be a more favorable perception of lower status peers than was previously held (Amir & Garti, 1977; Shaw, 1973). Such positive changes in interethnic relations are likely to occur under conditions of equal status, because they emphasize equal competence, similarity in ability and social norms, and they enhance attraction and friendship between children in the class regardless of ethnic background. Desegregation under the right conditions presents the opportunity for ethnic integration.

On the other hand, there are other aspects of status relations in the classroom that are frequently cultivated in schools, even those with a policy of ethnic integration, and that emphasize the inequality of the pupils' status in and out of the classroom—namely, processes of social comparison based on academic achievement or competition for grades, attention, and social standing. These processes can counteract the positive effects of equality of school policy and teacher behavior toward pupils (Aronson, Stephan, Sikes, Blaney, & Snapp, 1978; Katz, 1955; Sharan, 1980; Sherif & Sherif, 1953; Singer, 1964; Slavin, 1977).

There are also additional reasons why well-controlled contact between children from different ethnic groups in school can have positive effects on interethnic relations. Schools constitute a social setting that legitimizes and sanctions ethnic contact and as such are representative of the official social norms (Clark, 1953; Pettigrew, 1961). Moreover, the child engages in ethnic relationships under the authority of relevant adult figures. Exposure to this kind of social setting can teach children social patterns, even if the consequences and implications of such patterns are not spelled out explicitly but are nonetheless implemented in daily experience. If educational institutions are to realize the full benefits of ethnic integration in schools on the level of personal relationships among ethnically mixed pupils, thereby bringing about a sense of fuller acceptance of minority-group children into the mainstream of society, they will need to plan optimal conditions in which ethnic contact at the classroom level will yield positive results in terms of attitudes and relationships.

It should be pointed out that change in attitude or ethnic relations can occur in different social, cognitive, affective, and behavioral dimensions. Thus, ethnic stereotypes may not change following ethnic contact in integrated schools, even though pupils participate freely in ethnically mixed activities. Relationships between pupils on the behavioral level can change with or without a concomitant change on the affective–evaluative level (Aronson, 1972; Katz, 1976; Schofield & Sager, 1977). Furthermore, there are attitudes related to the contact situation itself (i.e., to what extent a person is willing to be a party to a mixed-ethnic group and to accept the fact of working together with someone from a different group). Desegregated classrooms may make an important contribution to ethnic integration by cultivating children's willingness to develop positive attitudes toward being placed together with others from different backgrounds, whatever the nature of their ethnic stereotypes. In Israel, whatever public opposition to desegregation has appeared in the community was mostly prior to implementation, rarely after desegregation had taken place. Once children were studying together, they and their parents appeared to accept the integration.

Findings from research studies in this field are not uniformly positive. To the best of our knowledge, the classrooms where attitudinal data were gathered generally failed to plan for the social conditions prevailing when pupils of different ethnic backgrounds came into contact with each other. Under such conditions it is not surprising that positive findings could not be detected.

Thus far, we have discussed only the effects of ethnic contact in desegregated classrooms on interethnic attitudes and relationships. What are the alternative methods of influencing ethnic orientation positively, other than meeting with members of the other group? One might point, for example, to methods of treatment aimed primarily at individuals, such as psychotherapy or counseling, but, obviously, individual treatment does not have wide social impact, in addition to which empirical results thus far indicate that individual treatment is not very effective in the field of ethnic prejudice.

There are also socially oriented approaches other than desegregation for changing ethnic attitudes, such as the dissemination of information about various groups in society by various means, notably channels of mass communication and the educational system (i.e., teaching children about the culture of other groups while children from those groups are not present in the classroom). These methods, too, have not been shown to be particularly effective (Ashmore, 1970; Lazarsfeld, 1940). The mere transmission of information, either through the mass media or in schools, brings about only limited improvement of perception of other groups and may have some effect on the attitudinal level, when combined with other techniques in an overall program for promoting positive ethnic attitudes and relationships (Harding, Proshansky, Kutner, & Chein, 1969).

In summary, it seems clear that desegregation in schools, carried out in a planned manner calculated to create positive conditions for ethnic contact (such as cooperative relationships that give every child an opportunity to participate in the classroom academic and social process), can yield positive results. However, in the absence of planned ethnic contact, desegregated settings may produce no change or even yield negative results in terms of attitudes and relationships.

SECTION III   SOME POTENTIALLY UNDESIRABLE CONSEQUENCES

A social change as complex as desegregation and encompassing such large numbers of people cannot possibly be implemented without raising many problems and risking undesirable consequences. As many as possible of these potentially negative outcomes should be anticipated and prevented, or, at least, minimized. Some negative effects may have relatively straightforward solutions, whereas others require sophisticated analysis and carefully conceived programs for their solution. Our purpose here is to point out some of the potential pitfalls that can undermine the value of ethnic desegregation in schools.

The Self-Concept

The effects of desegregation on children's self-concept can be divided into two sets of variables: those related to the macrosocial level and those resulting from events taking place at the microsocial level, primarily the classroom. At the macrosocial level one may anticipate that desegregation might be perceived by the minority-group children as enhancing their self-concept, because their group is thus officially accepted into institutions or social settings from which they had been previously excluded. Removal of this rejection at the official level should enhance their self-concept.

On the microsocial level (the classroom) we view potential changes in the minority-group children's self-concept as a function of at least two other crucial variables, namely, academic achievement and social relations among members of both ethnic groups (Coleman, Campbell, Hobson, McPartland, Mood, Weinfeld, & York, 1966; Hunt & Hunt, 1977; Hughes & Works, 1974; Stephan, 1978). If schools will take steps necessary to guarantee minority-children's progress and status both academically and socially, desegregation may have positive effects on their self-concept. However, most reports about desegregated classroom life indicate that schools have yet to take effective steps in this direction, both in the instructional and organizational aspects of schools with mixed-ethnic populations. Consequently, it is not surprising that some studies have reported a negative effect on the self-concept of minority-group children studying in desegregated classrooms, reasons for which have been discussed earlier.

To date, we are unaware of any theoretical argument suggesting that the self-concept of majority-group children would change positively or negatively as a function of studying in desegregated classrooms.

Loss of Cultural and Ethnic Integrity

The danger of assimilation into the majority-group's culture and consequent loss of cultural and historical integrity confronts many minority groups and is a problem that extends far beyond the domain of ethnic desegregation in schools. Nevertheless, schools cannot avoid attending to this problem that has many ramifications, some of which can be potentially harmful to the pupils' future adjustment, as well as to the interests of the minority group as a whole (Friere, 1970). One of the negative byproducts of desegregation in the realm of cultural identity may be the creation of a cultural vacuum among minority-group youth who lose their ties to their cultural or religious roots but are not adequately rooted in the majority culture or may even feel antagonistic toward this culture. This loss of identity and historical roots can lead to social alienation, marginality, and other forms of social malaise, as well as individual confusion and aimlessness. Lately, some societies and school systems have become aware of the need for a more pluralistic approach to education and to the teaching of cultural subject matter where mutual respect, rather than an assimilationist policy, serves as the guiding principle of ethnic integration (Chesler, Crowfoot, & Bryant, 1978; Forehand & Ragosta, 1976; Townsend & Brittan, 1973; Wellisch, 1977). Nevertheless, this issue will probably continue to occupy educators and policy makers for some time to come.

Erosion of Good Will and of Resources

Successful coping with the problems posed by desegregation on the classroom and school level requires the goodwill and active cooperation of many groups of adults in addition to that of the pupils themselves. If *desegregation* fails to lead to *integration,* and/or if the social and educational problems posed by desegregation are not treated adequately, each one of the groups involved can become disillusioned with desegregation and withdraw its cooperation.

Support for desegregation by parents and parent organizations can be eroded if children appear to receive unsatisfactory education or fail to become socially integrated into the mixed-ethnic population of the school. This is probably true for both lower and higher status parents (Israel Ministry of Education and Culture, 1979). If the former group feels that its children are not getting the attention and help they need and are not making progress or that their lower status in the classroom undermines their motivation to learn, they can lose their faith in desegregation as a means for integration. As a result they may oppose the desegregation of schools in middle-class neighborhoods and may even go so far as to leave the public school system entirely and enroll their children in private schools. If majority-group parents feel that their children are losing out, being "held back," or being exposed to "bad influences" in the wake of desegregation, they, too, may oppose this policy.

Opposition to, or even overt rebellion against, desegregation can stem from teachers as well as from parents. Confronted by ethnically, and, hence, academically heterogeneous classrooms, teachers may find themselves inadequately trained in instructional skills and lacking in curricular preparation to meet the wide range of abilities, interests, and needs of the pupils. Heterogeneous classrooms appear to require more varied instructional competencies than teachers may have at their disposal after years of teaching more homogeneous classes. Teachers will need to invest time and effort in acquiring new skills and changing old habits, as well as working with a broader range of learning tasks, in order to cope with the new demands made upon them in the classroom and to meet parents' expectations.

Desegregation also places administrative and financial burdens on the school system and on the community as a whole, particularly for providing the resources needed to implement the programs necessary for the success of desegregation. We have already mentioned the need for inservice teacher training, for changes in classroom teaching processes (which imply far more than just offering courses in new skills to teachers), and for the development of differentiated curricula. Busing for some of the pupils may also be necessary, and this is a very costly undertaking. Moreover, the school system may find it advisable to engage in an extensive public-relations effort in order to enlist support for and cooperation with the desegregation program on the part of the public. All these added expenditures can arouse public resistance and opposition to desegregation.

Finally, erosion of goodwill and willingness to persist in the desegregated setting may affect the pupils themselves if interethnic contact is accompanied by an escalation of tension, aggression, or violence, or even if the lower status pupils feel jealous and envious of their middle-class peers, due to a sense of economic inferiority and deprivation. The loss of status that the lower class pupil may experience can be attributed to a variety of sources: academic, social, and economic. A combination of these factors can cause the pupil to wish to withdraw from the desegregated classroom.

SUMMARY

We have argued in this study that a multiethnic society will be more successful in consolidating its population and in implementing a policy of equal educational opportunity on the macrolevel if it proceeds with the ethnic desegregation of its schools, than if it were not to do so. In the case of Israel, some may even wish to formulate this conclusion more forcefully by stating that school desegregation is a necessary precondition for building this nation's social solidarity. It appears that the ethnic desegregation of schools is a social imperative for Israel, where all the Jewish ethnic groups see themselves as an integral part of the Jewish nation and people, and where social policy and norms proclaim equal educational opportunity for all ethnic subgroups. Such a small nation, still in the earliest stages of assimilating a population comprised overwhelmingly of immigrants from all corners of the globe, can hardly sustain the atomizing effects of unequal distribution of its public resources in education. Thus, school desegregation appears to be one of Israel's central mechanisms for achieving macrosocial goals, as it would be for any society seeking to consolidate an ethnically diverse population.

Close examination of the impact that desegregation should have, in theory, on several microsocial and psychological variables leads to a less-unequivocal conclusion than that derived from considerations of goals and policies on the macrosocial level. Direct ethnic contact in the schools seems to be prerequisite for affecting ethnic attitudes and relationships positively, whereas alternative methods for influencing ethnic attitudes, such as public presentation of information about minority groups, or teaching children about the history and mores of different groups, have not proven to be socially effective. In the realm of academic achievement, it may be possible hypothetically to offer high-quality education in schools attended exclusively by minority-group children. Yet, in reality, desegregated schools have more chance of actually enjoying the benefits of superior or increased resources than lower class or minority-group schools. This is true despite the allocation of superior resources to schools for minority-group children, but, apparently, the delivery of services is not a direct function of their allocation.

We wish to emphasize that the psychological benefits mentioned here are *potential* contributions to desegregation. In order to realize this potential, society must make a social and political commitment as well as an appropriate invest-ment, often of substantial size and scope, in the programs and resources neces-sary to bring about ethnic *integration*. Without integration, desegregation can arouse considerable discouragement and frustration. Investment in well-con-ceived programs for fostering integration is the "price" that society must pay in order to reap the benefits of desegregation. It could even be claimed that unless this price is paid, and paid in time to implement the necessary changes in ethnic desegregation in schools, harsher ethnic reality may emerge from ethnic contact in schools than that prevailing in a segregated school system.

There appear to be additional "prices" to pay for ethnic desegregation, particularly in terms of children's psychological adjustment. In the traditional classrooms prevalent today, ethnic desegregation could entail some loss of self-esteem for minority-group children. There may also be a decline in the minority-group children's identification with their cultural and historical identity, a factor that also can have important psychological consequences yet to be explored. Desegregation may also be a causal factor in social maladjustment and loss of a sense of well-being if steps are not taken to insure that lower status children can be given supportive help to function well and succeed in school. Only proper planning and programming, including teacher training, can counteract the social forces that may bring about potentially negative outcomes in desegregated classrooms.

Thus far, we have depicted the success of ethnic integration on the macroso-cial level as less problematic and easier to achieve than that on the microsocial level—namely, at the level of ethnic contact in the classroom. This, however, does not imply that we agree that conditions will remain this way indefinitely. If the expected changes and progress in ethnic relations stemming from desegrega-tion are not forthcoming at the level of daily contact within a reasonable period of time and the process of integration is not seen to be making progress, in the long run (just what time-span constitutes "the long run" is not known) one may expect growing disaffection of the minority group with ethnic desegregation as a potential solution to the problem of inequality. Equal educational opportunity must be *experienced* by the lower status group at the school level in order for it to be perceived as operating at the level of national policy.

Reviewing the arguments we have presented in this chapter, we can state that ethnic desegregation of the schools can produce positive effects on the macroso-cial level even in the absence of special programming for treating the psychologi-cal and pedagogical problems arising from the creation of ethnically hetero-geneous classrooms, and from the meeting of high- and low-status groups in social and academic settings in the school. However, these benefits are likely to be forthcoming only in the short term. Failure to counterbalance negative out-comes of social and academic inequality in the desegregated school can undermine early gains and threaten to generate, in both the majority and minority groups, undesirable reactions whose exact nature cannot yet be foreseen. The view presented here is that desegregation provides the opportunity to realize important social, educational, and psychological goals that segregation cannot or is unlikely to achieve. Realization of this potential depends on the implementation of programs at the school and classroom level that will insure the creation of conditions needed to promote ethnic integration. If the societies that decide to desegregate their schools will make the political and social commitment, and will allocate the financial and professional resources needed, the theoretical perspective presented here seems to point toward positive outcomes.

REFERENCES

Allport, G. W. *The nature of prejudice.* Cambridge, Mass.: Addison–Wesley, 1954.

Amir, Y. Contact hypothesis in ethnic relations. *Psychological Bulletin, 1969, 71,* 319–342.

Amir, Y. The role of intergroup contact in change of prejudice and ethnic relations. In P. Katz (Ed.), *Towards the elimination of racism.* New York: Pergamon Press, 1976.

Amir, Y., & Garti, C. Situational and personal influence on attitude change following ethnic contact. *International Journal of Intergroup Relations,* 1977, *1*(2), 58–75.

Amir, Y., Sharan, S., Bizman, A., Ribner, M., & Ben–Ari, R. Attitude change in desegregated Israel high schools. *Journal of Educational Psychology,* 1978, *70,* 63–70.

Aronson, E. *The social animal.* San Francisco: W. H. Freeman, 1972.

Aronson, E., Stephan, C., Sikes, J., Blaney, N., & Snapp, M. *The jigsaw classroom.* Beverly Hills, Calif.: Sage, 1978.

Arzi, Y., & Amir, Y. Intellectual and academic achievements and adjustment of underprivileged children in homogeneous and heterogeneous classrooms. *Child Development,* 1977, *48,* 726–729.

Ashmore, R. D. The problem of intergroup prejudice. In B. E. Collins, *Social psychology.* Reading, Mass.: Addison–Wesley, 1970.

Becker, H. Social class variations in the teacher–pupil relationship. *Journal of Educational Sociology,* 1952, *25,* 451–465.

Biener, L., & Gerard, H. B. Effects of desegregation on achievement - relevant motivation. *Law and Contemporary Problems,* 1978, *42*(3), 121–150.

Brophy, J., & Good, T. L. *Teacher–student relationship.* New York: Holt, Rinehart, & Winston, 1974.

Byrne, D. Attitudes and attraction. In L. Berkowitz (Ed.), *Advances in experimental social psychology* (Vol. 4). New York: Academic Press, 1965.

Chesler, M. A., Crowfoot, J. E., & Bryant, B. I. Institutional changes to support school desegregation: Alternative models underlying research and implementation. *Law and Contemporary Problems,* 1978, *42*(3), 174–213.

Clark, K. Desegregation: An appraisal of the evidence. *Journal of Social Issues,* 1953, *9*(4), 2–76.

Cohen, E. Interracial interaction disability. *Human Relations,* 1972, *25,* 9–24.

Cohen, E., & Roper, S. Modification of interracial interaction disability: An application of status characteristics theory. *American Sociological Review,* 1972, *37,* 643–652.

Cohen, E., & Sharan, S. Modifying status relations in Israeli youth. *Journal of Cross-Cultural Psychology,* 1980, *11,* 364–384.

Coleman, J. S., Campbell, E. Q., Hobson, C. J., McPartland, J., Mood, A. M., Weinfeld, F. D., & York, R. L. *Equality of educational opportunity.* Washington, D.C.: U. S. Government Printing Office, 1966.

Cook, S. W. Desegregation: A psychological analysis. In W. W. Charters, Jr. & N. L. Gage (Eds.), *Readings in the social psychology of education*. Boston: Allyn & Bacon, 1963.

Crain, R. L., & Mahard, R. E. Desegregation and Black achievement: A review of the research. *Law and Contemporary Problems*, 1978, *42*(3), 17–56.

Epps, E. G. The impact of school desegregation on the self-evaluation and achievement orientation of minority children. *Law and Contemporary Problems*, 1978, *42*(3), 57–76.

Festinger, L., & Kelley, H. H. *Changing attitudes through social contact*. Ann Arbor: Institute for Social Research, University of Michigan, 1951.

Forehand, G., & Ragosta, M. *A handbook for integrated schooling*. Washington, D. C.: U. S. Department of Health, Education, & Welfare, 1976.

Friere, P. *Pedagogy of the oppressed*. New York: Seabury Press, 1970.

Gerard, H. B., Jackson, T. D., & Conolley, E. S. Social contact in the desegregated classroom. In H. B. Gerard & N. Miller (Eds.), *School desegregation*. New York: Plenum Press, 1975.

Gottlieb, D., & Tenhouten, W. D. Racial composition and the social systems of three high schools. *Journal of Marriage and the Family*, 1965, *27*, 204–217.

Harding, J., Proshansky, H., Kutner, B., & Chein, I. Prejudice and ethnic relations. In G. Lindzey & E. Aronson (Eds.), *The handbook of social psychology* (Vol. 5, 2nd ed.). Reading, Mass.: Addison–Wesley, 1969.

Hughes, R. E., & Works, E. The self-concepts of black students in a predominantly black high school. *Sociology and Social Research*, 1974, *59*, 50–54.

Hunt, J. G., & Hunt, L. L. Racial inequality and self-image: Identity maintenance as identity diffusion. *Sociology and Social Research*, 1977, *61*, 539–559.

Inbar, M., & Adler, C. *Ethnic integration in Israel: A comparative case study of Moroccan brothers who settled in France and in Israel*. New Jersey: Transaction, 1977.

Insel, P., & Jacobson, L. *What do you expect?* Menlo Park, Calif.: Cummings, 1975.

Israel Ministry of Education and Culture. *Report of the committee on the evaluation of Israel's school reform*. Jerusalem: Ministry of Education and Culture, 1979. (Hebrew)

Johnson, E. G., Gerard, H. B., & Miller, N. Teacher influences in the desegregated classroom. In H. B. Gerard & N. Miller (Eds.), *School desegregation*. New York: Plenum Press, 1975.

Katz, I. *Conflict and harmony in an adolescent interracial group*. New York: New York University Press, 1955.

Katz, I. Socialization of academic motivation. In W. J. Arnold & D. Levine (Eds.), *Nebraska Symposium on Motivation*. Lincoln: University of Nebraska Press, 1967.

Katz, I. Some motivational determinants of racial differences in intellectual achievement. In M. Mead, T. Dobzhansky, E. Tobach, & R. Light (Eds.), *Science and the concept of race*. New York: Columbia University Press, 1968.

Katz, Y. J. *An investigation of social integration and social attitudes of pupils after the establishment of junior high schools in the Israeli school system*. Israel: Bar–Ilan University, M. A. Dissertation, 1976. (Hebrew)

Klein, Z., & Eshel, Y. Toward a psychosocial definition of school integration. *Megamot*, 1977, *23*(3–4), 17–40. (Hebrew)

Kramer, B. Residential contact as a determination of attitudes toward Negroes. Cambridge, Mass.: Harvard University, doctoral dissertation, 1950.

Lazarsfeld, P. (Ed.). *Radio and the printed page*. New York: Duell, Sloan, & Pearce, 1940.

McConahay, J. B. The effects of school desegregation upon students' racial attitudes and behavior: A critical review of the literature and a prolegomenon to future research. *Law and Contemporary Problems*, 1978, *42*(3), 77–107.

Minkovitz, A., Davis, D., & Bashi, J. *Evaluation of educational achievement in the Israeli elementary school*. Jerusalem: The Hebrew University School of Education, 1977.

Orfield, G. Research, politics and the antibusing debate. *Law and Contemporary Problems*, 1978, *42*(3), 141–173.

Peres, Y. *Ethnic relations in Israel*. Tel–Aviv: Sifriat–Poalim, 1976. (Hebrew)

Pettigrew, T. Social psychology and desegregation research. *American Psychologist*, 1961, *16*, 105–112.

Pettigrew, T. F. *A profile of the negro American*. Princeton, N. J.: Van Nostrand, 1964.

Pettigrew, T. F. The Negro in education: Problems and proposals. In I. Katz & P. Gurin (Eds.), *Race and the social sciences*. New York: Basic Books, 1969.

Razel, O. *Compensatory education and welfare—for whom?* Jerusalem: Ministry of Education and Culture, 1978. (Hebrew)

Rich, Y., Amir, Y., & Ben–Ari, R. Social and emotional problems associated with integration in the Israeli junior high school. *International Journal of Intercultural Relations*, 1981, *5*, 259–275.

Rist, R. C. Student social class and teacher expectations: The self-fulfilling prophecy in ghetto education. *Harvard Educational Review*, 1970, *40*, 411–451.

Rokeach, M. *The nature of human values*. New York: Free Press, 1968.

Rosenthal, R., & Jacobson, L. *Pygmalion in the classroom*. New York: Holt, Rinehart, & Winston, 1968.

Schofield, J. Cooperation as social exchange: Resource gaps and reciprocity in academic work. In S. Sharp, A. Hare, C. Webb, & R. Hertz–Lazarowitz (Eds.), *Cooperation in Education*. Provo, Utah: Brigham Young University Press, 1980.

Schofield, J., & Sager, H. Peer interaction patterns in an integrated middle school. *Sociometry*, 1977, *40*, 130–138.

Schwartz, Z. Ethnic identity and interethnic contact. Israel: Bar–Ilan University, Master's dissertation, 1975. (Hebrew)

Sharan, S. Cooperative learning in small groups: Recent methods and effects on achievement, attitudes, and ethnic relations. *Review of Educational Research*, 1980, *50*(2), 241–271.

Shaw, M. Changes in sociometric choices following forced integration of an elementary school. *Journal of Social Issues*, 1973, *29*, 143–157.

Sherif, M., & Sherif, C. W. *Groups in harmony and tension*. New York: Harper, 1953.

Singer, D. The impact of interracial classroom exposure on the social attitudes of fifth-grade children (unpublished, 1964). Cited by E. Aronson, *The social animal*. San Francisco: W. H. Freeman, 1972.

Slavin, R. Classroom reward structure: An analytical and practical review. *Review of Educational Research*, 1977, *47*, 633–650.

Stephan, W. G. School desegregation: An evaluation of predictions made in Brown vs. Board of Education. *Psychological Bulletin*, 1978, *85*(2), 217–238.

St. John, N. H. *School desegregation outcomes for children*. New York: Wiley, 1975.

St. John, N. H., & Lewis, R. G. *Children's interracial friendships: An exploration of the contact hypothesis*. Unpublished paper, 1973.

Townsend, H., & Brittan, E. *Multiracial education: Need and innovation*. Schools Council Working Paper 50, London, England: Methuen, 1973.

Wellisch, J. *An in-depth study of Emergency School Aid Act (ESAA) schools: 1975–76*. Report for System Development Corporation, 1977.

Wellisch, J., Marcus, A., MacQueen, A., & Duck, G. An in-depth study of Emergency School Aid Act (ESAA) schools: 1974–1975. Report for System Development Corporation, July, 1976.

Wilson, A. Social stratification and academic achievement. In A. H. Passow (Ed.), *Education in depressed areas*. New York: Teachers College, Columbia University, 1963.

Winder, A. White attitudes towards Negro–White interaction in an area of changing racial composition. *American Psychologist*, 1952, *7*, 330–331.

2

School Integration in the Context of the Development of Israel's Educational System

Chaim Adler

INTRODUCTION

The primary purpose of this chapter is to provide an overview of the social-educational implications of Israel's ethnic composition. Some of the salient changes that occurred in the social and educational conditions prevailing among the various ethnic groups are also considered. These topics are discussed in terms of their relationships to school desegregation. Any analysis of school desegregation (i.e., the ethnic mix in the Jewish majority's schools and classrooms) should be conducted against the background of Israel's social structure and development. The education of Israeli Arabs and the possible integration of Jewish and Arab schools are discussed toward the end of the chapter. The chief ethnic division in Israel is between citizens of Western origin and those of Middle Eastern origin. The primary characteristic of this division is of a cultural nature. The Israeli case may thus shed light on the more general question of whether and to what extent the processes of modernization of peoples from non-Western countries may enfold successfully without disturbing in the process much of the indigenous traditional culture. The Jewish settlers of modern Palestine from the late nineteenth century up to the establishment of the State in 1948 were predominantly of European origin and Western culture. In fact, more than 90% of Israel's inhabitants in 1948 were of European background. At that time, mass immigration was instituted, doubling the population over the first 3 years of statehood, and tripling it over the first 12. It is the origins of the immigrants, however, and not their numbers, that are of interest here. Since independence, only about 50% of the new immigrants were of Western origin, the rest coming from Middle Eastern Jewish communities (mainly Iran, Iraq, Yemen, and North Africa). Toward the end of the 1970s, the proportion of Jewish citizens of Middle Eastern origin (whether born abroad or in Israel) was 45% of the total Jewish population (Statistical Abstract of Israel, 1977). Israel's independence coincided with, and probably encouraged, an on-going trend of Arab nationalism in practically the entire region. Consequently many of the Jews in the area felt insecure, some even encountered violence. Under these circumstances, many of these Jews naturally reacted favorably to the newly established State's call for immigration.

As the Jews of European background had mostly adapted to European cultural styles and institutional patterns, Middle Eastern Jews had been under the impact of Middle Eastern cultural styles and institutional patterns. Therefore, immigration for many, if not most, Middle Eastern Jews meant an encounter with, and transition to, an unknown and basically different social system. A market economy based on modern technology, a multiparty parliamentary democracy allowing for full participation of women were all new and alien to many of the immigrants from Middle Eastern countries. Hence, some of the characteristic features of the Jews from Middle Eastern countries of which the following three are outstanding examples constituted a priori obstacles to full social participation and integration. First, they had had little or no formal schooling; second, very few had undergone technological training congruent with the needs of a modern economy, and, finally, they arrived mostly in very large families and were ignorant of or opposed to family planning. It is almost self-evident that a group characterized by a confluence of these features would find itself in the lower social strata.

It would be wrong to attribute the gap in achievement between the two major ethnic groups entirely to the fact that the Middle Eastern Jews brought with them the "ingredients" of disadvantage. Some of the strategies of "absorption," even when applied universally, had a discriminatory effect on immigrants from Middle Eastern countries. The policy of "Population Dispersion," for example, which had valid demographic security and economic justifications, in fact facilitated the settlement of many Middle Eastern families in remote and arid areas and thus hindered their integration into the society (Cohen, 1969). Little if any allowance in absorption procedures in the early years of mass immigration was made for the fact that Middle Eastern Jews differed significantly from each other in education or the degree to which they were disadvantaged (Israeli, 1971). Thus, because many Middle Eastern immigrants had meager education and training, the well educated or highly trained among them suffered from a halo effect. For example, in job assignment or location of housing (which correlated highly to job opportunities), they were treated the same as the little-educated and ill-trained majority. Finally, institutional discrimination against Middle Eastern immigrants, intentional or unintentional, has been investigated in only a few studies, but they do seem to indicate that the disadvantaged socioeconomic position of Middle Easterners stemmed inter alia from the differential treatment by the official agencies during the initial period of "being absorbed" (Inbar & Adler, 1977; Smooha, 1978). The gaps in achievement between the two major ethnic communities may thus be attributed to an interaction between the a priori prevailing characteristics of the communities and the absorption policies of the relevant agencies at the time of immigration to Israel. Whatever the exact balance of these different factors in explaining the gap between the ethnic groups, its persistence has been a matter of great concern and has generated a wide area of public policies aimed at closing or at least containing this gap.

The underlying reason for this great concern over the issue has a number of roots, though from the point of view of public policy the need to understand exactly the historical sources of the gap may have diminished over the years, as the sons and even grandsons of the original immigrants have become the target population. Firstly, the founders of Israel, socialist visionaries who fused their quest for Jewish national revival with a search for a just and decent society had envisioned an egalitarian state. The institutional framework as initiated by the early settlers was aimed at keeping ascriptive differences between groups to a minimum. To this end, salaries, for example, were linked to family size; in the mid 1920s a sick fund to provide almost universal medical care was created by an extremely strong Federation of Labor; and simple housing patterns emerged, characterized almost exclusively by one- or two-bedroom apartments. In view of this the alarmingly wide and perhaps growing gap between Middle Eastern and Western immigrants which emerged in the early 1950s, was unacceptable and went against the grain of society's ethos. Furthermore an ethnic cleavage was intolerable, given the great need for national solidarity. Israel is not just a case of nation building where all forces tend to rally round the common interests of institution building and growth: The State was born out of a War of Independence and, in a short period of about 35 years since, has been exposed to five major wars. Under such circumstances, an ethnic cleavage would constitute a dangerous threat to the society's very survival. Finally, the ethnic gap is closely related to the quality of Israel's human resources: A very small nation of about 3.5 million, Israel, throughout the entire period of its existence, has been trying not only to grow economically and to increase its population through immigration, but also to take part in all spheres of modern industrial civilization. If a significant portion of the population remains under-resourced and hence neither a full participant in nor a significant contributor to these social, economic, or cultural endeavors, the desired goals of development may not be realized.

Let us now turn to the main policies that were developed in order to contain the gap and perhaps contribute toward diminishing it. Society provides housing, education, employment, subsidies for essential services and basic food, and welfare for those who need it. Throughout the entire period there has been almost full employment; free compulsory education (under the law adopted in 1949, compulsory education covered a span of 9 years—K through 8th grade; presently it covers K through 10th grade and is free through 12th); and insurance of births by the Institute for National Insurance (which enables working mothers who give birth to draw their salaries from the National Insurance over 3 months so they may take care of the baby). Some measures by the government aimed specifically at the Middle Eastern population, are, for example, the large family allowances or the great variety of compensatory educational programs that have been initiated (to be discussed later). Though there is no way to assess the extent and rate at which the gap would have increased without these policies, it clearly persists in spite of these measures and, in certain areas, has perhaps even increased slightly.

We have so far discussed "the gap" from the point of view of equality and participation and have looked at some of the strategies employed to enhance the prospects of an equitable distribution of resources (or at least prevent the further growth of ascriptive-based inequalities). The issue at hand is, however, of a cultural nature, as was mentioned previously when discussing the pattern of the large traditional family, or that the notion of women's equality was by and large alien to most Middle Eastern immigrants. The Israeli authorities' management of some of these premodern cultural and behavioral patterns under the label of "absorption" was indeed a major effort in modernization.

It seems that the concept of "cultural pluralism" does indeed imply that a meaningful process of modernization may occur while the affected people simultaneously remain steeped in their traditional culture. The contrary notion is that the cultural assimilation of the modernizing subgroup into the mainstream is required in order to achieve modernization.

It would appear that Israel has applied the latter model, especially during the initial era of mass immigration. The schools, for example, have quite effectively imparted uniform behavioral patterns, modes of expression, and even forms of speech. Similarly, and perhaps to an even greater extent, the army too served as an assimilating agent. Values and ideals or eating habits, as personified by commanders who, in the early years, were practically all of Western origin, were widely adopted. The mass media, which express cultural patterns, modes of behavior, ideas and values of a primarily Western type, had a similar impact. The family, protected in a way by intimate relationships and privacy, is perhaps the main focus of traditional Eastern patterns and modes. Yet the almost universally attended service of the well-baby clinics and the growing number of programs aimed at the family have become quite powerful interventions that most probably introduce new child-rearing practices of homemaking techniques into the privacy of the home. All this does not however imply the extinction of Eastern traditions and cultural patterns. It merely indicates the society's intent and perhaps illustrates the implicit goals of "absorption" (Eisenstadt & Zlocover, 1969).

Indeed, on drawing comparisons between the notions and attitudes of first- and second-generation Middle Easterns, a considerable degree of assimilation may be discerned. Witness for instance a trend of secularization among Middle

Eastern citizens (Herman, Farago, & Harel, 1976). There is also a clear tendency toward lower birth rates in the second generation: In 1955 the gross reproduction rate for Middle Eastern women was 2.77 compared to 1.28 for Western women; in 1975 it was 1.83 and 1.37, respectively (Statistical Abstract of Israel, 1976). There are several additional indications of a growing cultural similarity between the Western and Middle Eastern groups.

It remains to be seen, however, whether these developments are to be termed *successful absorption* or judged rather as obstacles to the process of social integration, inasmuch as the various ethnic groups may have less of a chance to make their unique contributions to the newly evolving culture in Israel. A look at some of the subjective reactions of Middle Easterners to the interethnic scene may perhaps indicate whether they themselves perceive these developments as a kind of "cultural imperialism." There seems to be conflicting evidence in this respect. On the one hand, researchers did not find evidence of interethnic tensions (Shuval, 1962). On the other hand, research established the emergence of self-rejection and even indications of self-hatred among Middle Eastern subjects (Peres, 1971; Shuval, 1966). At the same time one may encounter complaints about Western "cultural imperialism," mainly from certain Middle Eastern elite persons. Such trends could certainly be seen as obstacles to social integration.

It is appropriate to add, at this point, that this ethnic problem and the quest to integrate the entire Eastern population into the mainstream of Israeli society have so far been only slightly politicized. More precisely, there has been close to no Middle Eastern organization whose declared purpose is negotiation based on common ethnic interests. To be sure, there have been numerous political organizations on the local level, whose core comprises family groupings or ethnic associations, but on the national level there are almost none.

"Immigrant Absorption" in the early years, and more recently the gap between the ethnic groups in achievements and the rates of participating, have of course been issues of political discourse and controversy. All the political parties relate to the problem, designate people or departments to deal with the Middle Eastern electorate, and when in power seek to appoint able persons from this group to positions of representation or for administrative posts. But these measures appear to be preventive in nature and not an establishment reaction to grass-root political pressures. The question does arise of course of why there has been so little political engagement of the ethnic issue by representatives of the Middle Eastern communities. The answer is probably composed of several elements: The a priori intention, perhaps even desire, of many persons of Middle Eastern origin to be "Israelis" explains their far-reaching readiness to tolerate hardships in the process. Further, these tendencies were most probably encouraged by the external political military pressures that applied uniformly to all citizens. The rather effective social-welfare policies, which provided everyone's basic needs—housing, food, employment, health, education—had a profound impact in this realm: Even if the relative gap between the Middle Eastern and the Western subjects did not diminish, the very fact that the formers' absolute social and economic conditions tended to improve over the years inevitably had a mitigating impact. The expected rewards for success—educational, economic, or political—diminished the readiness to engage in deviant behavior or extraparliamentary politics.

This state of affairs, therefore, does not resemble the affirmative action model as developed in the United States. To be more precise, if affirmative action is defined primarily in terms of minority-group quotas to be filled irrespective of the candidates' qualifications or merit, then assuredly no parallel mechanism has evolved in Israel so far. If, however, affirmative action is defined as an overall policy aimed at providing minority people with a maximum opportunity for inclusion in the talent pool from which selection is made universalistically, then it does apply to the Israeli system as well. Schools and universities, the army, government departments and agencies all abide by this policy to different degrees. In this context, it is worth noting that so far, when the idea of Middle Eastern-promotion quotas have been proposed as a social strategy, it has been vehemently rejected by prominent members of that community. The Israeli circumstances thus seem to exert pressures on people of Middle Eastern origin to develop patterns of individually rather than collectively based mobility (Sowell, 1976, 1978).

The Magnitude of the Ethnic Gap in Select Social Institutions

It seems appropriate to turn now to some data that indicate the magnitude of the gap in a number of select areas. Table 2.1 presents the predominant trends in the ethnic composition of Israel's Jewish population since the establishment of the State in 1948. (The state of non-Jewish minorities is discussed separately.)

The table quite clearly indicates the upward trend in the rate of native Israelis and the decline of the rate of foreign born since the early 1950s. Similarly, there was a constant increase in the relative number of people from Middle Eastern origin in the general population until the late 1960s. Since then, the rate of this group has decreased and the group of native Israelis born to Israeli fathers has increased; the latter includes of course, people from Middle Eastern origin (about 50%).

Undoubtedly, ethnic gaps tend to be expressed first and foremost in the economic sphere. We turn first to income differentials; Table 2.2 presents the gap in monthly income between all Middle Eastern and all Western families. It shows clearly that the gap in income between the two major ethnic subgroups is constant, in the order of about .75; in the mid-1960s the gap is somewhat wider, with the income differentials tending to narrow in the 70s.

Turning next to data on poverty and its ethnic base, the following picture emerges: Studies conducted in the late 1960s show that between one fifth (Rotter & Shamai, 1971) to one quarter (Haviv, 1975) of the Israeli families were on or below the poverty line (as defined by indices of the Institute of National Insur-

TABLE 2.1
The Jewish Population of Israel by Ethnic Origin, 1948–1976
(Total Percentages)

Year	Total	Israel-born Father				Middle Eastern Born	Western Born
		Israel	Middle Eastern	Western	Total		
1948	716,700	—	—	—	35.4	9.8	54.8
1951	1,404,400	—	—	—	25.5	27.6	46.9
1957	1,762,700	—	—	—	33.9	29.0	37.1
1961	1,981,700	5.6	15.3	17.2	(38.1)	27.5	34.4
1964	2,239,200	—	—	—	39.4	28.7	31.9
1969	2,496,400	7.5	21.1	16.5	(45.1)	26.8	28.1
1972	2,723,600	8.7	22.7	16.5	(47.9)	24.9	27.2
1976	3,020,400	11.0	24.7	16.4	52.1	21.5	26.4

Note: Central Bureau of Statistics, The Israel Statistical Abstract, Vol. 17, 1966, Table B/16; Vol. 23, 1972, Table II/20; Vol. 28, 1977, Table II/21.

ance); the incidence of poverty among Middle Eastern families was considerably higher than among Western families—26% and 13%, respectively, indicating quite clearly that Middle Eastern families are significantly over-represented among the poor.

The picture emerging here is interesting: There seems to be a stubbornly persistent gap in income with the average income of Middle Eastern families at about 75% of the average Western family income. This average difference does not, however, seem to be unbridgeable. Indeed, in a number of studies that compared average family income of the two ethnic groups, the averages were adjusted, (i.e., education, length of stay in the country or occupation were

TABLE 2.2
Monthly Family Income (in Current Israeli Pounds) 1956 to 1977

	1956/7[a]	1963/4[b]	1967[c]	1971[c]	1975[c]	1977[d]
Middle Eastern	219	402	558	893	2292	4515
Western	300	640	925	1200	2783	5567
Index of equality[c]	73	63[f]	60	74	82	81

Note: This table has been adapted from S. Smooha (1978), Table 10, p. 282.
[a]CBS *Family Expenditure Surveys* 1956–7 and 1959–60—Special Series, 148, pp. cxxiv–cxxv.
[b]CBS *Saving Survey*, 1963–4, Special Series 217, pp. xxix (Table 5).
[c]CBS *Statistical Abstracts of Israel*, 1971, 22:182; 1973; 24:271; 1976, 27:261.
[d]CBS *Statistical Abstracts of Israel*, 1978, 29:303.
[e]This index is computed as a percentage that the income of AA families is of the income of EA families. Consequently, the closer the index is to 100, the smaller is the rate of inequality.
[f]According to a different source, the index of equality in this year was substantially higher—71 (CBS, *Family Expenditure Survey*, 1963–64, Special Series 200).

TABLE 2.3
Knesset Members 1949-1977

Knesset[a]	1st 1949	2nd 1951	3rd 1955	4th 1959	5th 1961	6th 1965	7th 1969	8th 1973	9th 1977
Total[b]	118	112	113	113	114	113	113	114	113
Middle Eastern	8	7	10	14	14	21	17	19	22
Western	110	105	103	99	100	92	96	95	91
% Middle Eastern	6.8	6.3	8.8	12.4	12.3	18.6	15.0	16.7	19.5
% Middle Eastern among 20+-year olds				32.65	33.89	39.48	40.76	41.74	42.2

Note: This table was adapted from S. Smooha (1978). Table 37. Sources: A. Zidon, The Knesset, Tel Aviv: Achiasaf, 1971 (Hebrew); Israel Government Yearbook; S. Weis, The ninth Knesset; Preliminary analysis of composition and recruitment patterns, State and Government, No. 11, Winter 1977 (Hebrew).
[a]At the beginning of each term.
[b]Excluding Arab members.

controlled for). The percentage of equality as calculated this way, in different years, was found to be between 80 to 95%. Yet it would seem that the high incidence of poverty in the Middle Eastern community is cause for greater concern and is much more alarming than is the gap between average incomes of the two groups.

For examining the ethnic gap in the realm of politics, the measures applied are the number (or relative representation) of Middle Eastern persons in different types of positions. In positions of political representation, the gap basically shows a tendency to decrease: In analyzing the Knesset (i.e., Parliament—)composition, one discerns that the proportion of Middle Eastern members increased from 6.8% in 1948 to 19.5% in 1977 (see Table 2.3).

In civil service and professional positions in Government the following trend emerges: Whereas there is a growing representation of Middle Eastern persons in middle and lower senior positions, no similar trend is evident in senior positions. For example:

TABLE 2.4
Rates of Middle Eastern Persons in Different Administrative
Positions, 1955-1970

	1955	1960/61	1965/67	1969/70
Police officers	3.6	7.0	13.6	20.4
Middle rank civil service	—	19.5	20.8[a]	—
Top position civil service	—	3.1	—	3.0
Army major generals	0	0	0	0

Note: Adapted from S. Smooha (1978). Tables 38, 40, 41.
[a]In 1961 there were no Israeli-born middle-rank civil servants. In 1967 there were 24.7%; undoubtedly a certain portion of those were from Middle Eastern background.

It seems plausible that as the educational status of Middle Eastern citizens improves, they will be better represented in top civil service and professional positions. (Though it may well be, that as in other similar situations, the further up people of Middle Eastern origin move, the more difficult it will be for many of them to compete for and assume top positions and offices.)

An interesting development along these lines can be observed in the assumption by Middle Eastern persons of leadership positions on the municipal level. Here again, the chances for there being Middle Eastern persons in locally elected leadership positions are greater the further one moves away from the political center of society.

It is important to take note of the fact that membership in city councils, and certainly mayorships, have become very important stepping stones for people of Middle Eastern origin to attain central leadership positions, for example in the Knesset, the executive committee of the Federation of Labor, or even the cabinet.

TABLE 2.5
Middle Eastern Representation in Municpal Councils and Mayorships
(Percentages)

	1955	1965
A. *Council Membership*		
Total	23.6	44.2
Councillors in large and middle-sized veteran cities	12.8	20.9
Councillors in other veteran settlements	20.3	39.4
Councillors in new local townships	39.8	61.9
B. *Mayorships*		*1969*
Total		32.7
Local authorities with Middle Eastern majority		63.4
Local authorities—mixed		15.9
Local authorities—Western majority		4.0

Note: S. Weis, *Local government in Israel and its leadership*, Ph.D. dissertation, Hebrew University, Jerusalem, 1968 (Hebrew) p. 356. Ben Zion Michaeli, *Israel's mayors*. Merkaz Hashilton Hamekomi, Tel Aviv, 1971 (Hebrew).

The picture that emerges from this brief discussion of the ethnic gap in the political realm is therefore mixed, as it was in the economic sphere discussed earlier. On the one hand there is a steady increase in the rate of people of Middle Eastern origin in political positions—quite remarkable on the local level, much slower in central positions—though even in the latter there is constant growth. Considering that this development is a matter of 30 years at the most and given the unequal initial positions, due to the disadvantaged background of most people of Middle Eastern origin, the development seems to be encouraging, pointing toward their growing political participation and thus greater equality in this realm too. Yet the alarming development from the social point of view seems to be that, again, there is a certain percentage of the population—overwhelmingly of Middle Eastern origin—that is politically passive (e.g., only two-thirds of the townships with a Middle Eastern majority have a Middle Eastern mayor). It seems a safe assumption that there is a high correlation between poverty, which as we have seen is highly concentrated among people from Middle Eastern origin, and political nonparticipation.

The Gap in the Field of Education

In turning to the field of education, which is our chief concern in this volume, we set out with a few introductory remarks. Israel's first compulsory free education law was passed by the Knesset in 1949, less than 1 year after the state was established. As we have already noted, this initial legislation applied to 9 years of schooling—kindergarten through 8th grade. It has been implemented effectively with 97% of the young peoples' population to whom the law addresses itself enrolled in schools. In 1968 compulsory school education was expanded by an additional year, and in 1978 by yet another, making a total of 11 grades, kindergarten through 10th. (In the same year, 1978, tuition fees were abolished, thus making for 13 years of free schooling).

The most remarkable feature of Israel's school system is perhaps its expansion: Whereas the country's Jewish population has just about quadrupled since the state was declared, its student population has grown about seven-fold. Since 1968, when compulsory schooling was extended beyond the 8-year elementary education, two developments have taken place: firstly, an ever-growing differentiation within the school system in terms of programs and curricula and, secondly, the launching of a school reform plan, one of whose basic features is that elementary education has been collapsed into 6 years, to be followed by 3 years of compulsory junior high school. By the beginning of the 1980s, about 50% of the system had been thus reformed. The other half still abides by the 8-year elementary and 4-year secondary system.

Israel's public school system, which embraces between 93 to 94% of the school population, is subdivided into two types—state schools and state religious schools. The latter, which emerged in 1953 as a political compromise and catered to parents who wish to complement the religious atmosphere of the home with that of the school, comprise about 20% of the public schools. The religious schools differ from the rest in their heavier Judaic Studies program and in school climate. (Six to 7% of the student population study in an ultraorthodox system, which is entirely independent.)

Since its very early years, the Israeli school system has been concerned with the gap in educational achievement between children from the two ethnic groups and the consequent gap in educational mobility. The educational system has basically accepted the general attitude that places on education the main burden of equalizing opportunities, integrating ethnic groups, and promoting the disad-

TABLE 2.6
Student Participation in Post Primary and Higher Education by Types of School and Place of Birth, 1956/7 to 1976/7[a]

		1956/57 Foreign Born	1966/67 Foreign Born	1966/67 Israeli Born	1976/77 Foreign Born	1976/77 Israeli Born
Total Post Primary						
Middle Eastern		13.0	37.9		53.8	
Western		40.9	68.6		70.6	
Index of equality:	Relative[b]	32.0	55.0		76.0	
	absolute[c]	−27.9	−30.7		−16.8	
Academic Secondary						
Middle Eastern		3.3	12.5		18.2	
Western		18.9	37.6		43.8	
Index of equality:	relative	19.0	33.0		42.0	
	absolute	−15.6	−25.1		−25.6	
Vocational Secondary						
Middle Eastern		2.2	15.3		35.6	
Western		6.6	16.7		26.8	
Index of equality:	relative	33.0	91.0		133.0	
	absolute	−4.4	−1.4		+8.8	
Matriculation Diplomas						
Middle Eastern			3.7		7.4[e]	
Western			24.3		31.7[e]	
Index of equality:	relative		15.0		23.0[e]	
	absolute		−20.6		−24.3[e]	
Higher Education						
Middle Eastern		0.2[d]	0.9	1.7	2.0[e]	2.8[e]
Western		2.3[d]	6.5	9.4	9.3[e]	13.8[e]
Index of equality:	relative	9.0	14.0	18.0	22.0[e]	20.0[e]
	absolute	−2.1	−5.6	−7.7	−7.3[e]	−11.0[e]

Note: Adapted from S. Smooha (1978).
[a]Student rates in post primary education are computed as percentages of the population of 14–17 year olds; rates for matriculation diplomas of the 17-year olds; higher education—of the 20–29 year olds.
[b]Computed as the rate of Middle Eastern from Western.
[c]Computed by subtracting the rate for Middle Eastern from that for Western.
[d]These are estimates (exact figures are available as of 1964/65).
[e]For 1972/73.

vantaged. Before embarking on an analysis of these efforts, let us examine some data defining the magnitude of the educational gap. When analyzing rates of participation (of different groups) in the Israeli educational system, postprimary and higher education are of particular interest, because primary education has always been compulsory and participation in it universal. Table 2.6 presents the rates of participation of the two major ethnic groups in postprimary education at three points in time. It should be noted that the bottleneck is evidently the academic high school and the acquisition of matriculation diplomas, which are necessary, even if not sufficient, for acceptance into higher education; the gap in participation in higher education is thus a direct consequence. There is little doubt that in the span of some 25 years reported about here, the chances of Middle Eastern youths to acquire a postprimary education have improved significantly: In 1956/57 the ratio of Middle Eastern to Western students was about one-third (32%); by 1976/7 it was about three-quarters (76%). Even in the selective secondary schools, a significant improvement has taken place—from a ratio of about one-fifth (18.9%) to more than two-fifths (43.8%). The data concerning secondary school matriculation obtained for a period of just 10 years (1966/67 through 1976/77), and it is thus all the more noteworthy that at this level too there has been growth—from 15 to 23% of Middle Eastern academic secondary school graduates out of the total number of Western graduates. (The rate of Middle Eastern students who successfully passed the matriculation examination from the entire Middle Eastern 17-year-old cohort doubled in those years—from 3.7 to 7.4%). Nevertheless, the gap has persisted due to the general educational expansion and changes in the patterns of educational participation among the Western students as well. In absolute terms, it has even increased (especially at the level of the academic secondary school). Thus, whereas the participation of Middle Eastern students in academic secondary schools has grown about six-fold, that of Western students has grown as well, though it has only doubled. In absolute measures, then, the gap that in 1956/57 was 15.6 percentage points grew to 25.6 percentage points in 1976/67. It appears, however, that the remarkable breakthrough that has taken place here is the consequence of the marked penetration of Middle Eastern students into vocational schools. But though opportunities for vocational school graduates are not identical to those available to graduates of academic secondary schools, there is a growing tendency for vocational school graduates to sit for matriculation examinations too; it may be assumed that over the next 20 years the opportunities open to the sons and daughters of Middle Eastern vocational school graduates will bear much more resemblance to those of their Western peers than was the case for their parents' generation.

The first signs of the educational gap were noted in the early 1950s. Soon afterwards the Ministry of Education started developing policies and launched intervention programs (to be discussed later) aimed at decreasing the gap. It soon became apparent, however, that the target population needed to be defined: Ethnic origin was rejected as the basis for definition, primarily on ideological national grounds. As we have already mentioned, the philosophy of "absorption" was couched in an ideological framework of national solidarity and uniformity. The emphasis on ethnic group identity by aiming a social policy at a particular ethnic group was, therefore, in contradiction to this ethos. Secondly, using ethnicity as a basis for defining "the disadvantaged" would have lent the problem a clearly ascriptive flavor, and that was unacceptable on social-ideological grounds: The definition was needed in order to single out those individuals who should be the target of rehabilitative or compensatory programs. Singling people out by an unalterable ascriptive characteristic, suspected by many to be the root of their disadvantage, was self-defeating. It could only serve to intensify the prejudice against Middle Eastern persons and encourage those forces in society that held that rehabilitative efforts were futile. Finally it was already evident at that early point that not all Middle Eastern students fall behind the norm in their educational achievements. Had ethnic origin become the basis of definition, Middle Eastern students with average achievement would have been afflicted with the generalized stigma. It was against this background that the concept of "disadvantaged" emerged. (It should be noted that the term in Hebrew carries a basically optimistic flavor: The target population are not defined simply as the "disadvantaged," but rather those who—if society will make the necessary decisions and allocations—stand a good chance of progressing educationally.) The definition, moreover, was applied to schools and not individual students, the reason being that the definition was sought primarily for the purpose of deciding where and to what extent to invest above the norm in compensatory educational resources. The target for such compensatory investments was obviously schools and not individuals. Disadvantaged schools were originally defined by the ratios of Middle Eastern students in the school population and their demonstrated scholastic achievements, but in 1974 a socially based index was developed by the Ministry of Education, which is composed of fathers' education, family size, and ethnic origin.[1] An analysis of Table 2.7 shows clearly that almost 95% of the disadvantaged students are of Middle Eastern origin, almost 90% of their fathers have primary education or less, and about 90% come from families with four or more children.

It is interesting to learn from the table that the major concentrations or "pockets" of disadvantaged students are in families with uneducated fathers and large families (four children or more). More specifically the table tells us that 44% of all the Israeli students—95% of all Middle Eastern students—were disadvantaged according to the criteria mentioned in Table 2.7. Algarebli reports that 60% of this group were enrolled in schools defined as disadvantaged (the rest being dispersed among regular schools). It follows, therefore, that not all Middle Eastern students are hard-core disadvantaged; these tend to be located in very specific sectors of the Middle Eastern population.

At this juncture it seems appropriate to introduce some of the relevant research findings, all of which point in the same direction: The powerful predictive quality of the father's education and family size on the student's achievement (or the likelihood of his being disadvantaged). About 10 years before the Algarebli study, Smilansky & Yam (1969), in an analysis of the data from the 1963 eighth-grade qualifying examination, showed that the predictive power of the father's education exceeds that of family size. In 1966 Litwin re-examined data of the

---

[1]The analysis of the achievements of students on a nationwide test administered to all eighth graders led to the definition of a school as disadvantaged if the majority of its students have less than 40% chance to score 70 points on the test. (The test incidentally was abolished in 1973.)

TABLE 2.7
Disadvantaged Students in Primary Schools by Father's Continent of
Birth, Father's Education, Family Size, and Type of School, 1971/72

	Percent of All Students	Percent of Disadvantaged Students	Percent of Disadvantaged Students in Category
Father's continent of birth—total	100.0	100.0	44.0
Africa	27.2	52.9	80.2
Asia	29.3	41.8	58.6
Europe	33.0	4.1	5.1
Israel	10.5	1.2	4.8
Father's education—total	100.0	100.0	44.0
None	11.6	26.8	100.0
Primary	49.8	62.1	54.9
Postprimary	35.9	11.1	13.6
College	8.7	0	0
Number of children in family—total	100.0	100.0	44.0
1–2	44.5	2.8	2.6
3	13.2	7.8	24.2
4	9.0	15.4	70.2
5	8.7	18.1	85.2
6	7.5	16.7	91.5
7	6.2	14.1	93.1
8+	10.9	25.1	95.1
Type of school—total	100.0	100.0	44.0
State	72.9	55.2	33.3
State religious	27.1	44.8	72.9

Note: Adapted from Algarebli (1975). Tables 1, 2, 3, 4.

eighth-grade achievement test for students in Jerusalem, following the Coleman model of analysis as closely as the data allowed (Litwin, 1971). He too established the predictive power of the home background (or SES) with respect to student achievements—father's education more so than family size. A longitudinal achievement study of 3600 fourth-through sixth-grade students also established that the gap between the ethnic communities was in the students' home environment—1.25 of a standard deviation (Lewy & Chen, 1977). The correlation between fathers' education and students' achievement was in the order of .39 to .47 with about one quarter (26%) of the variance in student achievements explained by home or SES factors. In total, 47.2% of the variance was explained; the additional variables were: School—3.5%; attitudes—8.8%; prior achievement (or an IQ equivalent)—11%. The most comprehensive study in this area is that of Minkovich, Davis, and Bashi (1977). Because this study used more sensitive definitions of the independent variables, it could easily locate the parameters of being disadvantaged. Accordingly, the most disadvantaged group were children in state religious schools whose parents had been born in Asia and Africa and had no education at all. Here again, the highest correlated variable with student achievements was found to be parents' education, to the order of .36 through .43; the correlation between student achievement and verbal interactions at home was in the order of .12 through .35.

Thus there is a convergence of all the relevant Israeli research as to the predominant predictive power of family variables, especially father's education, on student achievement. There is of course a high correlation between father's education and ethnicity, and ethnicity does indeed explain some of the variance in school achievement, independent of SES. These findings may have interesting implications for assessing the role of ethnicity in determining the educational gap and thus, as we see later, may have far-reaching policy implications.

Let us now turn to the gap in achievement proper. One of the early studies cited previously (Smilansky & Yam, 1969) that analyzed the achievement of eighth graders in 1963 reported an overall gap of .75–1.00 standard points between students from the two ethnic groups (equalling approximately one standard deviation). Ortar analyzed 12 years of the eighth-grade qualifying examination and also found the gap to be one standard deviation (Ortar, 1967). Lewy and Chen (1977) found that the gap between students from the two ethnic groups in home variables was wider than in scholastic achievement, with the latter at .8 to 1 of a standard deviation. The longitudinal aspect of their study consisted of testing students consecutively in all three grades, on identical items—"anchor items." In other words, they extracted from the fourth-grade curriculum items included also in the fourth-, fifth-, and sixth-grade tests; achievements could thus be compared across grades and across ethnic groups. In analyzing the data thus obtained, they found that on 50% of the "anchor items" the gap between the two groups was equivalent to one academic year; in 25% of additional items it was in the order of 2 years, and in the rest either less than 1 or more than 2. The Junior High School study reported almost identical findings about the achievement gaps (Chen, Lewy, & Adler, 1978). Finally, Minkovich et al. (1977) reported a gap in achievement between all students from the two ethnic groups on the order of .8 standard deviation.

We may conclude that the gap in scholastic achievements between the two main ethnic subgroups has not changed over the past 15 years. It has in fact tended to decrease somewhat: Whereas earlier research reported a gap of 1 S.D. between the groups, more recent studies report .8 S.D. (Minkovich, Davis, & Bashi, 1977).

In recent years a few studies were published that for the first time resorted to an intergenerational comparison of intellectual and educational achievements. The first study to address this issue was by Lieblich, Ninio, and Kugelmas (1972). They looked at children's IQ scores and compared them not only by ethnicity but also by generation, finding that second-generation Middle Eastern children (i.e., children whose fathers were born in Israel) scored 10 IQ points higher than first-generation children (i.e., children born in Israel, but whose fathers were born abroad); the scores being 101.3 and 92, respectively. Minkovich et al. also dealt with this issue: The achievement of second-generation Middle Eastern children is .50 of a S.D. better than that of first-generation Middle Eastern children. (As mentioned earlier "Second Generation" are Israeli-born children whose fathers were also born in Israel, as opposed to "First Generation"—who are Israeli-born children whose fathers were born abroad). Moreover, the achievement gap between second-generation Middle Eastern and Western students is somewhat smaller than it is between first-generation students from the two ethnic groups in the order of .10 S.D. These two studies, therefore, reinforce each other: Second-generation Middle Eastern children achieve better than first-generation Middle Eastern children; the gap in achievement between Western and Middle Eastern students decreases from the first to the second generation. One cannot, of course, rule out the possibility that selection factors are at play here: All the parents of first-generation Middle Eastern children immigrated during the nonselective waves of immigration that followed the emergence of the State of Israel; most grandparents of second-generation Middle Eastern children immigrated to Israel (then Palestine) in the pioneering-era of Zionism that preceded the foundation of the State. These early Middle Eastern settlers, most of whom had been ideologically motivated in their decision to immigrate, might have been culturally unique as a result of self-selection.

Finally, let us mention one developmental finding based on Chen and Lewy's longitudinal study. They found, interestingly, that the gap in achievement does not widen but remains constant at .8 S.D. Thus, in contrast to the "cumulative deficit" theory, the achievement gap did not grow between the fourth and sixth grades (Lewy & Chen, 1977).

In summary, the data we have been discussing suggests several generalizations concerning the gap in educational achievements. As in most other industrialized societies, in Israel too it was found that SES is the best predictor of both educational participation and educational achievement (Boudon, 1974; Coleman, Campbell, Hobson, McPartland, Mood, Weinfeld, & York, 1966; Jencks, Smith, Acland, Bane, Cohen, Gintis, Heyns, & Michelson, 1972; Mosteller & Moynihan, 1972). It seems that in the Israeli case, the predictive power of the father's education is especially high. Though the universality of the expansion of education in Israel has so far prevented the gap from diminishing, this expansion does however ensure that the next generation of Middle Eastern students will be children of fathers whose education is considerably better and more extensive than that of the current generation of Middle Eastern fathers. Assuming that the high correlation between fathers' education and children's achievements and participation in education will continue, there is great hope for significant diminishing of the gap over the next generation. In addition, this is the place to mention again the penetration of Middle Eastern students into vocational education, which, if nothing else, will increase and improve the education of the coming generations' fathers. The relative gap in educational participation, moreover, has decreased considerably, and the gap in achievement, which has also decreased, is now in the order of .8 S.D. There are also indications to the effect that the intergenerational gap in achievements has already shrunk. The intelligence study (Lieblich et al., 1972) and the longitudinal study (Lewy & Chen, 1977) reinforce each other: No difference was found in the structure of intelligence of subjects from both ethnic groups, and no educational tasks were found that Middle Eastern elementary school students—given sufficient time—would not be capable of undertaking. (Like many Continental school systems, Israel's is by and large inflexible as to the allotment of time. Each grade is expected to master a certain segment of a curriculum and little allowance is being made for different time needs that different students naturally have. The greater the heterogeneity of the student body, the more detrimental this state of affairs can be for the slow learner.) The data seem to indicate that the educational gap between ethnic groups in Israel, in spite of its persistence, is in flux and in fact heading toward a substantial decrease.

At the same time, there is an alarming and apparently not decreasing sector of severely disadvantaged students who are practically all of Middle Eastern origin. These are the children of parents with no schooling, who have four or more siblings. It stands to reason that the pockets of poverty discussed earlier are also the loci for the development of this severe educational disadvantage. It is this group that produces the school dropouts, and which is the reservoir for Israel's "unattached youth": those 10% of the secondary school age groups who are neither in school nor in the labor force.

It would thus appear that in all spheres of society, it is not the gap in average achievements or rates of participation between the ethnic groups that pose a threat to the sustained development of society, but rather the social and ecological concentrations of poor, nonparticipating, ill-achieving individuals who are practically all of Middle Eastern origin.

School Integration in the Context of Compensatory Education

We now turn to some of the strategies employed by the education system in its endeavor to promote students of disadvantaged backgrounds and thus contribute to the efforts toward decreasing the interethnic gap in social, political, and cultural achievements. As indicated before, the structure of the educational system in itself was a potent factor in coping with the problem. The effective implementation of the compulsory school attendance law or the process of rapid educational expansion are two most important examples of this. More specifically, however, we would point to a number of stages in the development of Israel's compensatory education, policies—designed expressedly for the educational promotion of disadvantaged students.

Initially, when it became evident that Israel's national independence brought with it not only an unprecedented population growth, but also an influx of immigrants from different cultural backgrounds, administrative measures were taken in an effort to cope with the emerging educational problems. For example, in many schools up to 50% of the students failed in their studies and were class repeaters (often as early as in the first grade), so that class repetition had to be abolished. The symptom indeed disappeared, but no real remedy to the problem had been offered. This was followed by a second stage of policy development, which focused on compensatory education, and within which several strategies may be distinguished. One was a major effort in the realm of early childhood education: Compulsory kindergarten attendance for 5- to 6-year olds has already been mentioned. It should be added that about 95% of the 4-year olds and about 85% of the 3-year olds in the country's economically depressed areas attend publicly funded nursery schools. Yet another strategy focused on the school, especially on the teaching of reading and writing in first and second grades. A series of intensive experiments in this area yielded reading techniques that dramatically improved the acquisition of these basic skills by first and second graders of Middle Eastern origin. Many other school-based compensatory efforts were much less effective. One such major effort that was studied in the 1960s was the long school day (Gutman, 1972b). Despite the great effort and expense invested in this plan, it was found to have no effect on disadvantaged students. An additional strategy, also introduced usually under compensatory education, consists of structural manipulations. The most widely practiced among these is ability grouping, a technique whose single most important effect was on teachers: A majority of them expressed satisfaction with ability grouping. (Teacher satisfaction is indeed an important factor, especially when they are confronted with the difficult task of educating disadvantaged students.) As in other countries, however, studies in Israel have demonstrated that ability grouping does not produce an effect on disadvantaged students (Gutman, 1972a).

In the mid 1960s, about 15 years after the initial efforts in compensatory education, there was a growing dissatisfaction with the educational system's efforts to bridge the gap. Some of the previously mentioned studies, which were published during those years, reinforced this sentiment. It was then that the first groups of Israeli-born Middle Eastern youth were reaching young adulthood. Many of these young people were of course more articulate and more sophisticated than their older brothers or fathers, and it goes without saying that such a group would not only be sensitized to its own continued disadvantage but would also put forth demands for a more equitable distribution of resources. These were also the years during which Israelis became familiar with school integration as advocated by educators and social scientists in the United States. The fact that many disadvantaged students attended de facto segregated schools became therefore all the more disturbing. In 1972 a report by Shmueli indicated for instance that only 8% of the Middle Eastern students studied in classes in which the rate of

Middle Eastern students did not exceed 35%, whereas approximately 40% studied in classes with a Middle Eastern population of 95% or more (Shmueli, 1972). (It should be noted that these de facto segregated schools are the function of people's tendency to segregate in their housing patterns, rather than a function of segregated school districting procedures.)

Against the background of these processes and data developed the awareness that the impoverished learning environments that these segregated classes constituted may have a retarding impact on disadvantaged students. It emerged that de facto segregation, rather than promoting or nurturing the Middle Eastern students, only served to exacerbate their disadvantage. This revelation brought about the third and main stage in the educational system's effort to equalize opportunities. (It should be stated clearly that this somewhat artificial division into stages does not imply that they exclude each other. In fact, rather, they coexist and the different strategies are being employed simultaneously.) The major national project of this third stage in which integration is a central element is the School Reform. The theme of the Reform is not only the aforementioned extension of compulsory school attendance (up to age 15), but also the formation of an integrated Junior High School. The principal assumption guiding the policy makers when this reform was instituted was that integration in and of itself will contribute to the formation of a common cultural fabric, to harmonious relationships across ethnic lines, and above all to the improvement of scholastic achievements. Similar assumptions guided a decision to launch in Jerusalem a pilot project of integrating schools at the elementary level. This project was of particular significance for several reasons. The fact that it was launched in the capital city of Jerusalem gave it national prominence. The project also involved a school that enjoyed considerable social prestige. Finally, the student body was composed of pupils who displayed very large differences in social background and academic achievement (See Chapter 7).

It seems worthwhile to add here, that whereas the policy decisions as outlined previously have initiated organized integration, a parallel uninstitutionalized process of integration has been evolving over recent years, and it may be assumed that the two processes reinforce each other. Thus when Minkovich et al. (1977) reported the relevant data for the early 1970s, they indicated a considerably higher degree of desegregation than did Shmueli (1972), whose data applies to the late 1960s. The former found that among second-generation Middle Eastern students only 9% studied in homogeneous classes (95% or more Middle Eastern students), whereas among first-generation Middle Eastern students—25% did so. On the other hand they found that there are hardly any Western students who study in homogeneous Western classes. Perhaps the most interesting finding of this study was that even within the sample under study the increased tendency for desegregation was discernible: Among the first graders in their sample, there was a lower degree of segregation than among the sixth graders. The most plausible interpretation of this finding is that young Middle Eastern parents are more socially mobile than their elders. It would seem that these findings supplement the picture that emerged throughout this chapter: Apparently, the one-third of hard-core disadvantaged students mentioned earlier in our discussion of school failure, poverty, and political nonparticipation is composed of approximately 25% of the first-generation Middle Eastern students, plus approximately 9% of the second-generation Middle Eastern students who study in homogeneous classes. In other words, whereas more than half (probably close to two-thirds) of the Middle Eastern students are being absorbed into the mainstream of education, participating and achieving reasonably well, about one-third of the Middle Eastern students are the hard-core disadvantaged and underresourced.

One as yet unresolved issue of both definition and policy in the realm of integrated education ought to be discussed here. In the American context, the term *integration* clearly refers to the mixing within a school or classroom of children from different ethnic (or social) groups by decree of law. Israel does not have a constitution, the interpretation of which could generate court-imposed integration. Integration, moreover, is expected to occur between the children of groups that are not as overtly separate either ethnically or socially as are the races in the United States. This gives rise to the question "who is to be integrated?" Not only are the differences between the ethnic groups less distinct than they are in the United States, but the general direction has been quite explicitly to blur ethnic differences and definitely not to use ethnicity as a basis of policy. Moreover, in line with the previous analysis, it seems to emerge that the potential impact of ethnicity per se as a handicap to individual mobility has been decreasing. At the same time, in contrast to all other compulsory measures, which may be directed primarily at disadvantaged students, as such, school integration must be seen in the ethnic context.

A few conclusions seem to follow from this state of affairs. Desegregation is the bringing together of people of differing ethnic backgrounds. It is clearly, in Israel as elsewhere, a strategy designed to generate social contact and interaction, sharing experiences and mutual respect. There is no reason to expect that such mixing of students in schools will in itself have a positive impact on the scholastic achievements of young people of disadvantaged origin. If, at the same time, ethnic desegregation is found to be correlated with improved scholastic achievement, this is an important finding. Even though, of course, no causal relationship should be inferred from such a finding, it is of great significance in social planning terms. Unfortunately the opposite seems to be the practice in Israel. Integration *per se* is expected to yield improved scholastic achievements among disadvantaged students. Yet, when integration *does* appear to be correlated with improved scholastic achievement, the policy implications thereof are being attenuated because the contributions of desegregation to pupil achievement is also highly correlated with student socioeconomic status. Thus controlling for SES in the analysis of achievement data underestimates the role of ethnic desegregation.

Limits Upon and Resistance to Integrated Education

In closing let us turn our attention to those sectors in Israeli society that, as we have mentioned, are and will remain reluctant about integrated education, or to which the policy does not apply in any event. Firstly, it should be mentioned that in consequence of the settlement policies (as for example the policy of "population dispersion" mentioned earlier) there are in Israel today a number of areas that are ethnically almost completely homogeneous. Most outstanding would be a certain type of cooperative agricultural settlement (Moshavim) and many of the new Development Towns. These ethnically homogeneous villages and towns have a total population of about half a million—almost entirely of Middle Eastern origin. (This figure does not include segregated neighborhoods in the larger cities, because people living there are not isolated from interethnic contacts.) Given that a massive program of busing is not enacted—a program that might not be technically feasible and that until now has not been the policy—it follows that certain segments of the Middle Eastern population cannot be introduced into integrated learning environments. As these areas are sometimes the most distinctly disadvantaged, the channeling of specific and intensive compensatory programs to them seems to be an important policy.

Another sector in society that has difficulty with integrated education is the religious sector. As was mentioned earlier, Middle Eastern students constitute about 70% of the students in state religious schools, whose student body accounts for about 20% of the total student population. Obviously, there can be no assignment of students to these schools that would produce any meaningful integration. It should be added that it seems that some parents from the Western "minority" within the state religious schools are reluctant to send their children to integrated schools because of apprehension that they be scholastically impaired. One way to overcome this state of affairs would of course be the fusion of the state religious with the regular state schools. Judging from past experience such a development would seem highly unlikely. Because this problem is purely political in nature, it is beyond the scope of this study.

The kibbutz movement is yet another case in point. The kibbutz, in many ways the embodiment of the original pioneer movement, is an integral part of the society's core. Thus, though Kibbutz membership accounts for only 3½% of Israel's total population comprised almost exclusively of Jews of Western background, its reluctance to expose its children to integrated education is of symbolic significance. This reluctance is not due primarily to the ethnic component of integrated education, as much as desegregation would require the busing of kibbutz children to regional schools. Under such circumstances it would become difficult to center the education of the younger generation around the kibbutz movement's goals and ideals. It is thus mainly due to ideological considerations that some segments of the Kibbutz Movement are reluctant to integrate their schools. It should be added that the kibbutzim today have more members of Middle Eastern origin than they had in past years, so that there is an element of ethnic integration even in their own semiautonomous educational system. Some kibbutzim, moreover, tend to facilitate the integration of their children with disadvantaged children of the region by turning their own schools into regional ones, and by other means as well.

Given these demographic, political, and social circumstances, school integration cannot be conceived as an absolutely universal policy for Israel. Whereas these pockets of nonintegration may complicate the dialogue with other groups that are reluctant about integration, they should not be seen as offering a viable alternative to integration. People are not likely to become religious or decide to join kibbutzim merely in order to avoid integrated education.

The education of the Arab minority of Israel and the integration in schools of this minority's students and those of the Jewish majority calls for consideration at this point. Israel's population includes about half a million Arab citizens (not including the West Bank and the Gaza Strip). They comprise about one-seventh of the State's total population, subdivided into an overwhelmingly 76% majority of Moslems, 15% Christians, and 9% Druze. The rate of natural increase among the Arabs of Israel is twice that of the Jews—37 as opposed to 17.6%. Naturally, this feature finds expression in family size: Whereas 57% of the Arab families have six members or more, only 13% of the Jewish families are of a similar size (Statistical Abstracts of Israel, 1976, pp. 19, 43, 687). It follows that about one-half of Israeli Arabs are now below the age of 15, as compared to 30% of the Jews (Statistical Abstracts of Israel, 1976, pp. 44–45, 50, 59–60). It need hardly be mentioned that Israeli laws and regulations pertaining to education apply equally to all parts of the population, irrespective of communal or religious affiliation. Not only does the law not discriminate, the equal treatment of all by the law was indeed a source of friction: In the early years of Israel's statehood, the universal implementation of the law of compulsory education met with considerable opposition within the Arab sector, especially from the rural population (which constituted the majority of Israel's Arab citizenry). The obvious inclusion of females was unacceptable to the local traditional Arab leaders. Educational disadvantage was, however, an issue in the Arab schools, as it was in the Jewish ones. Two main sources of this disadvantage could be traced: Firstly, a large segment of the adult Arab population was not literate and could hardly be supportive of the children's work at school; secondly, the Arab schools were staffed mainly by unqualified teachers, because a major part of the Arab intelligentsia—including almost all qualified teachers—had fled Palestine when Israel proclaimed statehood. In recent years, however, illiteracy is being curbed and most, if not all, of the untrained teachers have been replaced by a new generation of well-trained Arab teachers, many of whom have a sense of mission and are dedicated to their profession. The main institutional educational disadvantage that the Israeli Arabs encounter is at the level of higher education: All the Israeli universities operate in Hebrew, and though the language is taught in the Arab schools and high school students are quite well versed in it, Hebrew remains a foreign language to them. Hence, the policy of educational integration does not embrace the Arab population of Israel. Furthermore, at this point in Israel's history, this state of affairs may be assumed to reflect the interest and desires of both communities. This statement calls for some clarification: The school system that has been developed by the Jewish majority since the beginning of this century is based on the Hebrew language and founded on the essentials of Jewish culture. Indeed, one of the main elements of Israel's cultural success has been the revival of the Hebrew language, which became the prime vehicle for the adaptation of Jewish culture to the life of a modern people. From this point of view, it appears that Israel has a distinct advantage over many of the new nations to have emerged in the second half of this century: Culturally, it represents the perpetuation of an age-old civilization and is thus not engaged in creating a new culture or set of symbols. It is only natural that this evolving culture in general, and the revised language in particular, are central elements in the life and work of the schools. Any inclusion of Arab students in this type of educational experience would be an imposition and could not but be interpreted as such. At the same time, the Arabs of Israel, most of whom wish to remain Israeli citizens, also strive to maintain their religious, cultural, linguistic, ethnic, and mostly political identity. They are a largely Muslim minority within a Jewish majority, speaking the Arabic language, tied to Arab tradition and culture, and alligned—in varying degrees—to the political rivals of Israel. Under these circumstances, integrated education would surely undermine most of these elements of cultural, national identity.

Almost paradoxically, then, a moderate and liberal orientation would lead toward a policy of nonintegration. Those who advocate Arab–Jewish school integration are those that are insensitive to the probability of blurring the cultural identity of the Jews, as well as of Israeli Arabs. It is fair to assume that, as the region moves into an era of peace, association between Arab and Jewish children will increase. Even so, it is doubtful whether the integration of schools will be welcomed by either of the groups. The Jewish majority will still seek to foster a Jewish identity through the school curriculum, and to transmit Jewish civilization, history and culture to the next generation. It is to be assumed that Israeli Arabs will seek to harness their schools to have a comparable effect on Arab children.

It would thus seem that the model of a pluralistic society would apply much more in the case of the relationships of the Jewish majority and the Arab minority in Israel than in the case of the relationships of the different ethnic components within the Jewish majority. In the former case each group is culturally, linguistically, religiously, and politically distinct and may be expected to desire to remain so. In the latter, an a priori existing "umbrella" of a cultural–religious nature (i.e., Judaism) performs a unifying function; a potent ideology of nation building is, moreover, exerting assimilatory pressures on the different ethnic groups within the Jewish majority. It may therefore be assumed that the process of school integration will continue within the Jewish majority, which in turn will, under conditions of peace, be more attuned to the needs of the separate Arab school system.

REFERENCES

Algarebli, M. Indices for the characterization of the social composition of schools and a system for the allocation of budgets to schools with disadvantaged students. *Megamot*, 1975, *21*, 219–227. (Hebrew)

Boudon, R. *Education, opportunity and social inequality.* New York: Wiley, 1974.

Chen, M., Lewy, A., & Adler, C. *Process and outcome in education: Evaluating the contribution of the Middle School to the educational system.* Schools of Education, Tel–Aviv University and The Hebrew University, 1978.

Cohen, E. The dispersion of population and amalgamation of exiles as conflicting goals. In S. Eisenstadt & A. Zlocover (Eds.), *The integration of immigrants from different countries of origin in Israel,* 1969 (Hebrew).

Coleman, J., Campbell, E., Hobson, C., McPartland, J., Mood, A., Weinfeld, F., & York, R. *Equality of educational opportunity.* Washington, D.C.: Office of Education, U. S. Government Printing Office, 1966.

Eisenstadt, S., & Zlocover, A. (Eds.). *The integration of immigrants from different countries of origin in Israel.* Jerusalem: The Magnes Press, 1969. (Hebrew)

Gutman, I. *An experimental investigation of the effects of various grouping methods on the cognitive and psychosocial development of elementary school pupils.* Jerusalem: Szold, 1972. (Hebrew) (a)

Gutman, I. *Long school day.* Jerusalem: Szold Institute, 1972. (Hebrew) (b)

Haviv, J. Poverty in Israel 1964–1974, in view of development in the income maintenance system. *Social Security,* 1975, *8.* (Hebrew)

Herman, S., Farago, U., & Harel, Y. *Continuity and change in the Jewish identity of high school youth in Israel* (1965–1974). Jerusalem: Hebrew University, 1976. (Mimeo) (Hebrew)

Inbar, M., & Adler, C. *Ethnic integration in Israel.* New Brunswick, New York: Transaction Books, 1977.

Israeli, Y. Absorption policy: A principal cause of the ethnic gap. *Afiqim,* 1971, *4.* (Hebrew)

Jencks, C., Smith, M., Acland, H., Bane, M., Cohen, D., Gintis, H., Heyns, N., & Michelson, S. *Inequality: A reassessment of the effect of family and schooling in America.* New York: Basic Books, 1972.

Lewy, A., & Chen, M. Differences in achievement: A comparison over time of ethnic group achievement in the Israeli elementary school. *Evaluation in Education,* 1977, *1,* No. 1.

Lieblich, A., Ninio, A., & Kugelmas, S. Effects of ethnic origin and parental SES on WPPSI performance of school children in Israel. *Journal of Cross Cultural Psychology,* 1972, *3,* 159–168.

Litwin, U. The allocation of resources in education in the light of pupils' achievement in the "seker" examinations. *Megamot,* 1971, *18,* 166–186. (Hebrew)

Minkovich, A., Davis, D., & Bashi, Y. *Evaluation of the educational achievement of the elementary school in Israel.* Jerusalem: The Hebrew University, School of Education, 1977.

Mosteller, F., & Moynihan, D. (Eds.). *On equality of educational opportunity.* New York: Vintage Books, 1972.

Ortar, G. Educational achievements of primary school graduates in Israel as related to their sociocultural background. *Comparative Education,* 1967, *4,* 23–34.

Peres, J. Ethnic relations in Israel. *American Journal of Sociology,* 1971, *76.*

Rotter, R., & Shamai, N. Patterns of poverty in Israel—initial findings. *Social Security,* 1971, *1.* (Hebrew)

Shmueli, E. Problems in the area of social integration in education. *Social Security*, 1972, *3*. (Hebrew)

Shuval, J. Emerging patterns of ethnic strain in Israel. *Social Forces*, 1962, *40(4)*.

Shuval, J. Self-rejection among North African immigrants to Israel. *Israel Annals of Psychiatry and Related Subjects*, 1966, *4*.

Smilansky, M., & Yam, Y. The relationship between family size, ethnic origin, father's education and students' achievement. *Megamot*, 1969, *16*, 248–273. (Hebrew)

Smooha, S. *Israel-pluralism and conflict*. London: Rontledge & Kegan Paul, 1978.

Sowell, T. *Affirmative action reconsidered*. The Public Interest, 1976, *42*, 63–65.

Sowell, T. Are quotas good for blacks? *Commentary*, 1978, *46*.

Statistical Abstract of Israel. Jerusalem: Israel Government Printing Office, 1976, 1977.

3 Communities, Schools, and Integration

Jeff Halper
Moshe Shokeid
Alex Weingrod

In his recent anthropological study of a California school, John Ogbu makes the point that relationships between the school and the community are sporadic and limited in scope. Parent and community involvement in the schools, he writes, normally mean participation in such extracurricular programs as PTA, open house, and social entertainments rather than more vital matters such as "making decisions concerning the school curriculum or new programs" (Ogbu, 1974). This is a common pattern: The extent of community participation or control over the schools may vary, but, in general, parents and other community members are content to leave schooling to the teachers and school administrators (Fein, 1971).

This traditional separation between school and community often breaks down, however, when the schools become actively involved in contemporary social and political issues. Large numbers of parents or other groups may not organize committees or attend meetings when a mathematics or history curriculum is on the agenda, but they are aroused when the topics for decision include drawing school boundary lines or busing pupils. School integration—the deliberate placing of previously separate minority and majority groups within the same school building—is surely the prime recent example of how social and political issues bring the school and its various communities into a more direct relationship. As the literature indicates, community responses to integration programs vary from total opposition to active acceptance and cooperation, with a great many shades in between (Crain, 1968; Gerard & Miller, 1975; Mayer, King, Patterson, Mc-Cullough, 1974). Community opposition has included seeking legal restraints as well as organizing demonstrations—sometimes violent—whereas cooperation may mean minority- and majority-group members coming together in various proschool activities. Whatever the response, however, the normally passive school-community relationship becomes imbued with bursts of great interest and activity.

Most of the literature tracing the response of local communities to school integration concentrates on the experience in the United States during the past quarter century. Social scientists have analyzed the complex processes that accompany integrating previously segregated Black and White schools in both the North and the South. Not surprisingly, these studies have primarily explored the *political problems and processes* arising from school integration. This point is emphasized in a recent study of integrated schools. Rist (1979) states:

> School desegregation is anything but an apolitical event. The very fact that school desegregation is profoundly political is what gives it varying approaches and programs in different communities. The political realities, the necessary compromises, the manner of external intervention by the courts or other agencies of government, and the vested interests of different groups all impinge upon the desegregation effort [p. 11].

The most ambitious study along these lines is Crain and associates' monograph entitled *The Politics of School Desegregation* (1968). Focusing on an entire city rather than a particular district or neighborhood, the authors analyze the complex interplay among civil rights advocates, boards of education, school officials, and local political and business elites in 15 U.S. cities, as they struggle and bargain with one another while seeking to implement (or delay) voluntary or court-ordered school desegregation. The authors conclude, for example, that school boards are more important than school superintendents in developing integration policies, and that the "political style of the city" and its elites is particularly critical (Crain, Inger, McWorter, & Vanecke, 1968, pp. 358–359). This emphasis upon political processes is also apparent in Gerard and Miller's (1975) longitudinal study of the outcomes of Black–White school integration in Riverside, California. Hendrick's chapter on the "Historical Setting" describes a rash of meetings, demonstrations, boycotts, and violent episodes (a school building was deliberately set on fire) that accompanied the onset of desegregation in Riverside (pp. 30–44). However, the Riverside schools were quickly integrated, and the demonstrations and meetings came to an end. Indeed, the Riverside case exemplifies rapid community acceptance and cooperation. Gerard and Miller (1975) state: "School desegregation was simply a hard issue to oppose when it involved such a minimal inconvenience and cost to the majority community [42]." On the other extreme, Collins' (1979) description of integration in Memphis, Tennessee, and Scherer and Slawski's (1979) depiction of integrated schooling in a Northern city review prolonged periods of community crisis and mutual antagonism.

The Israeli experience in school integration shares certain similarities with the United States but also has some fundamental differences. Let us begin with the differences. Although prejudice is sometimes present in relationships between Western and Middle Eastern Jews in Israel (Amir, 1969, 1976; Shuval, 1954; Smooha, 1978), the scope and depth of prejudicial attitudes and behavior is much more limited than that generally reported for Blacks and Whites in the United States. There is no tradition of racism or discrimination in Israel, and legitimization was never granted to differences between Jewish ethnic groups. On the contrary, the powerful Zionist ideology of ''cultural assimilation'' sought to eliminate social and cultural differences between Europeans and Middle Easterners. We would expect, therefore, that the extent of intergroup antagonism or tension accompanying school integration in Israel would be much less than in the United States. This has indeed been the case—there were no instances of rioting or other forms of violence arising from government-sponsored school integration programs.

Moreover, some potential conflicts were diffused by maintaining the school's middle-class Western orientation: Western parents whose children were to be ''integrated'' received assurance by the Ministry of Education that their school's curriculum would not change and that ''standards'' would not be lowered. They would continue to serve as ''cultural models'' for the Middle Easterners, who would be expected to adopt their attitudes and behavior patterns (Halper, 1977; Lewis, 1980; Weingrod, 1965). Indeed, many Middle Eastern students appear to have accepted this situation and seek to behave accordingly (Halper, 1977). Hendrick's previously cited conclusion regarding Riverside, California is therefore also applicable to Israel. As Gerard and Miller (1975) have asserted: ''School desegregation was simply a hard issue to oppose when it involved such a minimal inconvenience and cost to the majority community [p. 42].''

Nevertheless, as with the American experience, school desegregation in Israel did at times provoke community opposition and lengthy political struggles. As described elsewhere in this volume, school integration was based upon the desire to eliminate structural inequalities in occupation and income between the Western and Middle Eastern segments of the population. Not all parents and community members agreed to use their neighborhood schools—or better, their own children's school—as a means to attain this goal, and consequently school integration sometimes led to intergroup political conflicts.

This chapter examines three Israeli cases of school integration in close detail. More specifically, we were interested in comparing the responses to integration in three different social settings: a Middle Eastern Jewish neighborhood in Jerusalem, a Moroccan (Middle Eastern) Jewish cooperative village in the Negev area (southern section of Israel), and a modern orthodox religious neighborhood in Jerusalem.[1] To be sure, these three instances represent only a small fraction of

---

[1]The data presented in this article grew out of three separate anthropological studies carried out by the coauthors, rather than as part of an overall comparative design. Halper's research was in Orot, Shokeid's in Romema, and Weingrod's in Yemin Shlomo. Each of the coauthors studied a variety of topics. However, in the course of the research each explored the local process of school integration and subsequently decided to utilize these separate studies jointly in this chapter.

the by now rich Israeli experience with school integration, and we make no claim that they are "typical" or representative. At the same time, however, these anthropological studies clarify some of the ways in which schools and society become articulated in the specifically Israeli context, and they point as well to trends that are likely to become more significant in the future.

THE NAVON SCHOOL: POLITICAL DISPUTE AND COMMUNITY APATHY IN A NEIGHBORHOOD OF MIDDLE EASTERN JEWS

The Navon school is situated in Orot, an older residential area located close to the center of Jerusalem.[2] The area is divided into several subneighborhoods, and the population is composed mainly of Israeli-born working-class families, whose historic origins are in southern Turkey, Iraqi Kurdistan, and Iran.

Historically, the issue of school integration did not arise in Orot, but rather in Shaarei Shalom, an adjoining neighborhood with a similar population. Shaarei Shalom's school district included a large, prestigious middle-class neighborhood called Gan v'Etz. However, children from these two neighborhoods did not attend the same elementary school but went to separate schools that shared a common playground.

This blatant segregation was obvious and disturbing to some of the Shaarei Shalom residents. Suspecting that their children were receiving inferior education, a number of parents turned to the leader of the neighborhood council that represented both Shaarei Shalom and Orot and demanded that he "do something" to integrate the schools. The local council head, Nissim Mizrachi, was a university graduate and personally dedicated to the "cause" of integration. In addition, as an elected member of the Jerusalem city council he was also in a position to campaign for desegregation within wider political circles. Mizrachi set in motion what proved to be a lengthy, bitter public dispute. Following some concessions to Gan V'Etz parents who opposed integration, the municipality, which had at first remained aloof from the dispute, recommended a plan for gradually mixing the classes.

Following his success in the Shaarei Shalom–Gan V'Etz conflict, Mizrachi decided to bring the school integration issue to the attention of parents in Orot. Surprisingly, he found that the same issue that had provoked the Shaarei Shalom residents into action received little response or attention. The Navon school had, in the past, served several generations of Orot residents; it was an accepted part of the community, arousing neither support nor condemnation. If it was a poor school, it did not differ from the expectations of the Orot residents. There was no superior Ashkenazi school nearby, and the only other comparisons were to

[2]All the names cited in this chapter are fictitious.

neighborhood religious schools whose levels were even lower. Although Mizrachi received passive support from many of the residents, integration or the quality of schooling never caught on as vital local issues.

At first Mizrachi turned to attacking the administration of the Navon school. The principal was a weak figure, but his weakness in responding to Mizrachi's attacks had the effect of blunting their force. On the other hand, the assistant principal was a forceful and energetic person who was respected by the Orot parents. Many of the teachers were also well liked: Navon presented the image of an institution valiantly seeking to cope with a difficult situation. Even though no one sprang to the school's defence, many of the residents were sympathetic to the school's problems and the efforts made to overcome them.

Mizrachi did not seem to be proposing a clear-cut program of school integration. Unlike the Shaarei Shalom–Gan V'Etz schools, there was no nearby Ashkenazi school that could be merged with Navon. Undaunted, Mizrachi suggested a different solution: The Navon school should be closed and the children bused to other, better schools in the city. Continuing his attack on the school administration, he demanded that Navon's principal be fired; this demand was rejected by the Teachers' Union. Mizrachi then publically demanded that the school be closed. At one point he even threatened to burn down the school if it were not closed! With the approach of the Knesset elections in 1973, Mizrachi, who had won a place on his party's list, distributed the following leaflet:

To the Citizens of Orot–Shaarei Shalom!

I came to Israel 37 years ago with my parents, married and have five children, and I share with you suffering and happiness. I know your needs and will struggle for you. We started a neighborhood council, and the struggle for better education was a big success. Our children who studied in backward schools now study together with the children of Gan V'Etz, and get impressive results. We must improve education at Navon, and try to replace it with a good modern school in which our children will study with children of Western origin and people who are well off. We hope that busing will be the answer.

Throughout his campaign against Navon, Mizrachi did not succeed in enlisting more than a handful of residents to support him actively. The issue of poor education at Navon was, however, an embarrassment to officials in the municipality and Ministry of Education. Under pressure from Navon's administration, the Knesset Education Committee appointed a subcommittee to investigate Mizrachi's charges. The committee held a series of hearings and submitted a report.

Their report substantiated Mizrachi's charges of poor education at the Navon school. Most of the blame was placed on Orot's "backward" population. The school administration was mildly criticized for not having developed fuller relationships with parents, and for their ineffectiveness in instructional methods. The local residents, including Mizrachi, were taken to task for their methods of protest, which, the committee charged, had undermined the morale of both pupils and teachers. The Education Committee did not recommend closing the school, as they claimed there was need for a school in the area but instead suggested some general reforms.

Nevertheless, the Navon school was in the process of being gradually phased out. Even though Mizrachi lacked grass-roots support in the neighborhood, he was influential in the Jerusalem municipality and his lobbying there had its effect. No clear decision to close the school was ever announced. Indeed, until the end there was uncertainty regarding the city's intention to maintain the Navon school. However, in 1974, the boundaries of the school district were redrawn and half the Orot neighborhood was combined with Shaarei Shalom and Gan V'Etz. By 1976 the student population at Navon, which had once stood at 1500, was reduced to 200. No new pupils were accepted for the first-grade classes that year, and students in grades two through four were reassigned to other Jerusalem schools. Finally, in 1977, the Navon school was closed entirely.

Just as they had previously accepted the school, so too the Orot residents accepted its closing without much comment or opposition. For many pupils, the educational situation had improved. This was particularly the case for those integrated with the Gan V'Etz school. Other pupils' schooling may in fact have become less effective. Many were bused to schools far from their homes, without any plans for social integration or educational assistance. On the other hand, the political agitation that had accompanied the integration conflict did subside. Mizrachi turned his attention to other issues and the neighborhoods regained their normal quiet. (For additional details, see Halper, 1977.)

FROM CONSENSUS TO CONFLICT OVER SCHOOLING IN A RURAL AREA

Located in the northern Negev, Romema is a moshav, or cooperative village, which was settled in 1956 by Moroccan immigrants from the Atlas Mountain region. Together with 11 other moshavim and a kibbutz, it composes a regional council whose responsibilities include providing education for the village children. There are four elementary schools in the region, all belonging to the national religious elementary system—three for children of the moshavim, and a separate school for the kibbutz youngsters. Together with the children of two other moshavim of North African immigrants, the Romema youngsters attended school at Gador, a nearby moshav of veteran Israelis, about two-thirds of whom were of Western origin. The teachers and administrators at this school were mainly Gador residents.

During their initial decade or so at Romema, the Moroccan settlers did not place special emphasis on questions of schooling or school integration. Their main concern was to succeed economically in agriculture, and they were also deeply involved in internal factional disputes. Throughout this period their children attended the regional school located at Gador. (For additional details of the Romema dispute, see Shokeid, 1980.)

The children of veteran Israeli settlers from Gador did not at first attend the local school but were instead bused to the nearby kibbutz school: In effect, the education of the children of North African immigrants was segregated from that of the children of Western veterans. Although at that time the Romemites did not protest, the national religious school authorities placed considerable pressure on the Gador parents to send their children to the local school, and, bowing to this pressure in 1966, the Gador parents agreed. However, within the school their youngsters were concentrated in a single class, and they also received additional tutoring and extracurricular activities. The arrangement adopted was one in which the Gador school included youngsters from three North African villages and from Gador itself, with the Gador children placed in a single class together with a few selected Moroccan youngsters.

This pattern prevailed for a decade. During this time important changes took place in Romema. The village became one of the most successful in the region; the earlier factional disputes were muted, and the community became increasingly stable and well managed. The village was also strikingly successful in the field of education; in 1976, more than 50% of those between the ages of 17 and 20 had completed 12 years of schooling. Quite a few of them went on to hold important positions in regional economic, organizational, and educational institutions.

It is against this brief historical background that the recent dispute between Gador and Romema regarding integrated education can be properly understood. The dispute focused on the composition of the first-grade classes. At the beginning of the 1976–77 school year, 60 pupils presented themselves for registration at the Gador regional school. Twenty-one were from Gador, and the remaining 40 came from the three North African villages in the school district. According to the agreement that had been reached 10 years earlier, all the Gador youngsters would be enrolled in the same first-grade class, whereas the others would be divided into two classes of 20 students each. In earlier years the Romema parents (as well as those in the two other immigrant villages) had accepted this, although with increasing reluctance as their economic and social status improved. By 1977 they strongly opposed this arrangement and demanded a different form of integration.

The education committee of the four villages held numerous lively meetings before the start of the school year, and two opposing plans were presented. The Gador representatives suggested that their children be divided equally into two first-grade classes, with each class having the same number of children "of good intellectual potential" from the neighboring villages. A third class would then be composed of children with a "lower intellectual level" from the other villages.

The representatives of the North African villages presented their counterproposal: Each of the three first-grade classes would have an equal number of children from each village. At the end of the school year, all the first-graders would be tested and then assigned to a second-year class.

The two sides were unable to arrive at a compromise or agree on an alternative plan. Feelings ran so high that the parents from the North African villages boycotted the school, thereby preventing the opening of the school year. The four education committees were summoned to the Ministry of Education in Jerusalem, where it was unanimously agreed that the Ministry would appoint a committee to investigate the entire matter.

Within a few days the committee met and announced its conclusions. It recommended that two equally advanced first-grade classes be established, that a third smaller class of less well-prepared first graders be set up, and that a special class also be formed for six "underdeveloped children." The committee also suggested that additional teachers be assigned, and that new educational equipment be made available for the less well-prepared students. According to this proposal, the student population of the two weaker classes would be composed entirely of North African children.

The committee's recommendations were deeply resented by the Romemites and the other North Africans. They accused the committee members of prejudice, because their conclusions were based solely on information supplied by the Gador school officials. Nevertheless, the report was finally accepted, the parents' boycott of the school was called off, and the school year began.

It is important to understand the range of attitudes expressed by the Romema parents. The older parents, particularly those who had come to Israel with young children, took a passive stance, accepting the decisions of the education committee and acting accordingly. In contrast, the younger parents, mainly persons in their 30s who had been at least partially educated in Israel, were extremely active in the dispute. The majority of these younger parents tended to favor a compromise with the Gador settlers. They acknowledged the efforts and resources invested by the people of Gador, both individually and collectively, in the education of their children. They also recognized that the environment in some Romema households was indeed such that their children were poorly prepared for school; these families were accused of slowing Romema's development. Aware of the deficiencies in their own education, these younger settlers were anxious to implement some changes, but not at the price of splitting the school. They believed that educational integration would compensate their children for the deficiencies in their own environment and provide them with equal opportunities. They often sought to calm the situation, and in meetings with Gador representatives they tried to dismiss the accusations of ethnic discrimination made by other Moroccans.

A third category was composed of men in their mid-20s who already held senior managerial positions. Most of them had completed high school in Israel, and a few had continued on to institutions of higher learning. Although their children were not yet of school age, they bitterly resented integration on Gador's terms and insisted on nothing less than complete integration. Indeed, they considered segregation preferable to a compromise that would imply that Romema students were socially or intellectually inferior. Well-acquainted with the values and techniques of higher education, and themselves "living proof" that Moroccans with their background could reach high office, they repeatedly accused the Gador committee and the ministry officials of being prejudiced and discriminatory. To be sure, the fact that their own children were not yet of school age may have served to make their attitude more extreme, but there is little doubt of the depth of their feelings.

Although the radical position in Romema advocated closing the school, radical opinion in Gador called for sending their youngsters back to the kibbutz school (even though they knew that in the kibbutz school their children would not enjoy the same high status as in the local school). Nevertheless, there were also those in Gador who had moral doubts about the village committee's refusal to have their children spread throughout the first-grade classes and asked themselves whether they had done enough to integrate their North African neighbors "into Israeli culture." In effect, the more extreme position held at Romema, plus the practical considerations of the Gador settlers, placed pressure upon the latter to agree to a compromise. In the following year both sides reluctantly agreed to assign all first graders to an appropriate class according to entrance tests. This agreement also involved some changes in the school administration, particularly the transfer of the principal who had been accused of siding with Gador. The compromise agreement has been followed by both sides.

IDEOLOGY AND INTEGRATION IN RELIGIOUS SCHOOLING IN JERUSALEM

The events surrounding the formation of the Neot school in Jerusalem's Yemin Shlomo district represents a classic instance of how parents become involved in school integration. The background to the Neot case can briefly be summarized as follows.

During the mid-1960s a small group of friends began discussing the formation of a new type of religious school. They were all young religious parents facing the problem of enrolling their children in school. Nearly all the men were associated with the Yeshiva Harav Kook, a religious seminary that combined religious training with Zionist ideology. Western and middle class in background, Israeli born and well-educated, these parents were themselves graduates of the state religious school system. They had, in fact, been among the first graduates of a special elite religious high school program. However, they did not feel that their experience in the religious school system had been entirely satisfactory; they were critical in particular of primary schools, because they considered them to be inadequate in religious terms. One alternative might have been the schools organized by the ultrareligious Agudath Yisrael; but the parents rejected this option, because the Agudath schools emphasize neither Zionist nor national ideals.

Following lengthy discussions these parents decided to create an entirely new school, called the Neot school. Their objective was to design a school that would provide a deep religious education coupled with secondary emphasis upon secular topics such as history or mathematics. In contrast with the state religious schools, which merely taught religious topics academically, Neot was to bring the "spirit of the Bible" and sense of religious community to everyday life. Not only would the religious curriculum be advanced and sophisticated, but the teaching staff would be deeply committed to religious practice and hence provide a constant model for students. In addition, Neot was to develop a positive identification with the Jewish people and a commitment to Zionist ideals. Finally, registration would be selective: Only students from properly devout homes would be accepted, creating a true community among students, parents, and teachers.

Energetic, imaginative, and idealistic, the tiny band of Neot supporters set out to create their own school. Neot was at first a private school, outside the framework of the national state-supported school systems. It is important to emphasize that in the early stages (between 1966 and 1970) the issue of school integration did not figure prominently in the minds of the school's supporters or their opponents. It was only later that integration became the focus of a bitter, prolonged controversy.

The Neot school drew its support primarily from the small *yeshiva* community located in Yemin Shlomo. A few religious families from other neighborhoods who shared the school's outlook also enrolled their children there. As the number of students increased, however, opposition to the school also mounted. Some of the religious residents of Yemin Shlomo whose children were enrolled in the neighborhood state religious school, the Maimon school, were strongly opposed to Neot. These parents disapproved of the strong religious emphasis (they favored a mixed religious–secular curriculum) and were also concerned about the selective, elite stance that Neot had adopted. Moreover, the Jerusalem Education Department and the Ministry of Education also opposed the school: They saw the formation of a private religious school as a precedent that might split the entire state religious educational system. The ensuing struggle to determine the new school's legitimacy continued for 10 years.

This is not the place to document or analyze the dispute itself (described in detail by Weingrod, 1981). The Neot parents and their supporters campaigned tirelessly and effectively in favor of the new school. Indeed, following a lengthy controversy they succeeded in having their school included on the list of state-approved schools. As a result, the school received substantial state financial support, although its curriculum was not supervised by the Ministry officials.

Neot continued to grow in size—and the issue of school integration then became more intense. The reasons for this are readily apparent. The Neot school mainly attracted students from middle-income Western families; it was among this population that the school's ideology and high-quality education had its greatest appeal. Moreover, the selective criteria employed by the school appeared to rule out children of Middle Eastern origin: Prospective students were screened for their religious orthodoxy, and Middle Eastern families were thought to be less rigorous in their religious practices and consequently unsuitable as candidates. This had an immediate effect upon the local Yemin Shlomo state religious school: Its Western registration declined, and the school enrolled Middle Eastern youngsters from adjoining neighborhoods to take their place. The Maimon school therefore became more integrated, whereas the Neot school was increasingly segregated.

It soon became clear, however, that the repercussions were far wider. As an "approved state school," Neot could legally enroll students from any neighborhood in Jerusalem. As a result, Ashkenazi youngsters from schools throughout the city began streaming there. In most instances these youngsters had been enrolled in neighborhood state religious schools that had a mixed or majority Middle Eastern population. This was, indeed, the crux of the controversy: Neot was accused of causing segregation in religious education throughout the entire city of Jerusalem.

Neot's opponents joined forces to fight the school's continued growth. A committee representing eight state religious schools, as well as some influential political figures, was organized to pressure the city and state authorities and to mobilize public opinion around the banner of integration in state religious schools. At one point this group went on strike to protest Neot's selective policies. The municipal and national school authorities also joined the battle. For example, the municipal officials refused to provide Neot with larger school facilities; they accused the school of not having an adequate proportion of "underprivileged" Middle Eastern students and rejected various compromise proposals put forward by the Neot leadership.

Certain of the justice of their cause and heartened by the constant flow of new students, the Neot supporters fought back vigorously and effectively. When the authorities were slow to provide classrooms, they staged a demonstration at the Jerusalem ministry offices and "taught" in front of the television cameras; the school's lawyers kept up a lengthy correspondence with the ministries protesting the treatment they received. Sensitive to the charges of segregation, the Neot leaders claimed that they were in fact enrolling substantial numbers of underprivileged Middle Eastern youngsters. The Neot leadership even proposed a plan according to which they would, in effect, take control over several religious prekindergarten classes in predominantly Middle Eastern neighborhoods and then recruit students from this pretrained population. (The residents of these neighborhoods rejected the plan.) In this way and other ways, they sought to deal with the accusations of discrimination. However, in softer voices and behind closed doors, the school leaders expressed the view that there were "values more important than school integration"—religious values in particular—and that parents should have the right to select their children's schooling.

In the end, Neot triumphed. One of the first acts of a new (religious) Minister of Education was the allocation of funds to provide adequate space for expansion of the school. In 1978, the Neot school enrolled close to 800 students from throughout Jerusalem. Many of the religious residents in Yemin Shlomo continued to support the school, and the local state religious school adapted itself to Neot's presence. Neot had succeeded in becoming an important force in religious education in Jerusalem, and for that matter, influential throughout the whole of Israel.

DISCUSSION AND CONCLUSIONS

Although we are mindful of the problems of generalizing from a small number of cases, several trends do emerge from our analysis of the data. We suggest six closely connected conclusions regarding school integration and community in the Israeli context.

1. From the Perspective of the Community, School Integration is a Political Process Involving Local- and National-Level Agencies and Officials.   In the earlier portions of this chapter, we noted the emphasis on politics in U.S. studies of the community and desegregation. Our Israeli data point in the same direction, involving political activism in each of the sample cases: At Navon the key political leader led the fight for school integration; in the Gador case the different villages mobilized as political pressure groups; and in the Neot example both sides made skillful use of various political tactics. In Israel as in the United States, opposed viewpoints, ideologies, and interests regarding school integration provoked lengthy political struggles.

There are, however, some important contrasts: In the United States these disputes tend to remain at city or local school-district level, whereas in Israel they rapidly escalate to include state agencies and national-level political organizations. For example, in Crain's study (Crain, Inger, McWorter, & Vanecko, 1968) of school integration in the United States, little attention is given to state or national-level state agencies; the key decision makers are local school-board members or important figures in the business elite. The courts at various levels are, it is true, involved in desegregation, but the issues tend to remain localized. This is in keeping with both the large scale and the power structure of U.S. society, as well as with ideological emphasis given to relatively autonomous school boards.

The Israeli pattern is, naturally, much different. Not only is the scale smaller and more compact, but state agencies and national-level political parties have considerable influence on local events (Eisenstadt, 1966). This is well exemplified in our case material. In the Navon example the Knesset Education Committee became directly involved in the dispute over local schooling, and at both Gador and Neot the Ministry of Education as well as national political party leaders took active roles in specific school-integration issues. In effect, in Israel there seems to be less distance between neighborhood and national levels.

How does this effect the Israeli school-integration process? State agencies such as the Ministry of Education are unequivocally in favor of school integration. The national political parties have also supported integration programs. Not only do these groups control crucial resources, but they are also able to generate public opinion in favor of school integration. Consequently, opponents of integration at the local level are immediately placed in a political confrontation with state-level officials, and conversely, the proponents of integration are able to enlist the active support of the government ministries and other allied agencies. This does not mean that what are essentially segregated schools cannot be established or sustained (the Neot school is a case in point). But these are probably unusual cases: The clear government prointegration policy, as well as the broad public consensus in favor of social and cultural assimilation, strongly favors the school-integration process.

2. The "Recipient" and "Applicant" Groups Differ Widely in their Success in Making Use of Political and Other Resources.   Generally speaking, those already receiving better education, the ''recipient groups,'' are of Western origin, whereas those seeking better education (or for whom such is sought), the ''applicant groups,'' are Middle Eastern in origin. Discussions of school integration often assume that there are major similarities within these categories. For example, the previously mentioned study by Crain and his associates suggests a certain uniformity among Blacks and Whites in the U.S. desegregation struggles (1968). However, the case material presented in this chapter shows that groups within the same category vary greatly in their access to political resources and the ways in which they employ them in particular political situations. For example, the Western parents at Neot succeeded in their battle against integration, whereas their peers at Gador failed. This is probably explained by the close ties between the Neot leadership and important national political leaders. Similarly, the Moroccan farmers at Romema successfully manipulated the religious political party as well as various national-level agencies in their battle for integration, and in this regard they resemble the Neot parents. We conclude that in conflicts over school integration both the applicant and the recipient groups are potentially able to mobilize significant support, and that the outcomes depend on particular combinations of motivation, leadership, and political skill.

3. In Certain Circumstances Applicant Groups Consider School Integration Irrelevant to Their Needs and Aspirations.   Our case material indicates that some insular urban communities are not much concerned with school integration. This is best exemplified in the case of Orot. Middle Eastern parents and community members in that neighborhood were indifferent to school integration even after having been harangued by their own political leaders and told that their children were receiving an inferior education. Within Orot, where ethnic and neighborhood social ties are powerful, feelings of relative deprivation were blunted by the self-contained nature of the neighborhood. This contrasts sharply with Shaarei Shalom, where equally strong local and ethnic ties were mixed with the realization that the children were attending an obviously segregated school.

How can this be explained? Orot's "insular character" is closely connected with its socioeconomic position: Many of its residents are occupationally linked with a series of local resources including taxi and truck driving, retailing in a large nearby open market, construction work, and the like. Entrance into these occupations is dependent on personal and family ties rather than formal educational certification. There was, therefore, no powerful incentive to insist upon school integration, and the residents themselves were not aware of the long-term importance of continuing education. For these reasons, school integration did not become a salient issue for them, and the residents rather passively accepted the proposals put forward by government education officials.[3]

4. Whereas There is General Ideological Support for School Integration, Particular Plans or Programs May Provoke Community Tension and Conflict. Our data show that an ideological commitment to integration need not prevent opposition to specific integration programs. The dispute at Gador illustrates this point: Many of the Romema students had achieved educational success before the issue of desegregation was even raised. Moreover, the Romema parents demonstrated a willingness to compromise throughout the lengthy negotiations. They also accepted the "concern for education" expressed by the Western Gador parents. Although accepting the ideology of school integration in principal, the Gador parents opposed the plan that would have distributed their children in classes with the Moroccan youngsters. In fact, they finally accepted a compromise, but the negotiations lasted more than a decade.

In this regard it is important to take note of the "educational quality" issue: In all our cases, those who opposed specific integration programs claimed that mixing the school populations would inevitably lower the quality of their children's education. Whether or not integration is detrimental to the achievements of the recipient group, the terms in which the issue is often debated are likely to provoke anxiety among Western parents. For example, the frequently discussed schooling problems of Middle Eastern children, or their designation as "culturally disadvantaged," convinces many middle-class people from Western origin

---

[3]The much stronger response of the Shaarei Shalom residents is probably explained by their close physical proximity to a middle-class Western neighborhood.

that there is little to be gained—and perhaps much to be lost—by integrating the schools. Leaving aside the merits of such concepts, a strategy that emphasizes the cultural differences and educational problems of one group of pupils is unlikely to allay the fears of others.

5. *Anti-integration Sentiments May also Receive Ideological Support.*   Not only have some communities opposed specific school integration plans, under certain circumstances this has also been provided with an ideological justification. This is demonstrated most clearly in the Neot case, where the emphasis given to "high religious standards" served to exclude many Middle Eastern pupils and, in effect, created school segregation. The mirror image of this position is represented in the Gador example. It is recalled that the younger, more successful Moroccan parents favored creating their own segregated school if their proposal for total classroom integration was rejected. In this case the ideological basis seems to have been that incomplete school integration would have a negative educational and psychological result, and that a high-level segregated school would therefore be preferable.

Although two cases do not necessarily signal a trend, ideological opposition to school integration may well become more insistent in the future. Discontent with the pace or results of desegregation may lead some groups to oppose continued school integration. Moreover, tensions between ethnic groups may also produce prosegregation ideologies. The process of school integration in Israel is far from complete, and any weakening of the ideological consensus will threaten the considerable progress that has already been made.

6. *Upwardly Mobile Middle Easterners Are Likely to Insist upon Total School Integration.*   Our data indicate that it is among this segment of the population that the demand for desegregation is especially powerful. This is best illustrated in the Gador case, where the younger, better educated Moroccans were unwilling to compromise on the integration issue. These young men and women were themselves successful graduates of the Israeli educational system, and they were affronted by the accepted pattern of segregation within the Gador school. This active concern regarding education signals a new situation, in which Middle Eastern parents will not be content with anything less than high-quality education for their children.

This is likely to be an important trend during the next decade; that is, closed urban enclaves such as Orot are becoming unusual as increasing numbers of Israeli-born Middle Easterners become absorbed within the broad Israeli middle class (Matras, 1981). Insofar as this also results in residential desegregation—and there is some evidence that this is the case—in the future many schools will become desegregated by virtue of their neighborhood population composition (Gonen, 1981). This is by no means an "automatic process," however, and it clearly depends on national and international economic, political, and social processes. Indeed, the process of upward mobility may itself sharpen tensions, as new demands and expectations are expressed by the mobile groups. The likelihood is, therefore, that school integration will continue to be an important social and political issue in the years ahead.

REFERENCES

Amir, Y. The contact hypothesis in ethnic relations. *Psychological Bulletin,* 1969, *71,* 319–342.
Amir, Y. The role of intergroup contact in change of prejudice and ethnic relations. In P. Katz (Ed.), *Toward the elimination of racism.* New York: Pergamon Press, 1976.
Collins, T. W. From courtrooms to classrooms: Managing school desegregation in a deep South high school. In R. C. Rist (Ed.), *Desegregated schools.* New York: Academic Press, 1979.
Crain, R. L., Inger, M., McWorter, G. A., & Vanecko, J. J. *The politics of school desegregation.* Chicago: Aldine, 1968.
Eisenstadt, S. N. *Israeli society.* New York: Basic Books, 1966.
Fein, L. *The ecology of the public schools.* New York: Pegasus, 1971.
Gerard, H. B., & Miller, N. *School desegregation.* New York: Plenum Press, 1975.
Gonen, A. *Some social geographic features of urban ethnic residential dispersion,* 1981. (Mimeo)
Halper, J. *Ethnicity and education: The schooling of Afro–Asian Jewish children in a Jerusalem locality.* Milwaukee: University of Wisconsin, Ph.D. thesis, 1977.
Lewis, A. *Power, poverty and education.* Ramat Gan: Turtledove, 1980.
Matras, J. *Intergenerational social mobility among different ethnic groups.* 1981. (Mimeo)
Mayer, R., King, C., Patterson, A., McCullough, J. *The impact of school desegregation in a southern city.* Lexington, Mass.: Heath, 1974.
Ogbu, J. *The next generation: An ethnography of education in an urban neighborhood.* New York: Academic Press, 1974.
Rist, R. C. *Desegregated schools.* New York: Academic Press, 1979.
Scherer, J., & Slawski, E. Color, class and social control in an urban desegregated school. In R. C. Rist (Ed.), *Desegregated schools.* New York: Academic Press, 1979.
Shokeid, M. An anthropological perspective on the crisis in education in a regional school. *Megamot,* 1980, *26,* 10–21. (Hebrew)
Shuval, J. Cultural assimilation and tension in Israel. *International Social Science Bulletin,* 1954, *8,* No. 1.
Smooha, S. *Israel: Pluralism and change.* Berkeley: University of California Press, 1978.
Weingrod, A. *Israel: Group relations in a new society.* New York: Praeger, 1965.
Weingrod, A. Rashomon in Jerusalem: Ideology and power in an urban dispute. *European Journal of Sociology,* 1981, *22,* 158–169.

4 Integration in Education: The Development of a Policy

Nachum Blass
Benyamin Amir

INTRODUCTION

This chapter examines the history of Israel's official, government-level treatment of the problem of ethnic integration in the nation's school system. The preparation of this chapter was guided by a historical–theoretical–analytical approach. In choosing our sources, we relied on our intimate knowledge of the educational system, and on our appraisal—in light of this knowledge—of the potentially significant sources reflecting the evolution of integration policy in Israel. We did not utilize quantitative methods of content analysis to determine the relative importance of the different objectives and attitudes that comprise this policy (although we did make use, inter alia, of statistical data in order to support various hypotheses). It is doubtful whether quantitative methods exist that can reliably calculate the relative importance of the various opinions within the system or overcome the problem of the intentional and unintentional bias of written sources. Moreover, there are situations of changing conditions in which nondecision or the absence of discussion (or available sources on such discussion) can also serve as an indication of a change in policy (or of loyalty to a previous policy, depending on the overall context). Nevertheless, in our estimation, the best, though not the only, way to study changes in policy orientation is by tracing and analyzing the available sources reflecting changes in behavior and decision making (whether published or internal and unpublished).

Accordingly, we reviewed the following sources: the Knesset Records, basic policy outlines of the different Israeli governments, government yearbooks, minutes of meetings of the executive forums of the Ministry of Education and other central forums of discussion, documents of the Ministry of Education on specific topics, circulars issued by the Director General of the Ministry, publications of the Central Bureau of Statistics, scientific publications on relevant topics, and newspaper clippings. We tried to review these sources in full, in order to avoid the need to devise a reliable sampling method for the qualitative content analysis we used. The quotations cited in support of various arguments were based on our own evaluation of the extent to which they expressed the main approaches and orientations, both in thought and in action, of the policy makers and of other elements that dealt with the subject of integration during the years studied.

Before we begin the discussion itself, we should clarify the use of the term *integration in schools* as used in this chapter. Simply put, according to Kleinberger (1973), integration in schools is the: "mingling and meeting of students of different social classes or different ethnic groups within a common academic framework—heterogenous schools and homeroom classes [p. 13]." This definition in fact describes only one aspect of the subject—the organizational-structural aspect of the encounter between different groups. This definition does not deal with other questions and analyses inherent in the concept. For example, two distinctions that could be made are:

1. What are the "different groups" involved in the integration process? There are several alternatives: ethnic groups (by country of origin of the student or his parents); socioeconomic groups (by economic level, professional occupation, parents' education, social status); and groups based on academic ability and achievement. We are well aware that these three basic alternatives were at various times infused with other shades of meaning, such as immigrant versus veteran Israelis, form of settlement (e.g., kibbutzim versus moshavim)[1] and geographical area (e.g., north versus south Tel–Aviv). We are also aware of the overlapping and the interrelationships among these three types of classification. We nevertheless chose the three criteria of ethnicity, SES and academic achievement for defining our groups because of their implications for educational policy.

We focus primarily on the ethnic aspect, which—in Israel at least—has always been among the most divisive factors in many social issues. Even recently, despite the growing percentage of Middle Eastern Jews in the Israeli middle class, the lower social stratum is still to a large extent composed of people of Middle Eastern origin.

2. Integration in the schools: means or end? Those that claim that integration is an end in itself view its attainment as an expression of the values of social equality and national unity. In order to realize these values, if only partially, they

---

[1]Kibbutzim and moshavim are two original and exclusive Israeli forms of (mainly) agricultural settlements based on collective production and consumption. The main difference between the two is the degree of collectivism (greater in the kibbutzim). Today there is also a marked difference in the socioeconomic structure of these two types of settlement, whereas the greater part of the Moshavim is populated by newcomers from Asia–Africa.

are willing to pay a certain price, should this prove necessary (whether on the emotional or cognitive plane with regard to the students, or on the economic or political plane for society at large). On the other hand, there are those who present the importance of integration in the schools primarily as a means for achieving a variety of goals, whether on the academic or psychological level, or for the future good of society. The proponents of this view examine integration in terms of gain and loss, and according to criteria of functional effectiveness. In other words, if it becomes apparent that under certain conditions integration does not achieve the expected gain, or that the other alternatives are more effective, they will not hesitate to propose the use of other methods in defacto segregated situations. Of course, this problem cannot be approached by such a dichotomous analysis. Because of the complexity of the problem and its social sensitivity, an integrated view has been developed which sees integration as both a means and an end. This integrated view has had certain implications on the course of action followed within the educational system.[2]

The present article is divided into two parts. In the first section, we shall present the development and changes which occurred in the Ministry of Education's policy with regard to integration in Israeli schools from a chronological-theoretical point of view. We shall indicate the three stages of this evolution—stages which represent fundamental shifts over the three decades since the establishment of the State of Israel in 1948. In the second section, we shall propose several hypotheses explaining how and why these changes occurred.

SECTION I: THE THREE STAGES OF POLICY DEVELOPMENT

A schematic description of the evolution of educational policy in Israel with regard to social integration reveals three major stages:

1. The "preliminary stage"—the period that predated the public awareness of the problem of integration.

---

[2]Viewing integration as a means leads to the development of tools which facilitate its effective use (curricula, teaching aids, pedagogical methods, etc.) and to the planning of activities in segregated populations, for whom integration is either ineffective or impossible (various programs for advancing disadvantaged students). At the same time, viewing integration as an aim leads, on the one hand, to the creation of basic integrated frameworks by organizational means (school districts, bussing, heterogenous homeroom classes) and, on the other hand, to the existence of segregated groups within larger integrated frameworks (grouping, slow classes, progressive classes etc.). The integrated approach apparently guided the public committee for examining the reform in the Israeli school system in 1979, as well as its recommendations (Israel Ministry of Education and Culture, 1979).

2. The "formative stage"—the period of the public committees.
3. The "stage of consolidation"—the development of the idea of integration as an essential and central element of educational policy.

In this section, we review the development of each of these stages and the transition from one stage to the next. We briefly describe the first two stages and dwell at length on the various factors in the development of the third stage.

"The Preliminary Stage" (1948–1962)

During the first 15 years of the state, the issue of integration in the schools did not occupy an important place in official policy. In fact it was virtually ignored by the educational system.

Only in the early 1960s is there some recognition of the problem of integration in the schools, together with an awareness that the social problems imposed upon the state by its ethnic composition could not be evaded. It is indicative that the first reference by the Central Bureau of Statistics to the ethnic factor in education was in a 1963 publication. This publication cites the breakdown of the school population by the students' country of origin from 1956. Data on fathers' place of birth are available only from 1962. Prior to this we find reference to problems of new immigrants versus veteran Israelis, but not by ethnic distribution. Only from 1964 on are there data on class composition by ethnic group. However, there was no consensus about the role of the school system in coping with this problem. The primary expression of this new awareness in the policy of the Ministry of Education was in the shift from the stage of "formal equality" to that of "fostering" (Smilansky, 1971, p. 125), reflected in the focus on bridging academic gaps and in concentrating activity within the disadvantaged groups.

"The Formative Stage" (1963–1968)

Such comprehensive and generic concepts as that of integration, with their far-reaching social and political implications, do not appear suddenly. As a rule, in tracing their emergence, early signs are found to exist even before people have fully realized that such ideas have taken root in society. This is also true of integration in the schools: The salient and tangible expressions of the concept of integration in official educational policy first appeared only in the late 1960s and developed gradually (first in the Educational Reform Program[3]), then in the

---

[3]The Educational Reform Program consists of a major overhaul of the administrative and pedagogic structure of the Israeli educational system. Its main element was the alteration of the former 8 + 4 system into 6 + 3 + 3 one, thereby creating a new administrative and pedagogic unit—the Junior High School.

From our point of view, the main element was that the new JHS purposefully drew pupils from different *socioeconomic status* composition by altering educational zones.

implementation of the Reform in the junior high schools, and finally in the extension of integration to other levels of education); but, in fact, signs of this new trend could already be distinguished in the early 1960s (Rimalt, 1971, pp. 41–43, 67; Protocol of meeting of the executive forum of the Ministry of Education, January 18, 1965).

The primary characteristics of the second stage are as follows:

1. In this period, the efforts of the Ministry of Education and Culture focused primarily on broadening and deepening the enrichment programs for the disadvantaged students. Concurrently, we witnessed the development of such programs as the extended school day and academic tracking, the preparation of special textbooks for disadvantaged students, and the expansion of the boarding-school program for gifted students. Whereas the early period was still marked by great momentum, the initial optimism began to give way to gnawing doubts and dissatisfaction with regard to the rate of progress of academic achievement and with the achievements themselves (Adiel, 1970, p. 25).

2. Whereas the political efforts of the Ministry were directed toward preparing the groundwork for implementing the Education Reform Program, the Ministry also began to formulate its views on integration. Gradually, the question of the ethnic composition of classes in the schools began to be raised. The idea of comprehensive schools, which was implemented in development areas, was one of the breakthroughs in integration. Although the comprehensive schools were located primarily in demographically homogenous areas (where the majority of the population was Asian–African in origin), the regional principle, as opposed to the neighborhood principle, meant that the possibilities for the integration of different ethnic groups and classes could begin to be foreseen. Nevertheless, when the parliamentary commission for examining Israel's educational structure began its work, integration was *not* the central issue. The main focus remained the improvement of the academic level of disadvantaged students and the narrowing of the educational gap among pupils of different social classes.

3. The concept of integration in educational policy received a further thrust in the course of the work of the Rimalt Committee[4] For a variety of reasons, this became one of the central issues in the commission's conclusions. The decision to reform the structure of the school system, as endorsed by such a large majority in the Knesset, may well have been prompted by the same process by which the idea of integration became a central national objective and an educational and social operative goal. The link thus created between the concept of integration and the Educational Reform Program had a mutually reinforcing effect: As already noted, the political–social arguments (in addition to and in support of the educational argument) strengthened the hand of those who advocated the reform

---

[4]A special parliamentary committee, headed by E. Rimalt, was appointed to investigate the problems of the structure of the Israeli school system (1966–1968). Its recommendations were the basis for the entire Educational Reform Plan.

TABLE 4.1
The Development of the Perception of Integration as a Means and
an End from Social and Educational Perspectives (1963–1968)

	1963	*1966*	*1968*
Social integration	General, "visionary", nonoperative idea	primary organizational expression (zoning, interethnic contact) and pragmatic approach: means for narrowing educational gaps	central end in itself in addition to a means for narrowing educational gaps
Narrowing educational gaps	The central goal of the educational system		

program; but, at the same time, the reform program elevated the issue of integration from the level of intra-Ministry discussions to the top of the public agenda, as well as according it a more prominent place on the Ministry's scale of priorities. Moreover, it is reasonable to assume that the call for integration in the elementary schools as well, and the beginning of its realization, are to a great extent attributable to the public discussion on reforming the structure of the school system and to the decision on the adoption and implementation of the reform program. This influence on integration within the school system continued to be evident in subsequent years. The identification between reform and integration was to reemerge in various discussions, giving rise to different reactions, both on the public level and within the school system.

4. This relatively short 6-year period marked the first turning point in the importance accorded to integration in educational policy. The evolution of the relationship between the concepts of "integration" and "narrowing educational gaps," and between integration as a means and an end, can be presented schematically, as follows in Table 4.1.

At first, the principle of integration was unrelated in practice to the programs of educational policy; rather it was confined to a general expression of the unity of the Jewish people and the integration of Jews from the breadth of the Diaspora, a goal that should be achieved as a matter of course and as a result of ongoing educational or social actions. The central goal was to narrow the educational gaps and to advance the disadvantaged groups.

At the middle of this period, in 1966, integration already played a part in the educational programs, with emphasis on the organizational aspect (regional schools that brought together children from an entire region in a single school), integration being viewed pragmatically as a means to facilitate the narrowing of academic gaps, and the advancement of the disadvantaged groups.

At the end of the period, in 1968, the social-ideological aspect of integration was given more explicit expression. There was a growing awareness that integration should be viewed as a national-social goal in itself, as well as a promising means—as expressed in the hopes of the Ministry of Education—of narrowing the educational gaps and improving the lot of the disadvantaged.

"The Stage of Consolidation" (1970s)

The recognition by Israeli educational leaders of the importance of integration as a guiding principle in official educational policy, which had already emerged in the second stage, was consolidated during the third stage, which lasted from 1969 until the end of the 1970s.

From the beginning of this period, the Ministry of Education began intensive action for the implementation of the reform program, including integration. Immediately after the Knesset's approval of the Reform Program, the "Committee for the Implementation of the Reform" was established, functioning officially until the end of 1970. The final report of the Committee revealed the growing centrality of the concept of integration in the policy of the Ministry of Education; whereas in the recommendations of the Rimalt Committee, the goal of integration was only one—and the last, at that—of three goals (being expressed in technical terms as "the bringing together of children within the framework of regional schools"). The Committee on the implementation of the Reform (Israel Ministry of Education and Culture, 1971) stated *two* central goals, of which integration was one and was formulated explicitly and unequivocally: "the acceleration of the process of social integration among the different ethnic groups and classes [pp. 17, 19]." Moreover, the Committee did not confine itself to a "statement of intent" but formulated operative directions for the implementation of this goal.

Indeed, in a later discussion the director general stated: "On the principles of integration and on integration itself, there is no debate; there are directives approved by the Knesset and we are acting accordingly."[5]

In other words, from as early as 1971, or at the least 1973, there was, at least officially, an unreserved acceptance of the principle of integration and a willingness to implement it within the educational system. But, in reality, the realization of desegregation as a social objective was accompanied by doubts, indecision, and difficulties, as is to be expected in such a fundamental change. We illustrate this in three ways: by a description of the legislative process, of the background and development of the "Nahlaot project," and by a review of the various discussions held within the Ministry of Education on desegregation.

---

[5]Protocol of the meeting of the executive forum of the Ministry of Education, May 30, 1973.

Legislation. One of the main instruments that the government posseses for carrying out any policy is legislation. An area in which legislation could be used directly to implement integration was in the determination of school districts. The recommendations of the parliamentary Committee for examining the educational structure, presented to the Knesset on May 27, 1968, and approved by it on July 29, 1968, stated (Rimalt, 1971): "A reexamination of elementary school districts in the cities and towns, and in the areas under the jurisdiction of the regional councils is desirable, in order that children of different ethnic and social strata should meet in elementary school education at as early an age as possible [p. 237]."

In their comments on the recommendations, the Committee said of the school districts (Rimalt, 1971):

> The regional junior high schools will serve as a meeting place for Israeli children of all classes and ethnic groups. The elementary school is usually a neighborhood school; that is to say, it is in most cases homogeneous with regard to the social and ethnic composition of the student population; the junior high schools will be 'regional' (in small towns, which are usually homogeneous in population) or 'district-wide' in the cities. The junior high school districts in the cities will be drawn in such a way that in most cases the student population in each will be varied and not of a single social fabric. The meeting of children whose parents come from different social classes and countries of origin, at least from age twelve, in a single school (paragraph 25h of the Rimalt Committee's recommendations) was viewed by the Committee not only as a necessary means for narrowing the educational gaps between Israeli children, but also as a national-educational value in itself [pp. 249–250].

The Knesset decision to endorse the recommendations of the Committee was not a "reform law" but an expression of the legislators' volition, instructing those directly concerned to introduce the proper changes in existing laws in order to implement the program. This recommendation was not lost on those responsible within the Ministry, but the procedures for amending the zoning regulations were apparently slow and needed a strong push (in the form of the ethnic demonstrations that followed in 1970/1971) for the decision to be implemented.[6]

In May 1971, the Deputy Minister of Education informed the Knesset of the Ministry's intent to study the question of readjusting the school districts (Israel Knesset, 1971, Vol. 61, p. 3545), and, in August 1971, the Minister of Education announced that "the Ministry is preparing a bill that will prevent parents in affluent neighborhoods from opposing the integration of their children's schools with those in deprived neighborhoods."[7]

---

[6]Based on an internal memo, dated July 18, 1981, prepared by the legal advisor and submitted to the Minister of Education, and on a memo dated September 6, 1977, prepared by the officer in charge of education administration and submitted to the Minister of Education.

[7]"Davar" newspaper, August 4, 1971.

Following a decision of the Ministry's executive forum on July 13, 1973, the Ministry's legal advisor prepared a bill entitled "Education Law (Integration of Students)," which was presented to the Minister on July 18, 1971. By granting the Minister very broad powers, the bill was designed to allow for the transfer of students from one school to another, to appoint teachers to integrated schools, to integrate schools, and to carry out any other measures that would promote integration. The primary motive for the implementation of integration, as expressed emphatically by the legal advisor, was social and not educational pedagogical.

But because of the radical nature of the proposal, the political dangers it raised, the doubts and lack of knowledge of the best and most suitable ways to implement integration, and the easy alternatives for achieving more limited goals—if more plausible goals, both educationally and politically—through secondary legislation, the proposal did not even reach advanced stages of discussion within the Ministry. An excert from a letter written by the legal adviser to the Ministry of Education 4 years later illustrates this: "At one time a draft bill aimed at achieving integration in the schools was circulated in the Ministry and was intentionally shelved, not because of a rejection of integration in elementary school education but because of the desire to avoid a formal discussion of the subject."[8]

At the same time, in July 1971, an ad hoc Committee was appointed to examine the regulations of school registration. The Committee was asked to take into consideration in its recommendations the "pedagogical and social principles involved in the determination of the student population in each school."[9] It presented its recommendations in October 1971. The most significant amendments proposed for school districts were contained in the statement that the criteria for determining school districts, aside from distance, would be based on a scale of priorities that would be made known to the public, with the option of placing more than one school in each district (the distribution of students between these schools would be determined by the local school authorities). This statement allowed any local school authority *that so desired* to determine ethnically and socially heterogeneous school districts, and to distribute the students among the schools as they saw fit. At the end of the year (December 29, 1971), it was also decided to introduce an amendment allowing geographically noncontinuous school districts, on condition that local school authorities provided the necessary transportation.

Thus at the end of 1971 we find explicit recommendations within the Ministry for changes in school zoning that would greatly facilitate integration, but these recommendations still had to go through the lengthy process of intra-Ministry debate (particularly with the religious education sector) and were only issued as

---

[8]Letter dated September 1, 1975, from the legal adviser of the Ministry of Education to the legal adviser of the Israel government.

[9]Committee's letter of appointment, July 9, 1971.

formal regulations 4 years later (Book of Regulations, no. 3388, page 2520, August 27, 1975).

What was the source of this delay?

First and foremost, it resulted from internal opposition, which continued even after the adoption of the Reform Program. But there was also another converse reason: The very success of the supporters of integration in an important court decision, allowing the Ministry of Education and the Jerusalem Municipality to prevent parents from sending their seventh-grade children to schools of their own choice (instead of to the designated junior high school), promoted the feeling that there was no urgent need to amend the legislation on school districts.

In 1975, legislation on integration was again discussed at the executive forum of the Ministry. Following this discussion, the legal adviser prepared a memorandum[10] whose principal points were as follows:

1. The existing regulations were sufficient to implement a policy of integration in the local school authorities *containing several school districts, when they so desired,* but they did not compel the authorities to carry out integration. (In fact, implementing integration was possible if the district director authorized to approve school districts was instructed to do so *only* when they complied with the policy of promoting integration.)

2. The regulations did not meet the needs of integration in some types of settlements (e.g., Kibbutzim).

3. In lieu of the previously mentioned, if the government wished to take positive action to impose integration, it was not sufficient to rely on the existing regulations or even their amendment; rather, integration must be required by law.

But the time was evidently not ripe for legislation. In January 1976, at a meeting with the Minister, it was decided that the law would not be amended and that the district directors would be instructed to take the element of integration into consideration when determining school districts. Following this decision, the legal adviser wrote on February 22, 1976: "The Minister decided not to initiate any legislation at this stage, but rather to direct the district directors to use their authority to promote integration as stated in the registration regulations and to inform the local authorities that they would do so."[11]

From a legislative point of view, the amendment of the 1975 regulations constituted the last stage in the evolution of the Ministry's actions. Although there was a growing demand within the educational system for a statement of policy and for effective operational measures of integration, in practice the

[10]Memorandum dated February 22, 1976 from the legal adviser of the Ministry of Education to the Director General of the Ministry.

[11]Letter dated February 22, 1976 from the legal adviser of the Ministry of Education to the deputy Director General.

Ministry did not yet take any course of action other than one of recommendation and guidance and continued to refrain from obligatory legal measures.

The Nahlaot Project. The Nahlaot educational experiment in Jerusalem is worthy of examination from a variety of aspects. We deal with it from the point of view of its treatment by the Ministry and of the evolution of the Ministry's approach to integration in the critical years of its formulation. We try to indicate how a unique experiment became the catalyst for the formulation of a committed attitude toward integration and was transformed over a short period of time into a symbol of commitment to integration on the one hand, and of the belief in its success on the other.

In May 1967, the committee of the Kurdish community and the committee of Nahlaot and Zikhronot—two poor neighborhoods—in Jerusalem, issued a sharply worded leaflet that shocked the Ministry of Education and the Jerusalem municipality. It included such statements as: "We will not forfeit our childrens' education . . . The education of our children is entrusted to schools the level of which is among the worst in the city. . . . What this means is that when our children grow up they will become unskilled laborers in the State of Israel." In addition, it urgently demanded the amendment of the school districts in such a way that would allow their children to attend the academically and otherwise prestigious schools of Rehavia (an adjacent affluent neighborhood). The assumption on which this statement was based was that if the children of Nahlaot were to attend schools with a high academic level, their academic achievement would thereby increase, thus bettering their chances for social advancement.

The leaflet, initiated by a group of parents in the process of upward social mobility who had personally experienced segregation among the children of Rehavia and Nahlaot, fell on attentive ears. The parliamentary committee for changing the educational structure was then at the height of its work, the early 1960s economic recession had reached a peak, and sensitivity to the ethnic problem had increased.

In the meantime, the Six Day War broke out, but this did not significantly delay the committee's work, and on November 22, 1967, in the wake of constant pressure, the Director General of the Ministry appointed the "first Nahlaot committee," which was instructed to examine the educational system in the Nahlaot area. No date was set for the conclusion of the committee's work, and the integration of the schools was not explicitly mentioned in the letter of appointment.

In the course of the deliberations of the "Nahlaot committee," serious apprehensions were expressed with regard to full and immediate integration (especially by the superintendents of the Ministry of Education). Information was cited from the Coleman study on the need to maintain a majority of advantaged students in the classroom; reports were submitted on other partial attempts that same year to achieve integration; and an attempt was made to distinguish between the problem of Nahlaot and the overall problem in Jerusalem. Political and social pressures were also reflected in the committee meetings. [12] Finally, despite differences of opinion, the committee unanimously reached an opinion and, after 4 months of deliberations, arrived at a series of conclusions and recommendations that ultimately led the Ministry of Education to embrace a more active policy of integration in the elementary schools. Although the committee did not view the introduction of basic changes in school districts as an overall solution to the problem, its central recommendation leaned toward gradual integration of the schools in the neighborhood, beginning in 1969. This recommendation was accompanied by a series of additional recommendations to ensure sufficient resources for the implementation of the project, to accelerate construction projects, to carry out community development programs, and to set up a task force to plan and direct the project. [13]

The committee report was approved by the Director General of the Ministry on April 11, 1968. It constituted a milestone in the changing attitude toward integration in the elementary schools. But this was only the first step. The implementation of the experiment began only a year and a half later. Throughout this period, heavy pressure was applied by parents of both sides, including threats of appeals to the Supreme Court of Justice and to international public opinion, and threats of violence. A special decision by the Minister of Education was required for the experiment to be put into effect. This decision to carry out integration was defined by the Minister's adviser as "a historic decision, since this precedent will undoubtedly be followed by other integration programs that will promote the success of educational reform. The Minister's decision was one of ethics and values, consistent with his policy in favor of ethnic integration in the school system." [14] The decision was also viewed similarly by the "Public committee for Zikhronot and Nahlaot." [15]

So, 2½ years after originally raising the issue, the parents of Nahlaot were able to send their first-grade children to ethnically integrated schools. But despite the extended period that had elapsed since the demand was first made, and even since its acceptance in principle, the experiment did not get off to a good start. In the view of those who implemented it, the Ministry of Education remained very sceptical in the first stages of the project. They felt that (Klein & Eshel, 1980): "integration in the project was a half-hearted political demonstration, based less on real commitment than on a response to demands of the moment [p. 17]."

---

[12]Minutes of the January 8, 1968 meeting of the committee for examining the school situation in the Nahlaot and Zikhronot neighborhoods in Jerusalem (from the archives of the Ministry of Education).

[13]For complete details, see the report of the committee for examining the school situation in the Nahlaot and Zikhronot neighborhoods in Jerusalem January 9, 1968 (stencil, from the archives of the Ministry of Education).

[14]*Al Hamishmar* newspaper, April 1, 1969, April 2, 1969.

[15]"Public Committee for Zikhronot and Nahlaot, letter no. 2, to the residents of Zikhronot and Nahlaot on the education of our children." Jerusalem, April 1969.

In our somewhat different view, there were already at that time (1969) important groups within the Ministry who viewed integration as a major and central part of the Ministry's activity; there were, however, other groups too. The hesitations and doubts of the latter were apparently partly political (approaching elections), partly ideological (the right and authority to impose integration), partly pedagogical (the uncertainty as to the propriety of this educational method), and partly organizational (the concentration of the Ministry's efforts on the junior high school reform program). It should be recalled that the main thrust of the Ministry's efforts was directed toward the implementation of the reform, which had been approved in mid-1968, and there were those who feared to extend the issue of integration so soon afterwards to another front—one that promised to be even more sensitive.

At the beginning of the second year of the project, there were indications that the Ministry of Education had decided to adopt the integrative approach in the elementary schools as well. On November 24, 1970, in the wake of social ferment in the disadvantaged neighborhoods (the Panthers), a committee was appointed to examine the elementary school system throughout Jerusalem. Unlike the Nahlaot committee appointed 3 years earlier, this committee's terms of reference made integration the central issue, stating that, while examining the elementary school system in Jerusalem, it "should also examine the division into school districts in order to integrate pupils of different ethnic and social groups in the schools."[16]

During that same period, the Ministry of Education reexamined the Nahlaot project and established clear operative guidelines for achieving integration. These included the affirmation of the principle of ethnic and educational integration, careful implementation ("moderate integration"), and emphasis on the need for pedagogical and administrative coordination."[17]

Thus, toward the end of 1971, we find a positive approach toward integration emerging at the highest levels of the Ministry, with the Minister and his deputy utilizing the forum of the Knesset to clarify their position. (Israel Knesset, 1971, Vol. 57, p. 2083; Vol. 60, p. 1373; Vol. 61, p. 3541). The project was ultimately adopted by the Ministry and was presented on different occasions as a symbol of its commitment to carry out integration and as an example of its possible achievement.[18]

Discussions within the Ministry Administration. With the Knesset's approval of the recommendations of the Rimalt Committee, the Ministry entered

---

[16]Report and recommendations of the committee for examining Jewish elementary school education in Jerusalem, July 23, 1971, p. 6 (stencil).

[17]Letter dated October 29, 1971 from the chairman of the committee of elementary school education in the Ministry of Education to the Director General (from the archives of the Ministry of Education).

[18]Statement by the Minister of Education before the Education Board on November 29, 1971 (from the archives of the Ministry of Education).

into the stage of intensive preparations for the implementation of the reform program, coming under heavy pressure from the Minister and all departments within the Ministry to begin implementation as soon as possible. The date of the program's approval by the Knesset—late July 1968—did not allow for the opening of significantly integrated junior high schools in the 1968–69 academic year. In that year, eight junior high schools were opened, but these were rather in the nature of workshops and were opened in areas where public sensitivity to the problem of integration was low. The 1968–69 academic year was therefore one of intensive discussions and preparations for the opening of 40 to 50 junior high schools the following year.

In the middle of the year, the first hints of opposition to the establishment of the planned junior high schools were heard. A meeting held in the Minster's office in May 1969 heard a report on difficulties encountered in the setting up of schools planned for 1970. The difficulties arose from opposition to the vacating of elementary schools, and from parental opposition to integration. Within 3 months, information was brought before the Ministry administration on nine planned junior high schools in which parents opposed integration. The Minister of Education, Z. Aranne, who had conceived and launched the idea of the reform and had achieved its passage in the Knesset despite the strong opposition of the teachers' union and a number of important parties, was not prepared for a head-on conflict with the parents. At the end of August 1969, just before the beginning of the school year, plans for the opening of four of the nine "problematic" junior high schools were cancelled.[19]

The first meeting of the new Minister of Education, Yigal Allon, with the Ministry executive forum in January 1970, was devoted to the problems of the reform program, with the issue of integration occupying a central place in the discussion. During three consecutive meetings, problems central to integration were discussed, including issues related to integration in general and to the religious schools in particular.[20] At these meetings several decisions were reached that continued to guide the Ministry for several years afterwards. These decisions implied that:

1. The Ministry was prepared to adopt a policy of integration.
2. The Ministry tended to avoid sharp conflicts and preferred to exhaust methods of persuasion rather than issuing orders—but at the same time did not shirk from taking necessary measures.
3. The Ministry recognized the need to carry out integration at a younger age than at the junior high school level.

---

[19]Protocol of meetings of the Board of the Ministry of Education on July 21, 1969, August 18, 1969, August 25, 1969 (from the archives of the Ministry of Education).

[20]Protocols of the meetings of the executive forum of the Ministry of Education on January 5, 1970, January 12, 1970, January 20, 1970 (from the archives of the Ministry of Education).

The success of local pressure in Nahlaot encouraged similar pressures in the Katamon area directed at the new, modern, comprehensive school built in the heart of this Jerusalem neighborhood. The decision to open a junior high school for the children of Katamon and adjacent advantaged neighborhoods led a number of parents in the advantaged neighborhoods to try to register their children in other selective schools. The conflict between the parents, the Ministry and the municipality, and among parents of the different groups reached a peak when several parents appealed to the High Court of Justice, demanding that their children be allowed to attend the schools of their choice. Despite warnings by its legal adviser, the Ministry of Education decided to stand by its position. The issue came up for discussion within the Ministry, and in a laconic report to its executive forum, the Director General reported in April 1971 "on the implementation of the Educational Reform in Jerusalem and on the decision to appear before the High Court of Justice, with the full knowledge that the law is not on our side, with the object of arousing public debate."[21] This report was in fact a further expression of the Ministry's fundamental and consistent support for integration at this time.

Despite talks relating in one way or another to integration, there was still a feeling within the Ministry that a fundamental discussion was necessary in light of continuing difficulties in carrying out the policy of integration. This discussion was held in the Minister's office in May 1973, where it became apparent that there was still a broad spectrum of opinions, questions, reservations, and doubts on the issue. The Minister summed up the meeting in a series of decisions aimed at strengthening integration in the school system on all relevant levels and at solving the problems encountered. Nevertheless, these decisions were based on the supposition that "there was no question of lowering the (academic) level as the price for integration" and that "we must find the appropriate solutions."[22]

After the Yom Kippur War there was a lull in discussions within the Ministry on integration, but conditions in the schools did not allow the issue to be dropped. From year to year, disputes related to integration became more aggravated. In Jerusalem, religious parents began increasingly to avoid the ethnically mixed schools. Elsewhere in the country as well (Petah Tikva, Tel–Aviv, Kfar Maimon, the Judean hills, etc.), problems arose over the desire—whether overt or latent—of advantaged parents to prevent their children from attending integrated schools, as opposed to pressure from lower class parents of Middle Eastern background to continue the implementation of integration.

---

[21]Protocol of the meeting of the executive forum of the Ministry of Education, April 25, 1971 (from the archives of the Ministry of Education).

[22]Protocol of the meeting of the executive forum of the Ministry of Education, May 30, 1975 (from the archives of the Ministry of Education).

The conspicuous event was the incident at the Ben Zvi school in Kfar Saba at the end of 1976. Following changes in the school population, several parents decided to transfer their children to other schools in the area. This caused an uproar in the community, with the Minister and the Kfar Saba municipality insisting that these children be returned to the school. The parents objected strongly and hired a lawyer who wrote to the Minister of Education on December 15, 1976, concluding: "I must note that no one is opposed to the idea of integrating children from good, cultured homes with children of underprivileged and problematic backgrounds; but what does this mean?—when the children from both types of homes live in the same neighborhood or at least in close geographic proximity and when the school is a reflection of the neighborhood in which it is located. But this goal cannot be achieved through an artificial mixing of children from different neighborhoods, without any social contact after school hours."[23]

But the Ministry of Education thought otherwise. At the end of December 1976, after the issue had passed through all the necessary stages, the Minister of Education took an unusually forceful step and issued a ministerial order requiring the parents to return their children at the beginning of the following year to the school from which they had removed them.[24] This act was the most forceful expression to date of the Ministry's commitment to the principle of integration. It deviated from the policy followed until then, which had been the exclusive use of persuasion in matters of integration, particularly in the elementary schools. Thus, real administrative expression was given to the position previously adopted, whereby the Ministry would utilize other means should persuasion prove inadequate.

After the change of government in 1977, disputes over integration continued in various parts of the country. The publication of the "Minkowitz–Bashi–Davis report," including a section on integration, (Minkowich, Davis, & Bashi, 1977, pp. 349–368) and the echoes aroused by this section meant that the issue remained on the public agenda. "Follow-up committees" were set up on the highest level, and after extensive work their recommendations were presented to the "Pedagogical Secretariat" of the Ministry. The Secretariat adopted a clear position on the implications of the Minkowitz report on integration in the elementary schools: "The standing committee of the Pedagogical Secretariat approves of the trend within the education system towards integration in the elementary schools." The Secretariat even recommended several operative steps for the implementation of this decision.[25]

---

[23]Letter dated December 15, 1976, from attorney Friedman to the officer in charge of education administration of the Ben Zvi school in Kfar Saba (from the archives of the Ministry of Education).

[24]Letter dated December 29, 1976, from the Minister of Education and Culture to the director general (from the archives of the Ministry of Education).

[25]Protocols of meetings of the Pedagogical Secretariat, May 5, 1980, May 12, 1980, May 19, 1980 (from the archives of the Ministry of Education).

Conclusion

Consolidation of the concept of integration in educational policy is characterized by the following three points:

1. The support of desegregation by official Ministry communiques, activities, and releases to the public regarding the essential importance of desegregation, apart from its instrumental value. Earlier, even the proponents of integration had stressed primarily its academic potential. There has been a growing perception of integration as an end in itself, rather than a means for narrowing interethnic gaps.

2. The utilization of the Ministry resources for the implementation of the Reform Program, in accordance with the Knesset decision, including integration in the junior high schools and the first attempts to extend integration to the elementary schools.

3. The clearly apparent tension between the desire to achieve integration and the objective difficulties involved (including lack of knowledge on how to do so successfully, budgetary difficulties, demographic and geographic problems, and ideological and public opposition).

SECTION II: EXPLANATIONS OF THE PROCESS

The material reviewed reveals that the issue of ethnic gaps, at least in education, emerged in the Ministry of Education as a central topic for discussion and programming in the mid-1950s, though primarily on the academic level. Integration became a subject for public discussion only in the mid-1960s.

Seemingly, there was a reason to expect that in the course of time interethnic tensions in Israel would decrease, because since the early 1950s, when mass immigration declined, there had been a steady rise in the absolute standard of living of the entire population, and a significant narrowing of gaps among people of different social classes in a number of important areas. For example, Asian–African Jews began to occupy an increasingly important place in local government, workers' unions, and even at the national level—in the army, political parties, the Histadrut (labor federation), the Knesset, and so on (Smooha, 1978). The percentage of ethnic intermarriage steadily grew: 11.8 in 1955, 13.8 in 1965, 18.9 in 1975, and 19.1 in 1976 (Israel Central Bureau of Statistics, Statistical Abstract, 1978, p. 80, Table c/12). Overcrowding declined: The percentage of families living under conditions of 3+ persons per room was 24.4% in 1957, 10.8% in 1967, 2.9% in 1977. The figures for the African–Asian population were 53.2%, 13.4%, and 5.5%, respectively (Israel Central Bureau of Statistics, Statistical Abstract, 1958, p. 25, Table 21; 1978, p. 315, Table A/21). In addition, the proportion of Asian–African students rose at all levels of education (Egozi, 1978, p. 17; 1980, Tables 25–26). Why, then, did public discussion of integration intensify in the mid-1960s, in spite of the overall improvement in conditions?

The question of what makes any issue a "social problem" is an interesting theoretical question that has been widely discussed in the professional literature (Blumer, 1971; Manis, 1974; Merton, 1971; Tallman & McGee, 1971). Despite the variety of definitions of the term *social problem,* there is a general consensus among social scientists on three necessary preconditions for the creation of a social problem:

1. The existence of an objective situation within a considerable segment of the population that contradicts the general values of the society that that population is part of.

2. Broad public awareness, expressed in the emergence of social and political organizations to correct this situation.

3. The recognition that this situation can be changed through social action—namely, that it is not an insoluble problem, but one that must and can be solved through social public action.

We now verify whether these conditions were fulfilled with regard to the issue of integration[26] and review several processes and phenomena that marked the period under discussion.

1. The Success of Educational "Propoganda."   Israel's population, including Jews of Asian–African origin, was convinced that education constituted the major instrument of social mobility. As long as the country had to cope with problems of physical absorption, and large segments of Israeli youth dropped out of the intermediate or higher levels of the educational system, the failure of the Asian–African groups to enter the more prestigious channels of social mobility could be attributed to this educational failure. By the mid-1960s, most of the elementary school children in Israel were native born. In 1967 the percentage of students of Asian–African origin in the ninth-grade age group was equal to their percentage in ninth-grade classes. Despite this increased attendance of Asian–African students in the school system, their academic achievement was found to be much lower than those of their peers of European–American origin. In addition, it was found that in the more prestigious courses of study (academic high schools, matriculation courses) the overwhelming majority were Israeli born or of European–American origin.

These data made it clear to anyone considering the problem that the efforts of the educational system had not yet achieved the desired goals. The data were particularly disturbing in view of the absolute rejection of hereditary explana-

---

[26]In this context of "social problem," the term *issue of integration* refers to the entire continuum, ranging from actual integration to lack of integration and segregation.

tions for such differences, and almost a decade of enrichment programs that had not achieved the desired results.

2. *The Success of Primary Absorption.*   According to Crenson (1971): "The failure of an issue to emerge into the 'political stratum' may indicate that there is simply no discontent about the subject, or it may signify that, although dissatisfaction exists, countless private distractions have diverted the citizens from registering their complaints with their political leaders [p. 5]."

In our opinion, the latter condition prevailed in the early years of Israel's statehood. Later, having coped with the primary difficulties of immigrant absorption and following the formation of a local leadership, the social situation could be examined more closely and critically. Eisenstadt (1969) wrote of this process: "A large segment of the immigrants and their children soon began to consider themselves part of Israeli society of the State of Israel. Although there is no precise data on this, many expressions serve as evidence that they began to consider themselves citizens with the right to demand complete equality and to develop fully within Israeli society [p. 10]."

It can be assumed that, whereas Israel Society was making much overall progress, Asian–African Jews felt they were being "pushed" to the lower levels of the employment and social-status scale. The fact that this was by no means the result of deliberate action did nothing to prevent this feeling. What is more, this situation in Israel was in stark contrast to the relatively higher social status of some of the immigrants in their countries of origin, as well as being incongruent with the values of equality and liberalism expressed by the leaders of the veteran Israeli community. Awareness of this gap was somewhat dulled by the economic prosperity of the late 1950s and early 1960s but intensified during the years of recession (1965–1967).

Indeed, several findings indicate that the development of such a feeling was justified precisely against the background of the successful primary absorption and social mobility of the Asian–African immigrants. They had improved their relative status in almost all areas more rapidly than had the Westerners: in income (Smooha, 1978), consumption of durable goods (Smooha, 1978), political integration (Peres, 1976), and education (Egozi, 1979). However: (1) Despite the rapid progress of the Asian–Africans in many fields, the absolute gaps not only did not narrow but became even wider; (2) entry of the Asian–African Jews into the higher status and income groups was accompanied by a growing ethnic homogeneity of the disadvantaged groups. The report of the Prime Minister's committee (1973) on disadvantaged children and youth stated that: "92–94% of all disadvantaged children come from families of Asian–African origin. . . . One of the most serious findings may be that all the children, without exception, from families of relatively deep and extensive (three-dimensional) deprivation are of Aisan–African origin [p. 8]." The Minkowitz–Bashi–Davis report stated that 97% of the children whose parents had no formal education were of Middle

Eastern origin (Minkowich, Davis, & Bashi, 1977, p. 68). The statistics show that, whereas in 1957 over 25% of families living in housing conditions of 3+ people in a room were of Western origin, the same group accounted for less than 10% of families living in such conditions in 1967 (Israel Central Bureau of Statistics, Statistical Abstract, 1958, p. 25, Table 21; 1978, p. 315, Table A/21).

3. Patterns of Population Distribution.   A third factor in the emergence of this problem in the 1960s was the change that occurred in the geographical distribution of the population. The official housing policy of the government was aimed at the geographical distribution and social integration of the population (Bacchi, 1968; Karmon, 1975). As a result of this policy, immigrants of all ethnic groups were directed largely to immigrant housing projects. For example, up to 1965, 55% of those directed by the Jewish Agency to Bet Shean were of Asian–African origin, and 45% were of European–American origin; the situation in Bet Shemesh was similar. Of those directed to Kiryat Gat, 78% were of European–American origin and 20% were of Asian–African origin. A survey conducted in 1956 among 450 families in Kiryat Yovel (Jerusalem) revealed that they originated from 17 different countries. But reality thwarted the efforts of the planners. Immigrants of European–American origin made every effort to move from outlying areas toward the center, and from less prestigious settlements with inferior services to settlements of greater prestige and better services. Thus, by 1965, 82.9% of householders in Bet Shean were of Asian–African origin, with a similar situation in Bet Shemesh. In Kiryat Gat, 51.5% were of Asian–African origin (Israel Ministry of Labor, 1966, 1967a, b).

The same applies to the immigrants who arrived in 1957–1959. Immigrants from European–American countries were settled at a "standard distance," relatively far from the center of the country: 77.3km in 1957, 82.3km in 1958, and 79km in 1959. For immigrants from the Asian–African countries the figures were similar: a distance of 69.2 km in 1957, 76.2 km in 1958, and 74.8 km in 1959. Nevertheless, in all cases the improvement in housing conditions—expressed in a shift toward the center—was slower among the Aisan–African immigrants than among the Western immigrants (Bacchi, 1968).

A similar picture emerges with regard to the ethnic composition of the medium-sized cities in 1961. New immigrants represented a large percentage of the population in these cities (varying from 68 to 88.3%). The percentage of Asian–African Jews in these same cities varied from 28 to 52.7%, but the majority of the veteran population and the Western immigrants were concentrated in the center of the cities, whereas the new Asian–African immigrants tended to live in the suburbs. However, even the suburbs were not homogeneously Asian–African in 1961, and the percentage of Asian–African residents varied from 36 to 89% (Gonen, 1972). There was on the one hand a constant process of assignment of immigrants by the authorities to distant settlements and suburbs and, on the other, a process of migration from these settlements to the center, led by those of European–American origin. As the relative share of immigration in population growth declined, and parallel to this, the proportion of spontaneous natural migration of the population increased, the ethnic homogeneity of the development towns and suburbs increased, becoming exclusive foci of settlements for Asian–African Jews. These processes, although they had existed previously, were now reinforced by the decline in the rate of immigration, the payment of German reparations to the European immigrants, and the integration into the economic life of the State of the prosperous segments of the population, regardless of ethnic origin.

In light of all this information, it seems reasonable to assume—although there are no explicit data to this effect—that in the early years after the establishment of the State a large proportion of Israeli cities and towns (large cities—especially suburbs, medium-sized cities, development towns, and agricultural settlements) were ethnically heterogeneous (although homogeneous with regard to number of years in Israel), and only in the late 1950s and early 1960s, with the improvement of Israel's economic situation, the input of German reparations, and the decline in immigration, homogeneity increased.

The growing homogeneity of cities and towns, particularly of individual neighborhoods, was accompanied by yet another process—the creation of new upper middle-class neighborhoods in close proximity to the disadvantaged neighborhoods: Savyon alongside Yehud, Ramat Eshkol alongside Shmuel Hanavi, Morasha alongside Neve Magen, and so on. As a result, a complex mosaic developed in the suburbs surrounding the metropolitan cities that was based on socioeconomic status and emphasized by ethnic distinctions (Gonen, 1975). This process was fostered by the rising prices of land in the large cities, the rising standard of living of the middle class (including vehicular mobility), and the desire to live in more comfortable homes and apartments. It is important to note that throughout these years, especially in the period of prosperity following the Six Day War, there was a growing presence of Asian–African Jews in prestigious neighborhoods and areas, but that this phenomenon, although promoting "natural integration" in these areas, led to the depletion of the "source neighborhoods," depriving them of their potential leaders and aggravating their social situation. The process described here created a situation that only served to emphasize the coexistence of homogeneous disadvantaged and prosperous neighborhoods.

4. Social Composition of the Schools.   A direct criterion related to social integration in education likely to foster a clash of social norms is the existence, in close proximity, of schools of homogeneous ethnic composition, not necessitated by local demographic composition, where a different distribution of students between the schools is possible. An extension of this is the existence of ethnically homogeneous classes within heterogeneous schools. Such a situation clearly existed in Israel, and a number of examples can be pointed out, such as

TABLE 4.2
Elementary School Classes and Pupils by Percentage of
Asian–African Pupils in Class

		0–24.9	25–74.9	75+
1964:	Classes	27.2	32.8	40
	Pupils	no data	no data	no data
1967:	Classes	18.9	33.6	44.2
	Pupils	21.4	37.5	41.1
1970:	Classes	16.2	34.3	46.5
	Pupils	no data	no data	no data
1973:	Classes	14.6	38.5	44.4
	Pupils	17.0	43.5	39.6
1977:	Classes	no data	no data	no data
	Pupils	17.4	52.42	30.3

adjacent neighborhoods within cities, and geographically proximate settlements with different lifestyles, such as kibbutzim, moshavim, and development towns.

Data from the Central Bureau of Statistics indicate that in the 1966–67 academic year 41.1% of the elementary school pupils in Israel attended classes in which 75% or more were of Asian–African origin, whereas 21.4% attended classes in which 75% or more were of European–American origin. Only 37.5% attended ethnically heterogeneous classes (see Table 4.2). However, it should not be inferred from this that 62.5% of the elementary school pupils in 1967 attended homogeneous classes that could readily be integrated: for a large part of the population concentrated in settlements with ethnically homogeneous populations, and in groups of special ideological character (e.g., the religious schools, kibbutz schools), where integration could not be implemented without complex manipulations (busing, etc.), and without conflicting with the then-accepted view of the importance of the school as a neighborhood institution, and without entering into controversies of far-reaching political implications. But, despite this, there was a fairly broad basis for the problem and for the emergence of a general social awareness of its seriousness.

There were also other phenomena in the area of education, which were indirectly related to the issue of integration, whether empirically or in the eyes of the public; for example, the difference in resources (particularly financial resources) and facilities made available to schools of different ethnic composition (see also Minkovich, Davis, & Bashi, 1977, pp. 99–124; Razel, 1978), and a continuing gap in academic achievement between students of different ethnic origin (Chen, Levy, & Adler, 1978; Levy & Chen, 1976; Minkovich, Davis, & Bashi, 1977).

These phenomena were in direct contrast to several basic values of Israeli society—first and foremost, those of equality and national unity, which were of supreme importance in a society that for many years defined itself as Zionist–Socialist in character. The commonly accepted ideology in Israel rejected outright the possibility that genetic differences between ethnic groups might contribute to the gap in achievement, viewing all children as having equal potential and deserving equal treatment. The mass immigration of Jews from all over the world, immigrant absorption, and the need to cope with external enemies heightened the need for national unity and ethnic integration. This value was threatened by the emerging reality.

5. Changes in the Social Environment and Political and Organizational Awareness.   If we may make some assumptions that have not been empirically examined, the following dialectic process can be said to have occurred in the wake of the Six Days War: The war demonstrated, to anyone still requiring proof, that the majority of the Asian–African Jews had become an integral part of Israeli society. So, on the one hand, there was no need to grant them special representation or treatment as an ethnic group (hence the decline in their representation in the Knesset and party lists), whereas, on the other hand, there could be no opposition to integration in the schools or to the appointment of anyone to a senior position because of Asian–African origin. Meritocratic principles again seemed—at least for a short time—to fulfill the needs of Israeli society.

Political salience of a problem in Israel can be measured by the frequency of its coming up for discussion in the Knesset, its inclusion in coalition negotiations, in party platforms, and in government guidelines, etc. Integration was recognized in Israeli political circles as an issue of primary importance. This was reflected in the discussions of the Rimalt Committee, in the Committee's recommendations, which were endorsed by the Knesset, in the plenary debates, and in the Knesset Education Committee. It can be said that awareness of the problem of integration was high on the political plane.

On the organizational level, the issue of educational integration did not give rise to a permanent body with the sole aim of advancing integration in the schools. The organizations that emerged were generally local ad hoc committees, mostly parents' associations or local action committees set up to promote or prevent integration in a specific location, and they were disbanded once a decision was reached. These organizations were generally short lived and almost never accompanied the implementation of integration once decided upon. Nevertheless, integration was often one of the central issues for various general bodies whose sole sphere of activity was education. Among these, we can list the Ministry of Education, local educational authorities, and education committees of public bodies (the Knesset, agricultural settlement movements, political parties, and so on). They dealt with the problems of integration both on their own initiative and as a result of the activities of the temporary local bodies.

6. The Influence of Research Studies.   The sixth contributing factor to the public discussion of integration was the publication of data on educational achievements in Israel and the influence of extensive research on this problem, particularly in the United States.

The results of a nationwide scholastic examination administered in the eighth grade to determine which pupils are suited for academic secondary education, together with data obtained in various studies, made it strikingly clear that despite considerable progress in material well-being, the educational achievement of students of Asian–African origin remained much lower than those of Israeli-born and Western students (Adar, 1956; Feitelson, 1953; Simon, 1957; Smilansky, 1957). The results of the national examination in particular, because of its comprehensiveness, regularity, and importance for the future of the pupils tested, contributed to the growing awareness of the interethnic gap.

Parallel to the flow of local data, a number of events and extensive studies published abroad focused attention on the problem of integration. In England it was the controversy over the comprehensive schools and the Plowden report (England, Department of Education and Science, 1967). In the United States there was the controversy over segregation versus integration in the wake of the Supreme Court decision (in the 1954 case of Brown versus the Board of Education), which declared segregation unconstitutional, and the famous Coleman study, which indicated the existence of a link between student achievement and social composition of the class (Coleman, Campbell, Hobson, McPartland, Mood, Weinfeld, & York, 1966). These two sources exerted much influence on the Israeli policy makers and intelligensia. Husen's research on educational reform in Sweden (Husen, 1961; Husen & Boalt, 1967) also influenced those involved in Israeli education to direct their thinking along the lines of comprehensive and integrated schools.

Studies in Israel focused primarily on the problem of interethnic gaps. Treatment of the issue of integration or of heterogeneous classes hardly existed at all. To the best of our knowledge, this situation also prevailed in the pedagogical activities of the institutions of higher education: There were no special classes, institutes, etc. focusing on integration. The studies in other countries, on the other hand, not only indicated the problem of the gap between different ethnic and status groups, but also the potential of integrative processes and settings as a possible solution for this problem. Israeli scholars and educational leaders who followed developments in educational and social research used this approach to influence the local educational system.

We have listed various reasons why integration became a "social problem" in the late 1960s. We do not examine here which of these was more important, and it is clear to us that additional reasons can be found to explain the phenomenon. The conclusion we reach is that, during this period, these factors gave rise to the three previously mentioned conditions that can transform any issue into a social problem.

Thus, after the issue of integration had been raised in the 1960s for the aforementioned reasons as a problem requiring serious consideration, it was then accorded recognition and dealt with at the highest level of the Ministry, in the Knesset, and in the press. It seems to us that the actions of the Ministry of Education in the area of integration—once it had finally decided that the issue should be actively pursued—were shaped by several factors.

The Educational Reform.   Although the issue of reform is not exclusively linked—in essence or in content—to the implementation of integration, it seems to us that the simultaneous development of these two topics, which of course was not coincidental (the same historical conditions gave rise to the demand for both), contributed to the advancement of each and to their interrelation both in theory and in practice. Support for the concept of integration served the support- ers of reform as a counterbalance to the opposition and doubts expressed by those who opposed other aspects of the reform, whereas the overt and latent opposition of parents to integration in the junior high schools could be overcome with the aid of massive investment in these new schools—in both construction and equip- ment, curricula and teachers. These investments were also designed to provide the answers to problems arising from the implementation of the reform program and the introduction of integration.

The Concept of Integration and Its Implications.   As already shown, integra- tion did not have unanimous support within the Ministry of Education. But even those who did support it sometimes did so for different reasons. Some viewed integration primarily as an instrument for achieving other goals, such as narrow- ing social and academic gaps, raising academic achievement, altering the indi- vidual's self-image, or fostering friendships between members of different ethnic groups. Others saw integration as an end in itself, namely, an operative ex- pression of ideological concepts of equality and national unity. Experience showed that the use of integration as an instrument to achieve certain goals did not always automatically result in their attainment; parallel to this, there was a growing tendency to view integration as an end in itself. (The alternative of abandoning integration was not considered.) The definition of integration as an end in itself, a goal grounded in the national consensus, provided an answer to those who judged it exclusively by its effectiveness as a means of achieving other goals. Moreover, the mere administrative implementation of integration—the seating of students side by side—marked, at least on the surface, the achieve- ment of the goal.

The Influence of Scholars and Research.   Changes in Israeli political leader- ship over a period of time gave rise to several processes that helped increase the influence of research and researchers on policy making.

The retirement of the ''founding generation'' also marked the end of the ''generation of dreamers.'' The new generation of leaders was faced not only with a vision of the future, but also with day-to-day problems, for which the solutions and ideas inherited from the previous leadership were not always adequate. Recognition of the deficiencies of such "traditional solutions," and the urgent need to cope with problems, opened the door to various elements whose background and abilities seemed suited to the formulation and consolidation of solutions. Among these, researchers played a prominent part.

A possible factor in this development was the close personal relations between people in a State as small as Israel, who grew up as friends or close acquaintances in organizations working for the establishment of the State (underground movements, Israeli army), in social groups (such as youth movements), and in political movements (parties) that were active in the preparatory and early stages of the building of the State. The same people later turned to different fields—politics, public administration, science—but the close ties among them permitted mutual influence—both in theory and in practice—among the various fields they represented. These personal ties greatly helped to bridge the gap existing in the other countries, and previously in Israel too, between research and government. Information channels were thus shortened, the chances of error in the transmission of messages were decreased, and the willingness for mutual assistance in science and government was enhanced.

This development, which occurred within the different sectors of Israeli leadership and administration, was also apparent in the educational system. The conditions just noted—the accumulation of knowledge on the one hand, and the creation of objective and social conditions on the other—led to the increased participation of social scientists in political decision making on integration and enrichment programs. This participation was reflected in the composition of the standing committee of the Prime Minister's committee on disadvantaged children and youth (Israel, Prime Minister's Office, 1973), in which 9 of the 14 members were full- or part-time academic faculty members, and of the educational planning committee for the 1980s initiated by the Director General of the Ministry of Education (Pelled, 1976). These two committees, which were charged with recommending educational policy principles for implementation, also touched— albeit only partially—on issues of integration. The growing participation of social scientists in the area of integration also found expression in the forming of various "committees of experts" to settle local controversies over integration, and in the appointment by the Minister of Education of the public committee for examining the educational reform in Israel (1978): Six of the 17 members originally appointed to this committee, including its chairman, were academic faculty members.[27]

---

[27]Even after a number of members resigned from the committee, for various reasons, there were 4 academicians among the 12 committee members (of whom 1 served as head scientist of the Ministry of Education) (See Israel, The Report of the Public Committee, Ministry of Education and Culture, 1979, p. 1).

In 1978–79, parallel to the work of the public committee, a group of investigators from different universities organized themselves, on their own initiative, as an interdisciplinary and interuniversity seminar on integration in the schools. The group decided to produce two documents: a collection of articles of an academic nature on various aspects of integration (of which this work is a part), and a kind of "manifesto" addressed to the policy makers, summing up the major findings of the seminar, to serve as the basis for or an aid in the formulation of educational policy (Inter-disciplinary Seminar, 1979). The willingness of the academic faculty to cooperate with members of the establishment was not one sided: The group was invited to present its views and evaluations at a special colloquium organized in the Knesset on November 20, 1979 (Israel Knesset, 1979).

The Evaluation of the Political Situation and the Public Reaction. Despite the general public consensus on the need for integration in principle, differences of opinion existed among various elements in the public, political, and party sectors as to methods of implementation (e.g., religious circles, kibbutzim, and middle-class parent groups). Against this background, and because of the delicate balance in the government coalition, it was necessary (as with any controversial issue) to proceed with care in the area of integration. The Ministry therefore refrained sometimes—though not always—from confrontations over integration when these could be avoided. Nevertheless, the Ministry adopted a position designed to prevent any regression in the efforts to advance integration, and to maintain the conditions necessary for their continuation.

It is clear that many of the day-to-day operative measures adopted by the Ministry of Education in the area of integration were determined largely by its evaluation of the relative political strength of the various groups that supported or opposed integration on the local level. This may explain the different decisions reached with regard to different educational settings, such as the yeshiva high schools and regional schools. In general, there was a greater willingness on the part of the Ministry to reach a compromise with nationally backed groups than with local groups of parents, but even in the case of individual schools, there was sometimes a marked reluctance to enter into sharp conflicts through the use of "ministerial orders."

The Lack of Information on the Methods of Implementation. The fifth factor influencing the Ministry's policy on integration was the lack of tested knowledge about how to implement integration, if viewed as an instrument to achieve further goals, or how to minimize possible adverse effects, if viewed as an end in itself. Because of this gap in our knowledge, the Ministry was in fact unable to mobilize broad professional authority in support of this important issue.

Political, Demographic, and Financial Pressures. Geodemographic conditions in Israel precluded general and large-scale actions for the rapid achievement of integration. The existence of two educational sectors, religious and secular (where the smaller of the two was composed largely of Asian–African students), the existence of large settlements in which the majority of the population is of Asian–African origin, and the existence of geographically circumscribed groups with distinctive ideologies (e.g., kibbutz) naturally limited the implementation of integration. Some of these difficulties could have been overcome by a massive input of resources whether for busing or for the building of superior integrated schools. However, after the need for integration became generally recognized (in the early 1970s), Israel entered into a period of economic difficulties following the Yom Kippur War, and such resources were no longer readily available.

In light of the factors listed here, it seems to us that the general policy of the Ministry of Education has been one of gradual, careful, but nevertheless, consistent implementation of integration as a self-evident necessity. Alongside far-reaching statements of intent on the national importance of integration and the readiness to fight for its achievement, the Ministry worked primarily by persuasion and tried to avoid sharp conflicts. However, when the very idea of integration was threatened, or when there was no choice and a decision had to be made, that decision was always in favor of integration (Nanlaot; the appeal to the Supreme Court on the Denmark school). In some cases—though not many—when sharp controversies emerged over the educational reform, the Ministry yielded on certain components of the Reform Program but maintained the general policy on integration. It is in this light that the compromises with the kibbutzim, some of the religious schools, and the junior high schools in Petah Tikva should be viewed. In all cases, the Ministry insisted that the principle of integration be accepted and honored, even when, because of its awareness of the difficulties involved, it was prepared to compromise on the extent and nature of integration. The formula according to which the ideal ratio between advantaged and disadvantaged students in a class was fixed at 60/40, attributed by its advocates to Coleman, was to a certain degree an obstacle. Reference to this formula encouraged parents whose children were to attend classes under different conditions to exert pressure to moderate or postpone the implementation of integration, and their efforts were often successful.

In conclusion, in our estimation it can be said that the Ministry of Education adopted the idea of integration as its guideline in the 1960s, especially since the end of that decade. Together with the recognition of the difficulties involved in implementing integration in different areas, there was a growing tendency within the Ministry to view integration as an end in itself. At the same time, because of political, public, budgetary, organizational, and professional pressures, the Ministry did not take drastic measures to apply integration throughout the educational system, and, although it was prepared to make compromises regarding the extent of integration needed, it insisted that the compromises should not render the policy void of all content, and that general progress in the implementation of integration should continue.

What were the operational expressions and the results of this official policy? Because of the need for compromise, the budgetary difficulties, and the lack of information—even among educational experts—on the most effective ways to achieve integration, the policy was implemented only partially or on a limited scale in certain areas (e.g., the preparation of textbooks, the development of suitable pedagogical methods, and the development of programs for social activities). Nevertheless, definite progress was made in the implementation of integration in several areas, in accordance with the Ministry's policy.

Class Composition. It is significant that the data on the ethnic composition in the schools was first published only in the early 1960s, indicating the level of awareness with regard to this problem at different periods.

The data of the Central Bureau of Statistics (Israel, Central Bureau of Statistics, 1973, Table 41; 1974, Table 12; 1977, Table 12) reveal the following picture: From this data we learn that: (1) There was a decline in the percentage of classes in which Asian–African pupils constituted less than 25% (from 27.2 in 1964 to 14.6 in 1973) and a rise in the percentage of integrated classes (from 32.8 to 38.5). On the other hand, there was a certain increase during these years in the percentage of classes where pupils of Asian–African origin constituted over 75% (from 40% to 44%). This table does not contain data on developments after 1973; (2) there was a marked decline in the percentage of pupils in homogeneous classes: From 21.4% in 1967 to 17.4% in 1977 in classes with up to 25% Asian–African pupils and in classes with over 75% from 41.4 to 30.3%. This was paralleled by an increase in the percentage of pupils in heterogeneous classes, from 37.5% in 1967 to 52.4% in 1977.

As noted, this trend was also visible in the junior high schools where direct action by the Minister of Education was greater: The percentage of junior high school students in heterogeneous classes in 1973 and 1977 increased from 42.7 to 47.2% (Israel, Central Bureau of Statistics, 1977, Table 13).

There is no doubt that the Reform Program strengthened integration in the schools to a certain extent. An analysis of the data of the Central Bureau of Statistics reveals that while in the sixth-grade elementary school 43.1% of the pupils in 1977 attended classes in which the proportion of Asian–African-origin pupils was between 25 and 75%, and in the seventh-grade junior high school classes to which they were transferred, 49.9% of the students attended such integrated classes. At the same time, this analysis indicated that for some populations and certain settlements, objective factors (such as the homogeneity of the population or sharp dichotomous polarity between a large minority and a small majority) preclude the implementation of integration (Egozi, 1978). In addition, internal selective mechanisms were found to exist within the junior high schools that led to the creation of homogeneous classes within the schools (Chen, Levy, & Adler, 1978). Such phenomena can be explained by the regulations that allowed for academic tracking, slow classes, and advanced classes, whether in response to pedagogical difficulties in heterogeneous classes, or as a result of situations of sharp polarity and wide gaps in the numerical ratio between the different groups, which in certain cases made integration difficult.

It is important to note that the development described here had its roots only partly in the integration policy of the Ministry of Education. Another source can be found in the changes in living patterns, which led to more heterogeneous populations in many neighborhoods. The relative weight of these factors is not clear. It can be assumed that those local authorities with a better grasp of integration policy (such as Jerusalem, Petah Tikva, and Ramat Hasharon) adopted policies of "zoning" that accelerated the natural processes of integration. We can also hypothesize that the two processes had a complementary effect: The policy of integrated zones lowered people's tendency to choose their place of residence on a segregative basis, and vice versa.

School Districts.   Another operational expression of the integration policy lay in the amendment of the registration regulations for elementary and junior high schools, and the directives issued on the basis of these regulations to the local authorities. This amendment permitted any local educational authority (e.g., city hall or town council) that so desired to determine broad districts containing several schools, and to divide the students among the schools in accordance with the desired composition of the school population.

Indeed, in the wake of these new regulations, appropriate directives were issued to the local authorities, and meetings were held with the directors of municipal education departments to convince them of the fairness of the directives and to guide them in carrying them out.

Pedagogical Methods.   Another operational expression of integration policy in the Ministry of Education was its concerted efforts to find ways of coping pedagogically with the heterogeneous-integrated classes. In recent years, financing has been provided for research as well as for experimental training and pedagogical programs aimed at identifying problems and finding solutions to them.

Official Pressures.   Finally, it should be stressed that the Ministry of Education demands that schools—and the public bodies that support them—that do not comply with the principles of integration should nevertheless attempt to cope with the problems inherent in it. Through constant pressure exerted on the kibbutzim, yeshiva high schools, unofficial and experimental educational institutions, and various local educational authorities, compromises have been reached in which the principles of integration, whereas sometimes softened, were ultimately upheld. Thus, we find that today all these bodies include growing percentages of Asian–African students (though, of course, Asian–Africans should not necessarily be identified as disadvantaged students).

Conclusion

With a certain degree of generalization, we can indicate two main axes of change in the continuing development of the Ministry of Education's policy on integration:

1. The first axis is the very recognition of the need for integration. This occurred in the mid-1960s. The primary reason for this change, in our estimation, was the creation of social conditions that differed from those that had existed previously, resulting in the greater prominence of the ethnic problem and the feeling that integration might be one of the primary solutions to this problem. During the early years of statehood there was an overriding need to overcome such basic problems as housing, economy, labor, and security. Social gaps existed, but the main dividing line was between new immigrants and veteran Israelis, not necessarily between different ethnic groups. Because of the change in the ethnic composition of later waves of immigration, the greater mobility of Western Jews, and other factors already discussed at length previously, by the mid-1960s the most striking social dividing line was that of ethnic origin.

2. the second axis of change in the Ministry's policy was the ongoing process focusing on the changing perception of integration. Whereas in the late 1960s and early 1970s integration was seen both as an end in itself and as a means for solving problems of ethnic gaps in academic achievement and improving interethnic relations, toward the end of the 1970s there was a tendency to place greater emphasis on integration as an end in itself. This is an example of what is known in organizational literature as "goals displacement." This phenomenon has been described in different contexts: when there is an objective change in the functions of an organization; when difficulties arise in the implementation of original goals; and when it becomes apparent that the fixed goals are unattainable at the present stage—it then becomes necessary to fix interim goals and examine other relevant objectives (Blau, 1963; Etziony, 1968; Wildavsky, 1979). In general, this does not mean absolutely abandoning one goal for another, or rejecting one approach in favor of another, but rather a change in the order of priorities and a shift of emphasis. The shift of emphasis in integration policy in the direction of social values enabled the Ministry: (1) to point to achievements (achievement of the goal of placing children of different ethnic groups in the same class); (2) to support continued activity toward integration, even when some of the original goals had not been fully achieved (such as central goals, of such supreme national values as national unity and equality, alongside the continued coping with academic problems, such as academic achievement and teaching in heterogeneous classes).

The practical expression of the policy change previously described was twofold: on the one hand, the Ministry continued to press for the implementation of integration as a national goal, and on the other, greater effort was made than in the earlier stages to find educational methods that would ensure the success of integration as a means of achieving other goals.

One of the factors in this change of policy and emphasis was the experience gained in the implementation of the Reform Program and the establishment of the junior high schools—the organizational framework that first declared integration as one of its goals. Difficulties encountered in the implementation of the reform in several places were of a public nature, with opposition directed against the imposition of integration. Hence—due to the ideology of the Ministry heads, the pressure exerted by the disadvantaged public, and the need to cope with the real focus of opposition—the Ministry tended to emphasize the values of integration at the expense of its instrumental aspect.

A second factor related to the first was the flow of information that began to reach the upper echelons of the Ministry from evaluative studies, symposia, and discussions with prominent educational researchers. This information emphasized that: (1) The public at large viewed the idea of integration positively, and even where there were difficulties at first, the principle was ultimately accepted. (Compare with similar findings from the United States, such as Orfield (1978) and Sharkansky & Edwards (1978); (2) desegregation per se, although yielding no significant academic improvement for the disadvantaged students, is not harmful to the advantaged students; (3) there are signs that, where integration was accompanied by suitable educational activity, all groups involved recorded higher achievement.

This information found expression in research studies (Amir, Rich, & Ben–Ari, 1978; Chen, Levy, & Adler, 1978; Klein & Eshel, 1980; Minkovich, Davis, & Bashi, 1977), in symposia at the Knesset, academic discussions (Inter-Disciplinary Seminar, 1979; Israel Knesset, 1973, 1979), and some of the previously mentioned committees. In many cases, and on many occasions, scholars stressed the analytical distinction between viewing integration as an end and a means, and, when external conditions permitted, this distinction began to take root in the minds of the upper echelons of the Ministry. This is not to imply that there was no awareness of this distinction previously, but rather that it was legitimized by the consensus among social scientists.

Finally, we refer to two additional points that are noteworthy:

1. Although it has already been stated in many different contexts, it is worthwhile reiterating the essential difference between integration in Israel and elsewhere in the world. In the United States and England, racial differences are accepted and integration is sought in the name of principles of liberalism, human dignity, a sense of guilt for historical injustice, and so on. In Israel the basic unity of the Jewish People is not questioned by any segment of the population. Efforts to achieve integration were designed to prevent dissolution and to in-

crease existing solidarity, not to create solidarity where none existed. Even at times of greatest ethnic tension, there is no question of dissociation or of a fundamental refusal to live together. Hence, in our estimation, the chances for the success of integration in Israel are much higher than in other countries where the problem is essentially racial.

2. Although integration has in recent years become a prominent public issue, in general it has not been at the focus of specific programs or at the top of the Ministry's operational goals. Even when it gained prominence in educational policy, it was accompanied by problems, doubts, and difficulties. We have seen that the discussion of this issue in the highest ranks of the Ministry was delayed for 2 years (from 1971 to 1973), and the amendment of the school registration regulations took 5 years. Interest in the Ministry of Education focused diverse techniques for the advancement of disadvantaged students, the narrowing of gaps, the training of teachers, and the preparation of curricula. Over the course of time, there were changes in the relative weight of the principle of integration in educational policy. The direction and force of these changes and the degree to which they were extended to other levels of the Ministry were affected by the extent of external pressure, by the political and social conditions prevailing at different times, and—perhaps decisively—by the level of personal commitment of those at the head of the educational system (Adiel, 1970; Pelled, 1976; Shmueli, 1972, 1975).

Although the issue of integration was not at the top of the list of priorities of the educational system, it can clearly be called a "real" issue. Integration is an expression of a serious social situation in which the ethnic problem plays a prominent part. In the eyes of large sections of the population, withdrawal from the commitment to the concept of integration would seriously undermine social achievements and obstruct further progress. The strong political significance of identifying integration—in the layman's view—with academic and other achievements, as well as with social mobility, precludes—from the political perspective—any openly declared withdrawal on the issue of integration, and requires those at the head of the educational system to continue to implement it, whereas at the same time striving to solve the problems inherent in it.

In view of all the factors discussed here, it seems evident that the issue of integration will continue to be a component of educational policy for a long time to come. As long as there is identification between disadvantaged groups within the population and ethnic origin, and as long as Israeli society rejects the idea of hereditary inferiority and remains imbued with the need—both historical and concrete—to achieve unity, social and political pressure to find solutions to the problems inherent in this effort will continue. One of the important solutions will undoubtedly lie in integration.

REFERENCES

Adar, L. Toward a study of learning difficulties of the immigrants' children. *Megamot*, 1956, *7*, 139–180. (Hebrew)

Adiel, S. A decade of fostering the disadvantaged. In S. Adiel, G. Bergson, E. Rokach, & A. Stahl (Eds.), *A decade of fostering the disadvantaged*. Jerusalem: Ministry of Education and Culture, 1970, 9–26. (Hebrew)

Amir, Y., Rich, I., & Ben–Ari, R. Problems of social integration in junior high school: Gain and loss to pupils, and proposed solutions. *Studies in Education*, 1978, *18*, 15–36. (Hebrew)

Bacchi, R. *Population distribution and internal migration in Israel*. Project H-I (Third Ford Grant), 1968. (Mimeographed)

Blau, P. M. *The dynamics of bureaucracy*. Chicago: University of Chicago Press, 1963.

Blumer, H. Social problems as collective behavior. *Social Problems*, 1971, *18*, 298–306.

Chen, M., Levy, A., & Adler, C. *Process and outcome in education: Evaluating the contribution of the Middle School to the educational system*. Schools of Education, University of Tel–Aviv and Hebrew University, Jerusalem, 1978. (Hebrew)

Coleman, J. S., Campbell, E. Q., Hobson, C. J., McPartland, J., Mood, A. M., Weinfeld, F. D., & York, R. L. *Equality of educational opportunity*. Washington, D.C.: U.S. Government Printing Office, 1966.

Crenson, M. A. *The unpolitics of air pollution—A study of nondecision making in the cities*. Baltimore: The John Hopkins University Press, 1971.

Egozi, M. *The socio-cultural mixture in the junior high schools*. Jerusalem: Ministry of Education and Culture, 1978. (Hebrew)

Egozi, M. *Statistical data on the Israeli educational system*. Jerusalem: Ministry of Education and Culture, 1979. (Hebrew)

Egozi, M. *The educational system in a numerical mirror*. Jerusalem: Ministry of Education and Culture, 1980. (Hebrew)

Eisenstadt, S. N. The aborption of immigrants, the amalgamation of exiles and the problems of transformation of Israeli society. In S. N. Eisenstadt (Ed.), *The integration of immigrants from different countries of origin in Israel*. Jerusalem: Magnes Press, 1969, 6–15. (Hebrew)

England, Central Advisory Council for Education. *Children and their primary schools*. London: Department of Education and Science, 1967.

Etziony, A. *The active society*. New York: The Free Press, 1968.

Feitelson, D. Causes of failure in first-grade pupils. *Megamot*, 1953, *4*, 37–63, 123–173. (Hebrew)

Gonen, A. *Mass immigration and the spatial structure of towns in Israel* (Research Report No. 1). Jerusalem: Institute of Urban and Regional Studies, The Hebrew University, 1972.

Gonen, A. Location and ecological aspects of urban public sector housing: The Israeli case. In G. Gappert & H. M. Rose (Eds.), *The social economy of the cities*. Beverly Hills, Calif.: Sage, 1975, 279–297.

Husen, T. *School reform in Sweden*. Washington D.C.: U.S. Office of Education, 1961.

Husen, T., & Boalt, G. *Educational research and educational change: The case of Sweden*. Stockholm: Almquist & Wiksell, 1967.

Inter-Disciplinary Seminar. *Integration and promoting the goals of education in Israel*. November, 1979. (Mimeograph) (Hebrew)

Israel Central Bureau of Statistics. *Demographic features of kindergarten and grade-school Pupils, 1964–1970* (Special Publications Series No. 389). Jerusalem: Government Press, 1973. (Hebrew)

Israel Central Bureau of Statistics. *Information on educational statistics: Demographic features of pupils in elementary and junior high schools*. Jerusalem: Government Press, 1974. (Hebrew)

Israel Central Bureau of Statistics. *Information on educational statistics* (No. 82). Jerusalem: Government Press, 1977. (Hebrew)

Israel Central Bureau of Statistics. *Statistical abstracts of Israel* (Vol. 1–29). Jerusalem: Government Press, 1950–1978.

Israel Government Yearbooks. Jerusalem: Government Press, 1950–1978.

Israel Knesset. *Integration policy in the educational system.* Minutes of public hearings at the Knesset, 26 February, 1973. (Mimeograph) (Hebrew).

Israel Knesset. *Integration and promoting the goals of education in Israel.* Minutes of public hearings at the Knesset, November 20, 1979. (Mimeograph) (Hebrew)

Israel Knesset. *Protocols of the Knesset meetings.* Jerusalem: Government Press, 1948–1978. (Hebrew)

Israel Ministry of Education and Culture. *Circular of the director general of the Ministry of Education and Culture.* Jerusalem: Government Press, 1955–1978. (Hebrew)

Israel Ministry of Education and Culture. *The junior high school—Principles, guidelines and directives* (2nd ed.). Jerusalem: Government Press, 1971, 1948–1978. (Hebrew)

Israel Ministry of Education and Culture. *Report of the public committee investigating the educational reform in Israel.* Jerusalem: Government Press, 1979. (Hebrew)

Israel Ministry of Labor. *Survey of manpower in Beit–Shemesh.* Jerusalem: Government Press, 1966. (Hebrew)

Israel Ministry of Labor. *Survey of manpower in Beit–Shean.* Jerusalem: Government Press, 1967. (Hebrew) (a)

Israel Ministry of Labor. *Survey of manpower in Kiryat–Gat.* Jerusalem: Government Press, 1967. (Hebrew) (b)

Israel Prime Minister's Office. *Report of the Prime Minister's committee on youth under stress.* Jerusalem: Prime Minister's Office, 1973.

Karmon, N. *Attaining social goals through housing policy: The evolution of the aspiration and an empirical study of the implementation.* Unpublished doctoral dissertation, Technion—Israel Institute of Technology, Haifa, 1975. (Hebrew)

Klein, Z., & Eshel, Y. *Integrating Jerusalem schools.* New York: Academic Press, 1980.

Kleinberger, A. Social integration as a main purpose and justification of the educational policy in Israel. *Policy Planning and Administration in Education,* 1973, *3,* 11–25 (Hebrew).

Levy, A., & Chen, M. Reducing or increasing educational achievement gaps in the primary schools. *Studies in Educational Administration and Organization,* 1976, *4,* 3–52. (Hebrew)

Manis, J. G. Assessing the seriousness of social problems. *Social Problems,* 1974, *22,* 1–15.

Merton, R. K. Social problems and sociological theory. In R. K. Merton & R. Nisbet (Eds.), *Contemporary social problems* (3rd ed.). New York: Harcourt Brace Jovanovitch, 1971, 793–845.

Minkovich, A., Davis, D., & Bashi, J. *Evaluation of educational achievement in the Israeli elementary school.* Jerusalem: School of Education, Hebrew University, 1977.

Orfield, G. Research politics and the anti-busing debate. *Law and Contemporary Problems,* 1978, *42*(4), 141–173.

Pelled, E. *Education in Israel in the 1980s.* Israel: Ministry of Education and Culture, June 1976. (Hebrew)

Peres, Y. *Ethnic relations in Israel.* Tel–Aviv: Sifriat Hapoalim, 1976. (Hebrew)

Razel, O. *Fostering and welfare for whom? A reanalysis of the allocation of inputs in elementary education.* Jerusalem: Ministry of Education and Culture, 1978. (Hebrew)

Rimalt, E. *The report of the Parliamentary Committee for the examination of the structure of elementary and secondary education in Israel.* Jerusalem: The Knesset, 1971. (Hebrew)

Sharkansky, I., & Edwards, G. C. *The policy predicament, making and implementing public policy.* San Francisco: W. H. Freeman, 1978.

Shmueli, E. Problems of social integration in the educational system. *Social Security,* 1972, *3,* 33–44. (Hebrew)

Shmueli, E. Busing as a means of educational desegregation. *Social Security,* 1975, *8,* 77–84. (Hebrew)

Simon, A. On academic achievements of the immigrant children in the Negev. *Megamot*, 1957, *8*, 343–368. (Hebrew)

Smilansky, M. The coping of the Israeli educational system with the problems of the disadvantaged. In C. Ormion (Ed.), *Education in Israel*. Jerusalem: Ministry of Education and Culture, 1971, 121–140. (Hebrew)

Smilansky, S. Children who failed at the beginning of school, and their families. *Megamot*, 1957, *8*, 430–445. (Hebrew)

Smooha, S. *Israel: Pluralism and conflict*. Los Angeles: University of California Press, 1978.

Tallman, I., & McGee, R. Definition of a social problem. In E. O. Smigel (Ed.), *Handbook on the study of social problems*. Chicago: Rand McNally, 1971.

Wildavsky, A. Strategic retreat on objectives: Learning from failure in American public policy. In A. Wildavsky (Ed.), *The art and craft of policy analysis*. London: The MacMillan Press, 1979.

5 Integration as a Situational Contingent: Secular Versus Religious Public Education

Joseph Schwarzwald

INTRODUCTION

In Israel, the religious sector of public education has enjoyed a legal status equal to that of its secular counterpart due to the provisions of the State Education Law in 1953. Under that law, State supervised schools—religious in orientation, curriculum, and staffing—were made available to parents who wished to provide their child with a religious education. These schools were open to any student willing to adhere to basic behavior codes both in and out of school. Currently, about 19% of the entire Jewish school population have registered their children in the first grade of the public religious school.[1]

The Educational Reform Act strove to achieve social integration between Middle Eastern and Western students in an atmosphere of equal, advantageous educational opportunity (See Chapter 2). Comparison of the impact of this reform in the contrasting settings of religious and secular schools can illuminate central factors contributing to the success or failure of ethnic school desegregation. The theoretical literature has suggested a number of objective conditions where interethnic contact may facilitate or hamper the goal of integration. The two parallel educational sectors in Israel offer a natural laboratory for assessing the degree to which these theoretical factors are indeed relevant to the impact of integration.

A recurrent thesis in this chapter is that integration is situationally contingent. Social contact theory argues that the success or failure of desegregation is directly contingent on such situational factors as equality of status, supportive

---

[1]Based on the *Educational Statistical Bulletin*, 1983.

social climate, and intimate contact. Examination of the contrasting school sectors illustrates the manner in which these contingent factors are translated into objective field conditions, influencing the outcomes of desegregation.

This chapter is divided into three main sections. In the first, an analysis is made of objective conditions from the perspective of integration theory, which distinguishes between the religious and secular schools. In the second, results from evaluation studies in the two school systems are summarized in order to assess the actual relevance of these theoretical distinctions. In the concluding section, the socioeducational implications of the Israeli desegregation experience are explored in regard to social-contact theory and current desegregation practice.

OBJECTIVE CONDITIONS IN VIEW OF SOCIAL INTEGRATION THEORY

Desegregation was implemented concurrently in both the religious and secular public schools. Social integration theory and practice point to at least four objective conditions related to successful integration where the religious schools were at a disadvantage. These conditions include:

1. The proportion of advantaged to disadvantaged students.
2. The extent of the academic gap between students from the two ethnic groups.
3. The geographical dispersion of students.
4. The distinctive religious way of life characteristic of the different ethnic groups.

In the following sections, each of these four conditions is discussed in light of current theoretical literature and their differing socio–educational implications for the two school sectors.

Proportion of Advantaged and Disadvantaged Students

The desegregation literature has dealt with the manner in which relative proportion of advantaged to disadvantaged students in the classroom may influence the outcomes of desegregation. Two parallel sets of arguments have been advanced to support the view that advantaged students should constitute the class majority. One of these arguments focuses on the issue of classroom climate, the other deals with the influence of class heterogeneity on instructional level.

In regard to classroom climate, a number of researchers (Jencks, Smith, Acland, Bane, Cohen, Gintis, Heyns, & Michelson, 1972; Klein & Eshel, 1977;

Miller, 1980) have stressed the need to impart educational norms and values to disadvantaged students in a congenial climate. When advantaged students form the class majority, the general learning climate is thought to benefit. The advantaged students' high educational standards and personal example can serve as a model, motivating the disadvantaged student to greater effort. At the same time, the academic climate for the advantaged students is not necessarily effected by the presence of pupils from the minority ethnic group.

A sharply contrasting picture of academic climate is projected when disadvantaged students are in the majority. In that case, interethnic contact may fail to achieve the desired results, because the learning atmosphere will be dictated by the lower educational norms and standards of the disadvantaged group. Under these conditions, interethnic contact may actually be detrimental to the more advantaged students without benefitting the disadvantaged slower group.

In addition to its ramifications for classroom atmosphere, the proportion of advantaged and disadvantaged students can also influence the teacher's level of instruction. Miller (1980) argues that the teachers must adapt out of necessity to the class average. In integrated classes where the disadvantaged form the majority, the instructional level after integration will show little or no improvement over the past. Yet for their advantaged classmates, the instructional level will be significantly lowered. Only when advantaged pupils constitute the majority will instructional levels remain appropriate for advantaged students and provide enrichment for the disadvantaged.

Recommendations by experts in the field regarding the optimal ratio of advantaged and disadvantaged in interethnic contact concur with these theoretical arguments for insuring a majority of the advantaged. Pettigrew and Pajonas (1964) recommended that a proportion of 60 to 80% advantaged students should optimally promote positive integration. The material presented by the U.S. Commission on Civil Rights (1967) also pointed to the benefits of a high ratio of advantaged students in a mixed-ethnic class. However, it must be recognized that some scholars dissented from this view, claiming that the issue of ethnic proportions is not pertinent to academic achievement in desegregated classes (Amir, 1977; Minkovich, Davis, & Bashi, 1977; Zirkel & Moses, 1971).

Studies in Israel and the United States offer empirical support for the relevance of ethnic ratios in determining the academic outcomes of desegregation. Smilansky and Shephatiah (1977) analyzed the effect of class composition on academic achievement and found a clear link between the two variables. Their study revealed that when less than 50% of the students in a class were disadvantaged, their achievement levels were raised without any impact on that of the advantaged students. However, when the disadvantaged students formed the majority, the academic achievement of the advantaged students declined. A similar pattern emerged in the study by Chen, Lewy, and Kfir (1977), who found that the proportion of the slower and average students going on to secondary education was much higher in classes with a Western majority than in classes with a majority of Middle Eastern origin. Recently, Egozi (1980) reanalyzed data from earlier studies in Israel (Chen, Lewy, & Adler, 1978; Minkovich et al., 1977). In this reanalysis, Egozi demonstrated that class composition exerts a significant influence on achievement.

Miller (1980) argued that the satisfactory results of desegregation in Riverside, California, as opposed to the poor outcome in Pasadena and Inglewood, California, were a product of differences in the classroom ethnic ratios. In Riverside, the instructional level appeared to correspond with the standards of the more advantaged students who formed 80% of the classroom populations. In Pasadena and Inglewood, teachers were forced to lower instructional levels because disadvantaged students composed 50% of those classrooms.

A review of conditions in Israel reveals that providing for a majority of advantaged students in the classroom poses serious difficulties for the religious schools (Egozi, 1977). Although the religious sector deals with only 20% of the Israeli school population, it encompasses over 37% of the disadvantaged population. As a result, the disadvantaged are actually the majority group in religious schools (approximately 63%), but only a minority in the secular schools (approximately 32%).

The direct socioeducational implication of the differing ratios in the two sectors is that secular schools can indeed implement integration under the favorable classroom conditions of an advantaged majority and disadvantaged minority. In contrast, the religious schools must implement desegregation in which disadvantaged students form the classroom majority. Under this latter condition, there is a serious risk that the learning climate and instructional level will be dictated by the slower students. This may be detrimental not only to the disadvantaged but also to the advantaged students. On the basis of this analysis, it could be expected that the academic achievement of both advantaged and disadvantaged students would be lower in the religious sector than in the secular sector.

The Gap Between Advantaged and Disadvantaged Students

The gap or distance between advantaged- and disadvantaged-student groups is along such basic dimensions as socioeconomic status, basic skills, and academic achievement. Theoretical analysis of this issue reflects in part the previous discussion of the effects associated with differing ratios on classroom climate and instructional level. Clearly, wide socioeconomic or academic gaps heighten the underlying meaning of heterogeneity and magnify the effects associated with different ratios of classroom ethnic composition.

Contact theory (Amir, 1969; Cook, 1969; Miller, 1980; St. John, 1975) introduces a powerful perspective on the issue of the status gap. According to this approach, status equality and similarity are considered essential bases for successful interethnic contact. Marked gaps in socioeconomic level or academic achievement are considered inimicable to positive change in group stereotypes, intergroup friendships, and self-concept.

According to contact theory, equality of status—particularly in areas where society evaluates individuals—is thought to strongly influence the attitudinal bases of intergroup relations. Encounters between equals provide an opportunity to discover that many stereotypic beliefs have no basis in reality. The ensuing discrepancies between stereotypic expectations and reality upset the participants' cognitive balance. These discrepancies stimulate attitude change, at least toward group representatives in the encounter (Aronson, 1976). However, when there is no equality in status, prejudicial stereotypes may be reinforced and social rejection and aloofness encouraged (Amir, 1976).

In addition to its direct effect on stereotypic attitudes, status equality may also have an indirect effect on intergroup friendship. Byrne (1969, 1971) argued that encounters between equals emphasizes the similarity between participants and thereby facilitates mutual affection. Empirical support for this thesis was provided by Hadad and Shapira (1977), who found that friendship between students is strongly influenced by the degree of similarity in their academic achievement. Others (Maruyama & Miller, 1979; Schwarzwald & Cohen, 1982; Schwarzwald & Yinon, 1977) have expressed similar views regarding achievement as a status criterion in school and its influence on student relationships.

Status equality has also been thought to be important for self-concept among minority-group members. As individuals generate expectations about their own ability in forming a self-concept, they are strongly influenced by social feedback and self-initiated social comparisons (Ziller, 1973). Encounters between unequals may sharpen shortcomings and thereby undermine the self-esteem of low-status-group members. In the case of disadvantaged students, the negative outcomes of social comparison may further upset a level of self-esteem that is already depressed (Coleman, Campbell, Hobson, McPartland, Mood, Weinfeld, & York, 1966; Pettigrew, 1964; Schwarzwald, 1979a).

Armor (1972) argued that the impact of status inequality on self-concept may worsen its effect on intergroup relations. Encounters between social unequals may lead disadvantaged students to see themselves as different and inferior, causing them to lose interest in social integration. This disinterest is further fueled by the frequent rejection of majority students, whose stereotypes of differences may match reality.

Academic gaps may foster negative self-concept in much the same manner as socioeconomic differences. Research findings in Israel and the United States (Armor, 1972; Arzi & Amir, 1977; Gerard & Miller, 1975; Miller, 1980; St. John, 1975) have shown that integration between ethnic groups is best achieved when academic levels are similar. Otherwise, the encounter often arouses feelings of personal disappointment and failure in the poorer student, which is fertile ground for developing a negative self-concept.

The demographic realities of Israeli education indicate that, here too, religious schools fare more poorly than secular schools. The literature suggests the practical necessity of reducing socioeconomic and academic polarization in classrooms in order to reap the potential benefits of improved social relations and avoid the dangers of lowered self-concept. However, disadvantaged students in the religious sector come from considerably lower social classes than the disadvantaged in the secular sector (Algarebali, 1975). Moreover, these students generally display much lower academic achievement than their secular counterparts (Lewy & Chen, 1976; Minkovich et al., 1977; Schwarzwald, 1979c).

The socioeducational implications of the accentuated gap in the religious schools bode poorly for desired advances in that sector. First, both advantaged and disadvantaged students in the religious schools are less likely than their secular counterparts to achieve a high level of mutual social integration. Moreover, the disadvantaged in the religious sector are more likely than the secular disadvantaged to display lowered self-concept as an outcome of the integrational experience.

Geographic Dispersion of Students

The geographical distribution of social groups within a school system has been seen in the past as an influential factor in the integration process. Jencks (Jencks et al., 1972), for example, makes the distinction between natural integration and integration through busing. Natural integration occurs when students of different ethnic groups, but of similar socioeconomic background, live in nearby areas and study in the same schools. In contrast, integration by busing often involves bringing together students of different ethnic groups and socioeconomic classes from geographically disparate areas. An early finding by Jencks was that naturally integrated black students fare better academically than segregated blacks or those integrated by busing.

In addition to academic advantages that appear to accrue from natural integration, it is possible to identify potential social benefits as well. Geographic distance between students often hampers opportunities for social contact before or after school, precluding intimate social meetings. Consequently, the basis for close friendships is sharply reduced when the pupils live far apart and desegregation takes place by busing.

Differences in geographical distance also have ramifications for parental acceptance of integration and support for its continued implementation. For parents whose children are bused long distances, integration poses an imposition and exacerbates antagonisms. For parents whose children are bused long distances, integration may represent a threat to the assessed quality of education. Studies in Israel (Max, 1972; Schwarzwald, 1979c, 1980a) revealed that parents tended to dichotomize between reputable and disreputable schools. Their judgments were based primarily on the proportion of advantaged students studying in the school. In school systems where advantaged students are in a minority, busing reduces this proportion, thereby impugning the school's reputation and decreasing parental satisfaction.

In Israel, the religious school population constitutes a minority within the wider school population and is very thinly distributed over broad geographic areas. Whereas 70% of the students in the secular sector live in ethnically mixed communities, only 20% of those in the religious sector live in communities with an ethnic composition favoring desegregation (Chen, Lewy, & Adler, 1978; Chen, Lewy, & Kfir, 1977; Egozi, 1975). In other words, the religious sector is forced to bus children from a large district, a fact that rarely allows desegregation in favorable proportions.

These differences in geographical dispersion of the religious versus the secular populations tend to accentuate the disparities, cited earlier, in the proportions of disadvantaged students in the two sectors. As can be seen in Table 5.1, over 70% of the schools in the secular sector have a favorable majority of advantaged students. Yet in the religious sector, over 80% of the schools have a majority of disadvantaged students. In effect, the poor conditions of geographical dispersion would be expected to accentuate the negative socioeducational outcomes for religious school children that we described earlier in this chapter.

Another socioeducational implication of the differing patterns of geographical dispersion for the two sectors is an increase in parental dissatisfaction with religious schools. Religious parents have a greater chance of seeing their child being bused to a school whose proportion of disadvantaged students would make it seem "disreputable" in their eyes. The wide status gap among pupils in the religious sector would be likely to further exacerbate this judgment. Yet, by law, parents cannot decide in which school their child is placed, only in which school sector (religious or secular). As a result, parents in the religious sector are often caught in the conflict of giving their child a religious education or an academically "reputable" education.

In sum, the socio–educational implications of geographical dispersion are relatively positive for the secular schools but not for the religious. Due to greater

TABLE 5.1
Percentage Range of
Disadvantaged Students in
Junior High Schools by Sector

Range in Percent	Secular	Religious
0–30	48.9	6.0
31–50	21.9	10.2
51–70	16.7	6.9
71–100	12.6	76.9

Note: Adapted from Israeli Statistical Year Book, 1978, pp. 673–674.

dispersion, the religious schools must make more extended use of integration by busing, thereby paying a price in reduced social and educational benefits and more negative parental attitudes toward integration.

Distinctive Religious Way of Life

As noted earlier, contact theory suggests that factors that heighten similarity or status equality between social or ethnic groups increases the possibility of positive intergroup relations. Conversely, factors pointing up group inequality or dissimilarity tend to hinder social integration. Unfortunately, the religious way of life—a factor that would seem to unify participants in religious public education—appears to act as an added source of interethnic dissimilarity and an obstacle to desegregation and integration.

There are major differences in the religious way of life as observed in the different Middle Eastern and Western communities. These differences can be seen in religious ritual practices and values, and especially in religious customs where religious law is translated into daily life. These variations find expression in the ritual melodies, in the text and chant of daily prayers, and in other aspects of life of great weight to an observant person.

From an educational perspective, a central area of contrast between the Middle Eastern and Western traditions appears in regard to educational ideals and methods for studying the Bible and other religious texts. Whereas Middle Eastern communities emphasize the ideal of the holy or righteous man, Western communities stress the scholar. Similarly, where Middle Eastern educational styles favor repetition and memorization, the Western educational styles favor richness of thought and breadth of understanding (Deshen, 1977; Goldschmidt, 1968, 1970; Ron, 1970; Simon, 1957; Stahl, 1969, 1976, 1977).

Within the religious public schools, preference was given to the Western tradition, whereas the Middle Eastern tradition was disparaged. Although this preference for Western as opposed to Middle Eastern cultural values is apparent in secular schools as well, it is amplified in the religious school due to the crucial importance of the religious traditions in the process of self-identification and social evaluation.

The different religious traditions and the valuations placed upon them suggest a variety of negative socioeducational effects for the disadvantaged Middle Eastern students. First, the preference and prominence awarded Western tradition over their own Middle Eastern background would seem to be a focal point for alienation from the school and increased social distance from the advantaged Western student. Second, the disparagement of the Middle Eastern tradition is a potent influence contributing to self-esteem for the Middle Eastern students, who find themselves culturally as well as economically deprived.

The differences in religious tradition would appear to have important ramifications for parental satisfaction as well. As shown in Table 5.2, advantaged parents are more religiously observant, demanding stricter adherence to tradi-

TABLE 5.2
Degree of Religious Observance (In
Percentages) of Parents with Children in
the Religious Sector by Type of School

Degree of Religious Observance	Advantaged Schools	Disadvantaged Schools
Highly strict	22.00	11.16
Strict	56.13	42.08
Moderate	20.45	36.75
Some	1.42	10.01
None	0	0

Note: Schools in which the percentage of disadvantaged students was less than 30% were defined as advantaged, whereas those with a greater percentage were defined as disadvantaged (Schwarzwald, 1979c).

tional practices from themselves and their children. Disadvantaged parents tend to be less strict in their concern for religious observance. As a result, desegregation is likely to pose a source of dissatisfaction for the advantaged parents who fear the adverse influence of alternate religious practices on their children's behavior and attitudes.

Theoretical Bases of Situational Contingency: A Summary

The theoretical examination of diverse conditions in the Israeli educational system points up the need to see integration as situationally contingent. According to this approach, the effects of integration are seen to be highly dependent on the manner in which field conditions interact with such basic psychological processes as social comparison. In line with this view of situational contingency, the analyses of the proportions of integrated groups, the extent of the interethnic gap, their geographic dispersion, and their distinctive ways of life all lead to differential expectations regarding the educational, social, and emotional outcomes of integration in the religious and secular educational sectors.

In particular, the analysis indicates that integration in the religious, as opposed to secular sector, will result in: (1) Lower academic achievement for all students; (2) Depreciated self-concept for disadvantaged students; (3) More sharply stereotypic social attitudes among all students; (4) Reduced parental satisfaction with the school, particularly among advantaged parents.

Evaluation Studies of Integrational Reform in Israel

Since the introduction of the educational reform a decade ago, which created the junior high school, several studies evaluated the desegregation enterprise. Selective examination of this body of work provides important empirical data bearing on situational contingency in the religious and secular schools. These deal with such core issues as reform implementation and its effect on academic achievement, the impact of desegregation on self-concept, and on parental satisfaction. Findings about these issues are described in the following sections.

Implementation and Academic Achievement

The reason for addressing the implementation of desegregation in junior high schools is an outcome of the dramatic evaluational findings in this area. Oftentimes, school reform did not lead to true integration but rather to "pseudo-integration." Although disadvantaged and advantaged populations were formally brought together within *schools*, ethnic mix did not always occur at the classroom level. As a result of different selection policies, students in desegregated schools often found themselves in segregated rather than in desegregated classrooms. Examination of this phenomenon illustrates an interesting dynamic in Israeli desegregation and bears directly on the analysis of academic outcomes in the religious versus secular sectors.

Bringing together students from defined geographical districts to centralized schools presented junior high school principals and teachers with the problem of teaching a school population that was distinctly heterogenous in academic achievement and background (Lewy & Chen, 1976). For fear that the great disparity in academic skills would interfere with instruction, principals were given the option of tracking students by academic level into classrooms for instruction in a limited number of core courses. Thus for some courses, students studied in classes with relatively homogenous academic level, whereas in others they were taught in heterogenous classes. Due to the high overlap between achievement, ethnicity, and social status, the practical result of tracking was continued partial segregation. The academically more advanced students, primarily from advantaged Western backgrounds, studied core courses with students of similar background. Likewise, the academically slower students, predominantly from lower class Middle Eastern homes, studied core courses with students with socioethnic backgrounds much like their own.

The Junior High School Study (Chen, Lewy, & Adler, 1978) revealed relatively extensive pseudodesegregation, whereby students were tracked into homogenous classes for all subjects. In this format, desegregation was implemented at the school level only and not in the classroom itself. This policy, though never officially approved, was employed primarily in the religious sector. However, it also appeared in those secular schools where disadvantaged students formed a majority.

As the Junior High School Study shows, tracking had a significant impact on academic achievement as well as on classroom composition. In general, higher track students (primarily of advantaged, Western origin) made significantly greater progress in core material than the lower track students (predominantly from disadvantaged, Middle Eastern origin). In other words, tracking had results directly contrary to those desired for integration. Instead of narrowing the academic gap, "pseudointegration" policies contributed to its widening.

The religious schools' use of tracking in all courses reduces the importance of any conclusions that one might have wished to draw from the changes that occurred in pupils' academic achievement, in both the religious and secular sectors, following desegregation. However, examination of the reasons behind the institution of these practices does provide some insight into the question of whether people in the schools felt that desegregation was differentially hampering academic achievement. In this regard, there is substantial evidence that teachers in the religious sector did indeed sense that their students may suffer academically from desegregation.

In the Junior High School Study (Chen et al., 1978; Inbar, Adler, & Resh, 1977), teachers indicated their attitudes toward tracking as well as their preference for social integration or academic achievement as a goal of integration. Teachers in the religious schools advocated the institution of tracking and a preference for academic achievement goals more frequently than their colleagues in secular schools. It is important to note that a similar tendency toward "pedagogical conversatism" was expressed by teachers in secular schools with a high proportion of Middle Eastern students. It would appear that this conservatism in the religious sector was a "defensive" response to a perception that academic achievement was threatened by the disproportionate number of disadvantaged students found there.

Similar defensive concerns appear in principals' explanations of their decision to institute selection policies such as tracking when schools were desegregated (Chen et al., 1978). These explanations included a desire to insure enriched instruction for more advanced students, an interest in reducing the load of overly heterogenous classrooms, and an attempt to increase school prestige by drawing better students to their "select" classes. The authors attributed these motivations, when expressed by principals of secular schools, to defensive concerns for academic achievement. Yet in explaining similar expressions by religious school principals, they invoked religious ideology. A more parsimonious conclusion would be that defensive concerns motivated both groups. Thus, it would appear that the greater tendency to employ selection policies in the religious sector was an outcome of the school staff's feeling that academic achievement was being more severely threatened there than in the secular sector.

The Impact of Desegregation on Pupils' Self-Concept

A series of studies (Arzi & Amir, 1976, 1977; Schwarzwald, 1978, 1979a, 1980b) offer convergent support for the hypothesis that a marked gap between the groups in desegregated classrooms in the religious sector would lower the self-concept of disadvantaged students. These studies focus on four divergent, yet interrelated, aspects of self-concept: self-esteem, personality adjustment, evaluations of own and other ethnic groups, and identification with one's own religious group.

Students' self-esteem was examined by Schwarzwald (1979a) using Fitts' (1965) self-concept scale. In this study, comparisons were made between advantaged and disadvantaged students, in integrated versus segregated schools, within either the religious or secular sector. On all components of overall self-evaluation except for physical self-image, students in desegregated schools had higher levels of self-esteem than their peers in the segregated schools. This result is not surprising, because segregated schools were composed almost entirely of disadvantaged students, whereas the integrated schools had larger numbers of their advantaged peers.

Direct support was obtained for the expectation that the self-esteem of the disadvantaged religious school student would be particularly threatened by desegregation. In the secular schools, no differences were found between the self-esteem of the primarily advantaged Western students and the predominantly disadvantaged Middle Eastern students. Yet in the religious schools, a strong contrast emerged between the high self-esteem of the Western students and the low self-esteem of their Middle Eastern peers. In fact, the self-esteem of these Middle Eastern students in the desegregated religious school was even lower than that found for their Middle Eastern counterparts in segregated schools.[2] In short, this pattern of results is highly consistent with the hypothesis that polarization as a result of desegregation would hamper the self-esteem of members from low-achieving groups.

Comparing self-adjustment ratings derived from the Fitts' scale leads to a similar conclusion. In the secular desegregated schools, no differences in adjustment appeared between Middle Eastern and Western students. Yet in the religious desegregated schools, Middle Eastern students did exhibit problems in adjustment, unlike their Western peers.

Further evidence for the conclusions that it is the gap in academic achievement that upsets adjustment during desegregation can be gathered from the findings by Arzi and Amir (1977). The latter study differentiated between advantaged and disadvantaged Middle Eastern students in their sample. They found that when there was a wide gap in academic achievement between the two groups the disadvantaged pupils displayed a sense of frustration and failure (on the Fitts' adjustment scales). In contrast, when there was no gap in academic achievement between the two groups, the disadvantaged remained well adjusted. These results

---

[2]Other studies, dealing only with academic concept, have also found a decline in the self-concept of disadvantaged students in the integrative setting. However, these studies (Chen et al., 1978; Eshel & Klein, 1977) are not cited in the text, because none made systematic comparisons between the religious and secular sectors.

regarding the impact of a wide achievement gap on adjustment are similar to those found in the United States (Armor, 1972; Gerard & Miller, 1975).

Evaluations of one's own and other ethnic groups were assessed in another study (Schwarzwald, 1980a) dealing with the effects of the achievement-gap concept. In this study, these evaluations were derived from asking junior high students to describe four Israeli figures, using a series of statements describing bipolar traits, the Western secular, the Middle Eastern secular, the Western religious, and the Middle Eastern religious Israeli. Factor analysis of the bipolar statements yielded two major evaluational components: social standing (including traits such as backward–advanced, successful–unsuccessful, intelligent– unintelligent) and friendliness (including traits such as warm–cold, selfish–unselfish, considerate–inconsiderate). Both components were attributed to ethnic origin.

In regard to social standing, the Middle Eastern Israeli—whether religious or secular—was given a lower rating on social standing than his Western counterpart. Moreover significant patterns emerged in how the Middle Eastern Israeli was rated in the religious and secular desegregated schools. Religious Western students assigned the Middle Eastern figures lower social standing than the secular Western students did. Most importantly, religious Middle Eastern students also evaluated the figures representing their own membership group significantly lower than secular Middle Eastern students. In other words, the relatively large gap in achievement between the two ethnic groups in the desegregated religious school resulted in having disadvantaged Middle Eastern students there express lower levels of self-evaluation. At the same time, the academic gap lead the Western students in these schools to express more sharply stereotypic views of the Middle Eastern groups.

A very different pattern of results appeared in the analysis of friendship ratings. Here, both Middle Eastern and Western students tended to view the Middle Eastern figures as more friendly than Western ones. Although the religious students in desegregated schools attributed lower social-standing scores to the Middle Eastern figures, they did not give them lower scores on friendliness. The difference in the two patterns seems to stem from the gap in academic achievement. Although social standing is closely related to inequity in status, friendliness is not a relevant aspect of status polarization.

The impact of the achievement gap in desegregated settings can be observed in findings on religious identification. In a study conducted only in religious schools (Schwarzwald, 1978), junior high students from Western and Middle Eastern communities were asked to express attitudes bearing on their solidarity and identification with their own religious group. The responses revealed that religious Middle Eastern students in desegregated schools showed less ethnic solidarity than their Middle Eastern peers in segregated schools. In fact, the religious Middle Eastern students from the desegregated schools showed clear signs of alienation from their religious membership group. This finding about identification with one's religious group converges with previous results about self-esteem, adjustment, and group evaluations, showing depreciated self-concept in desegregated religious school with a wide achievement gap between the two ethnic groups.

Integrational Impact on Parental Satisfaction

Studies on parental satisfaction (Chen et al., 1978; Inbar et al., 1977) support the hypothesis that religious parents would be less favorable toward integration than their secular counterparts. During interviews in the Junior High School Study (Chen et al., 1978), parents of students in the religious schools expressed more opposition to integration than parents whose children attended secular schools. Because the study did not distinguish between Western and Middle Eastern parents within the religious sector, we cannot know if there were differences in satisfaction between the two groups. However, the reported finding that Western parents as a whole expressed less satisfaction than Middle Eastern parents suggests that it was indeed the Westerners who were less satisfied in the religious sector.

Further support for this inference appears in a letter sent to a number of social scientists by the director of the Department for Religious Education. As supervisor of the implementation of desegregation, he reported that:

'Ashkenazic' (Western) parents in the religious sector are subject to the serious fear that desegregation in such proportions (30 percent Western children and 70 percent Middle Eastern children) sharply lowers the level of education, in comparison with the education children would receive in segregated schools. This view of desegregation is reinforced by the information channeled through the media regarding optimal ratios for successful integration.

These fears of religious parents do not appear to be related to religious ideology per se, as suggested by Chen et al. (1978) but seems rather to reflect a more basic concern for the quality of education in desegregated schools. Active opposition to desegregation was expressed by secular parents whenever the majority status of advantaged students in their children's school was threatened. Thus, the signal difference in the level of dissatisfaction between the two school sectors appears to be a direct outcome of the achievement gap and of the less-favorable proportions of ethnic mix in the religious schools.

Educational and Social Implications of Situational Contingency

The social and educational implications of viewing desegregation outcomes as situationally contingent clusters around three main topics. The first, already dealt at length, has been that the effect of integration on children and parents is dependent on objective field conditions. Yet, situational contingency also appears to have important ramifications for both the atmosphere of integrational implementation in the past as well as for the character of desired practice in the future.

Both the theoretical analysis and the empirical findings reaffirm the view that desegregation does not lead to simple uniform results for children. Rather, the effects for children are dependent on objective conditions prior to desegregation. The gap in basic skills and achievement creates difficulties for learning in the desegregated classroom. The inevitable comparisons in achievement and social status that group contact accentuates are deleterious to the lower status group's self-concept. Finally, wide geographical dispersion of social groups hinders intimate contact after school hours.

Certainly, there is a need for caution in drawing conclusions from the Israeli experience with desegregation in both the religious and secular sectors. Many of the studies conducted to date did not necessarily investigate hypotheses dictated by theory. Hence, expectations regarding such topics as interethnic attitudes and social relations were either not examined or the relevant variables were not studied. In fact, many of the findings reviewed here were often byproducts of studies with other purposes.

Clearly, situational contingency goes beyond the consideration of simple school conditions and forces one to deal with the broader cultural dimension. In fact, the Israeli example offers an ideal illustration of this dimension. As Miller (1980) argued, when different cultures are not given suitable representation in the school program, the goals of desegregation are not achieved. Unfortunately, the culture of the Middle Eastern Jewish community has not been adequately represented in either the secular or the religious sectors (Stahl, 1976). Cultural distortion is particularly marked in the religious sector where it is compounded by the issue of religious tradition. The Middle Eastern students in the integrated religious schools were dissatisfied with and unreconciled to their cultural heritage. This alienation goes hand in hand with difficulties in adjustment. As Frankenstein (1962) noted, a lack of continuity between cultural values at home and school may ultimately interfere with the religious school goals of fostering the internalization of religious values and observance.

The complexity of religious diversity in the desegregated schools affect parents as well. When core aspects of a given cultural heritage are threatened by intergroup contact, parents express fears and dissatisfaction. Thus cultural diversity heightens resistance to interethnic contact.

Dealing with studies in the field leads one to recognize that situational contingency has crucial influence on the implementation and climate of desegregation. In this regard it is important to focus on two issues: the issue of defensive strategies, or pseudointegration, and pedagogical conservatism. Neither phenomenon bodes well for successful integration.

The instructional problems posed by integration and conditions in the school system were apparent to the administration of the Ministry of Education from the outset. As a defensive countermeasure to cope with desegregation, a large number of schools instituted tracking. In secular schools, where the objective conditions for desegregation were more conducive, tracking was implemented in core courses only. When conditions were especially difficult, as in the religious sector, tracking was actually extended to all courses. In effect, differences in the degree of pseudointegrational policies were situationally determined.

Clearly, the recourse to even moderate forms of tracking by academic level is inconsistent with the goals of desegregation. On the one hand it attaches formal stigma and status to academic differences, thereby sharpening the interethnic gap. On the other hand, by allowing students to progress in core subjects at their own rate, it actually widens academic gaps. In effect, pseudointegration violates the desired goals of social integration and academic equalization, particularly when carried to its extreme.

In retrospect, tracking appears to be only one part of a broader picture of pedagogical conservatism. This conservative dimension expressed in a preference of academic over social goals in education (Chen et al., 1978) is in and of itself counter to integration. For the academically slower students this climate may lead to an avoidance of those highly prized learning tasks in which they are likely to fail. The emphasis placed on academic success may arouse fears in exactly those areas where they are least confident.

Whereas pedagogical conservatism stands in opposition to integrational goals, it is clearly dependent on the objective conditions found in schools where desegregation is implemented. Pedagogical conservatism was found to be most marked in schools whose proportion of disadvantaged students posed the greatest threat to academic objectives. Thus, pedagogical conservatism appears to be as situationally contingent as its implementational derivative—pseudointegration.

In summing up the implications of situational contingency for desegregation, it is clear that the desired goals cannot be attained by simply bringing students of different social groups into contact, at least under extant conditions. Without deliberate intervention the desired goals cannot be achieved. Because many crucial conditions such as ethnic proportions, the academic gap, geographical dispersion, or cultural diversity cannot be changed, other avenues for improvement must be explored.

The literature does not provide many examples of alternate paths for success. Yet even the sparce information available has not been exploited. One promising approach is to replace the widely used traditional method of frontal instruction, known to be competitive in nature (Aronson, Blaney, Stephan, Sikes, & Snapp, 1978), with pedagogical methods emphasizing students' interdependence and cooperation. This cooperative learning approach has been shown to improve intergroup relations and academic achievement (Aronson et al., 1978; DeVries, Edwards, & Slavin, 1978; Johnson, Johnson, & Scott, 1978; Sharan & Sharan,

1976; Slavin, 1977, 1980; Weigel, Wiser, & Cook, 1972). Expectation training (Cohen, 1972, 1973) may also be promising in this regard, because it aspires to promote greater status equality and defuse perceptions based on stereotypes (See Chapter 10).

A second broad approach to altering the basic conditions of desegregation that is particularly relevant to Israel is to implement it at the earliest stages of education. One reason behind the educational reform at the junior high level was the realization that equal educational opportunities had not been provided at the elementary school level. Thus, a direct benefit of desegregation at earlier stages in the educational process would be to rectify these inequalities in basic opportunities. In addition, such a step would bring young children together before social stereotypes and academic gaps had become firmly entrenched.

ACKNOWLEDGMENT

The author would like to express his gratitude to Michael Hoffman for his aid and comments in the preparation of this chapter.

REFERENCES

Algarebali, M. Indices for the characterization of the social composition of schools and a system for allocation of budgets to schools with disadvantaged students. *Megamot*, 1975, *21*, 219–227. (Hebrew)

Amir, Y. Contact hypothesis in ethnic relations. *Psychological Bulletin*, 1969, *71*, 319–342.

Amir, Y. The role of intergroup contact in change of prejudice and ethnic relations. In P. A. Katz (Ed.), *Toward the elimination of racism*. New York: Pergamon Press, 1976.

Amir, Y. Ethnic interaction and intergroup attitudes and relations: A review and reevaluation. *Megamot*, 1977, *23*, 41–76. (Hebrew)

Armor, D. J. The effect of busing. *Public Interest*, 1972, *28*, 90–126.

Aronson, E. *The social animal*. San Francisco: W. H. Freeman, 1976.

Aronson, E. Blaney, N., Stephan, C., Sikes, J., & Snapp, M. *The jigsaw classroom*. Beverly Hills, Calif.: Sage, 1978.

Arzi, Y., & Amir, Y. Personal adjustment and scholastic gains of culturally deprived children in homogeneous and heterogeneous classrooms. *Megamot*, 1976, *22*, 279–289. (Hebrew)

Arzi, Y., & Amir, Y. Intellectual and academic achievements and adjustment of underprivileged children in homogeneous and heterogeneous classrooms. *Child Development*, 1977, *48*, 726–729.

Byrne, D. Attitudes and attraction. In L. Berkowitz (Ed.), *Advances in experimental social psychology* (Vol. 4). New York: Academic Press, 1969.

Byrne, D. *The attraction paradigm*. New York: Academic Press, 1971.

Chen, M., Lewy, A., & Adler, C. *The junior high school study*. Jerusalem: Ministry of Education and Culture, 1978. (Hebrew)

Chen, M., Lewy, A., & Kfir, D. The possibilities of interethnic group contact in the junior high schools: Implementation and results, *Megamot*, 1977, *23*, 101–123. (Hebrew)

Cohen, E. Interracial interaction disability. *Human Relations*, 1972, *25*, 287–304.

Cohen, E. Modifying the effects of social structure. *American Behavioral Scientist,* 1973, *16,* 861–878.

Coleman, J. S., Campbell, E. Q., Hobson, C. J., McPartland, J., Mood, A. M., Weinfeld, F. D., & York, R. L. *Equality of educational opportunity.* Washington, D. C.: U. S. Government Printing Office, 1966.

Cook, S. W. Motives in a conceptual analysis of attitude-related behavior. In W. J. Arnold & D. Levine (Eds.), *Nebraska Symposium on Motivation.* Lincoln: University of Nebraska Press, 1969.

Deshen, S. Public religious education in its natural environment: Four proposals. *Bisdeh Hemed,* 1977, *20,* 206–211. (Hebrew).

DeVries, D. L., Edwards, K. J., & Slavin, R. E. Biracial learning teams and race relations in the classroom: Four field experiments using Teams–Games–Tournaments. *Journal of Educational Psychology,* 1978, *70,* 356–362.

Egozi, M. *Pupil population in the elementary school according to ethnic origin and family size: 1972 vs. 1975.* Jerusalem: Ministry of Education and Culture, 1975. (Hebrew)

Egozi, M. *Pupils' composition in the elementary education according to ethnic origin, father's education and family size.* Jerusalem: Ministry of Education and Culture, 1977. (Hebrew)

Egozi, M. *The influence of class composition on academic achievements of students differing in social background.* Jerusalem: Ministry of Education and Culture, 1980. (Hebrew)

Eshel, Y., & Klein, Z. School integration, academic self-image, and achievement of lower-class elementary school pupils. *Megamot,* 1977, *23,* 134–145. (Hebrew)

Fitts, W. H. *Tennessee self-concept scale.* Nashville Counselor Recordings and Tests, 1965.

Frankenstein, C. The school without parents. *Megamot,* 1962, *12,* 3–23. (Hebrew)

Gerard, H. B., & Miller, N. *School desegregation.* New York: Plenum Press, 1975.

Goldschmidt, J. On the religious custom. *Bisdeh Hemed,* 1968, *9,* 168–172. (Hebrew)

Goldschmidt, J. Advancement problems and the religious education. In S. Adiel, G. Bergson & A. Stahl (Eds.), *A decade in the advancement enterprises.* Jerusalem: Ministry of Education and Culture, 1970. (Hebrew)

Hadad, M., & Shapira, R. Commanding resources and social integration. *Megamot,* 1977, *23,* 161–173. (Hebrew)

Inbar, D., Adler, C., & Resh, N. Ethnic composition, integration, achievement and "school climate." *Megamot,* 1977, *23,* 230–237. (Hebrew)

Jencks, C., Smith, M., Acland, H., Bane, M. J., Cohen, D., Gintis, H., Heyns, N., & Michelson, S. *Inequality: A reassessment of the effect of family and schooling in America.* New York: Basic Books, 1972.

Johnson, H. B., Johnson, R. T., & Scott, L. The effects of cooperative and individualized instruction on student attitudes and achievement. *Journal of Social Psychology,* 1978, *104,* 207–216.

Klein, Z., & Eshel, Y. Towards a psycho-social definition of school integration. *Megamot,* 1977, *23,* 17–40. (Hebrew)

Lewy, A., & Chen, M. Closing or widening the achievement gap: A comparison over time of ethnic group achievement in Israeli elementary schools. *Studies in Educational Administration and Organization,* 1976, *4,* 3–52. (Hebrew)

Maruyama, G., & Miller, N. Reexamination of normative influence processes in desegregated classrooms. *American Educational Research Journal,* 1979, *16,* 273–283.

Max, D. *School as viewed by parents.* Jerusalem: The Hebrew University, M.A. thesis, 1972. (Hebrew)

Miller, N. Making school desegregation work. In W. Stephan & J. Feagin (Eds.), *School desegregation: Past, present and future.* New York: Plenum Press, 1980.

Minkovich, A., Davis, D., & Bashi, J. *An evaluation study of educational achievement in the Israeli elementary school.* Jerusalem: The Hebrew University, 1977.

Pettigrew, T. F. *A profile of the Negro American.* Princeton: Van Nostrand, 1964.

Pettigrew, T. F., & Pajonas, P. J. *Social psychological considerations of racially balanced schools.* Unpublished working paper prepared for the New York State Commissioner of Education, 1964.

Ron, A. On several educational problems in the religious public education. *Bisdeh Hemed,* 1970, *23,* 3–17. (Hebrew)

Schwarzwald, J. Problems of the reform program in the religious school system. *Studies in Education,* 1978, *19,* 107–122. (Hebrew)

Schwarzwald, J. The self-concept of junior high school students in its significance to religious education. *Megamot,* 1979, *24,* 580–588. (Hebrew) (a)

Schwarzwald, J. Parents' perception of the Israeli elementary school: I. Satisfaction of intrinsic and extrinsic components. *Studies in Education,* 1979, *24,* 61–76. (Hebrew (b)

Schwarzwald, J. *Teachers' and parents' attitudes and expectations regarding the elementary education.* Jerusalem: The Ministry of Education and Culture, The Religious Sector, 1979. (Hebrew) (c)

Schwarzwald, J. Parents' perception of the Israeli elementary school: Academic subject level and values imparted by school. *Studies in Education,* 1980, *27,* 105–130. (Hebrew) (a)

Schwarzwald, J. Relatedness of ethnic origin to the stereotypes of the Israeli in the eyes of junior high school students. *Megamot,* 1980, *25,* 322–340. (Hebrew) (b)

Schwarzwald, J., & Cohen, S. The relationship between academic tracking and the degree of interethnic acceptance. *Journal of Educational Psychology,* 1982, *74,* 588–597.

Schwarzwald, J., & Yinon, Y. Symmetrical and assymmetrical interethnic relations. *International Journal of Intercultural Relations,* 1977, *1,* 40–47.

Sharan, S., & Sharan, Y. *Small-group Teaching.* Englewood Cliffs, N. J.: Educational Technology Publications, 1976.

Simon, U. "East and West"—Recognizing religious diversity in Israel. *Hachinuch,* 1957, *28,* 423–433. (Hebrew)

Slavin, R. E. Classroom reward structure: An analytic and practical review. *Review of Educational Research,* 1977, *47,* 633–650.

Slavin, R. E. Cooperative learning. *Review of Educational Research,* 1980, *50,* 315–342.

Smilansky, S., & Shephatiah, L. Socio-cultural integration and other classroom variables as related to achievements in grades one and two. *Megamot,* 1977, *23,* 79–87. (Hebrew)

Stahl, A. The modern school in the eyes of the religious Middle Eastern parent. *Bisdeh Hemed,* 1969, *12,* 265–269. (Hebrew)

Stahl, A. *Culture integration in Israel.* Tel–Aviv: Am Oved, 1976. (Hebrew)

Stahl, A. Religious education and the disadvantaged student. *Bisdeh Hemed,* 1977, *20,* 3–7. (Hebrew)

St. John, N. S. *School desegregation outcomes for children.* New York: Wiley, 1975.

U. S. Commission on Civil Rights. *Racial isolation in the public schools.* Washington, D. C.: U. S. Government Printing Office, 1967.

Weigel, R. H., Wiser, P. L., & Cook, S. W. The impact of cooperative learning experiences on cross-ethnic relations and attitudes. *Journal of Social Issues,* 1972, *28,* 1–19.

Ziller, R. C. *The social self.* New York: Pergamon Press, 1973.

Zirkel, P., & Moses, E. G. Self-concept and ethnic group membership among public school students. *American Educational Research Journal,* 1971, *8,* 253–265.

6 Integration and School Variables

Dan Inbar
Nura Resh
Chaim Adler

To what extent do school-wide variables, such as teachers' role behavior, school size, and school policy, exert effects on the outcomes of ethnic desegregation in the school? This question emphasizes the role of school-wide variables as mediating the effects of desegregation on a host of pupil outcomes, in the personal, academic, and social-interactive domains.

For the purpose of the present discussion, the different variables are divided into four categories: structural variables, variables of role behavior, affective variables, and variables relating to goals and values. Even though these categories may overlap to some degree, they are helpful for organizing the discussion that follows. The following discussion is based on recurring trends in research results, and on empirical findings of a number of studies in the area of educational integration conducted in Israel in the 1970s. One set of sources consists of the three comprehensive studies that focused on educational outcomes in elementary and junior high schools in Israel. The first study evaluates the Reform of the Israel school system in which school integration is one of the main components (Chen, Lewy, & Adler, 1978). The second study is an evaluation of elementary schools that, whereas focusing primarily on academic achievement, also examined several questions relating to school variables including school integration (Minkovich, Davis, & Bashi, 1977). The "Nahlaot" experiment, which concentrated on the effect of integration on academic achievement, is the third source in this group (Eshel & Klein, 1977, 1978; Klein & Eshel, 1973, 1980). The second group of sources consists of qualitative and quantative studies evaluating integration in different schools (Amir, 1977, Amir, Rich, & Ben–Ari, 1978; Chen, Lewy, & Kfir, 1977; Gat, 1972; Rosenstein & Gat, 1975), and an in-depth study based on a case analysis of five schools (Resh, Adler, & Inbar, 1980). From this material we can suggest a number of hypotheses with regard to the effects of different variables on integration. The third group of sources consists of a number of quantitative empirical studies that focused on specific problems in the process of integration in Israel (Amir, 1968; Arzi & Amir, 1976; Bashi, 1977; Chen & Kfir, 1979; Chen, Kfir, & Lewy, 1976; Dar, 1977; Gutman, Gur, Kaniel, & Wall, 1972; Inbar, 1975, 1981; Levin & Chen, 1977; Smilansky & Shephatiah, 1977; Stahl, Agmon, & Mar–Haim, 1976). A fourth source is provided by studies that examined the link between the organizational climate of the school and teaching methods (Inbar, Adler, & Resh, 1977; Zak, 1981).

Structural Variables

There is no clear explanation about the nature of the links between structural school variables and the various results of desegregation. Desegregation invariably implies a more academically and socially heterogeneous student body. Large schools were found to provide opportunities for more differentiated programming than smaller schools, such as the use of a greater variety of curricular alternatives, special educational projects, and the use of alternative instructional techniques like cooperative learning in small groups (Resh, Adler, & Inbar, 1980). From this point of view, large schools have been viewed as providing the conditions necessary for successful ethnic integration. On the other hand, the larger the school the greater the number of problems perceived by the teachers. The greater academic heterogeneity of the pupils seems to be the most prominent of these problems. In addition, increased school size results in increased bureaucratization, the loss of a sense of intimacy in the school, greater institutionalization of roles, and ultimately in alienation. Greater organizational complexity found in larger schools seems to result in the fact that the programmatic opportunities available in larger schools are not exploited effectively and, hence, do not lead to an improvement in teachers' perceptions of the school in terms of its ability to cope with the challenge posed by desegregation. Thus, school size exerts a dual effect with contradictory trends.

Another group of structural variables are those of teachers' background, such as age, sex, education, length of teaching experience, and country of origin. No evidence was found of a relationship between length of teaching experience and approaches and attitudes toward integration (Chen, Lewy, & Adler, 1978; Minkovich, Davis, & Bashi, 1977). On the other hand, the level of education and type of previous teaching experience were found to be significant variables in determining school climate (Zak, 1981), and attitudes toward integration (Chen, Lewy, & Adler, 1978). In general, it can be said that teachers who had taught in elementary schools before they transferred to junior high schools tended to be more inclined toward social integration. They are usually graduates of Teacher Colleges rather than of universities. However, the decisive factor here is not their educational background but rather their previous teaching experience in elementary schools (Amir, Rich, & Ben–Ari, 1978; Resh, Adler, & Inbar, 1977).

This points once more to a paradox: One of the accomplishments of the school Reform in Israel (which established desegregated junior high schools) was to raise teachers' educational level, whereas at the same time to recruit new university graduates as teachers for the 7th, 8th, and 9th grades. The percentage of teachers with an academic education in these grades in the junior high schools is consequently significantly higher than that of their colleagues who teach in grades 7–8 in elementary schools (Chen, Lewy, & Adler, 1978). The academization of teachers may provide some assurance of a higher level of training and knowledge, but it does not constitute a guarantee of favorable attitudes toward integration, or of teachers' ability and readiness to cope with a heterogeneous student population. It is possible, therefore, that academization, in itself, may lead to an increased emphasis on academic achievement perhaps even at the expense of integration. Some changes in teacher training may thus be necessary in order to avoid this negative consequence of academic background.

The teachers' country of origin is a demographic variable that obviously takes on special importance in desegregation studies. Teachers' assessment of students' chances to succeed academically in school were studied. Teachers of Middle Eastern origin seem to be less optimistic than their Western colleagues with regard to Middle Eastern students' chances of improving their achievement level in desegregated schools. However, they are more optimistic about interethnic social relations and the expected adult social status of students of Middle Eastern origin who graduate from desegregated schools (Chen, Lewy, & Adler, 1978).

It was also found, however, that the ratio of teachers of Middle Eastern to Western background in schools was correlated with schools' "policy of selection," which is closely allied with a policy of segregation (Resh, Adler, Chen, & Inbar, 1979). The larger the ratio of teachers of Middle Eastern to Western background, the greater was the tendency to introduce homogeneous homeroom classes, the higher was the schools' dropout rate, and the higher was the tendency to employ ability grouping (over and above the ability grouping sanctioned by the Ministry of Education) (Chen, Kfir, & Lewy, 1976). It may thus be the case that teachers of Middle Eastern background are primarily concerned with students' academic achievements, and therefore they view school integration from that vantage point only. Consequently, they are pessimistic about disadvantaged students' chances to improve their levels of academic achievement due to integration. Similarly, the Middle Eastern teachers are more insistent on pupil selection processes, based on the notion that the better students among the disadvantaged should be separated and that extra effort should be made to advance them.

The school background variable most significantly correlated to selection policies is the schools' religious affiliation.[1] The religious public schools display a significantly greater tendency than the secular schools to adopt an internal

---

[1] In Israel there are *two* public school systems, secular and religious, (see Chapter 2 in this book).

selective policy. Teachers in religious public schools, in line with age-old Jewish tradition, tend to place a high premium on academic achievements. Religious teachers were thus found to stress achievement over integration, as were teachers of Middle Eastern background.

Israel's junior high schools were thus found to display the following: In the religious schools there is a greater tendency toward selectivity; religious teachers and teachers of Middle Eastern background tend to attach more importance to achievement than to integration; in the religious schools there are more teachers of Middle Eastern origin. In addition, the religious schools contain a much higher percentage of disadvantaged students, and in schools with a high percentage of disadvantaged students (religious and nonreligious), there are more teachers of Middle Eastern origin. One can see here a situation where a network of school characteristics, teacher characteristics, teachers' attitudes, and school policy combine to create a climate that is not conducive to social integration. Ironically, neither is it conducive to better academic achievement!

Educational studies in Israel also revealed information about the impact of integration on teachers' attitudes. It was found that the heterogeneity of a school's student body was correlated with teachers' perceptions of the existence of problems in areas of discipline, social intercourse, and curriculum and textbooks (Resh, Adler, & Inbar, 1982). In other words, teachers perceive the teaching of students in heterogeneous classes and the promotion of social integration to be complicated and difficult to implement. Teachers also feel that there are insufficient means and support for this task (Amir, Rich, & Ben–Ari, 1978; Chen, Lewy, & Kfir, 1977; Gat, 1972; Rosenstein & Gat, 1975; Stahl, Agmon, & Mar–Haim, 1976). It is thus to be expected that the difficulties inherent in dealing with heterogeneous classes will bring forth teachers' pressure toward homogeneous classes and/or greater reliance on ability grouping.

Interestingly enough, evidence has been found that such heterogeneous classes can serve as a catalyst for the teachers to seek new methods of instruction and reveal a greater degree of acceptance of educational innovations (Eshel & Klein, 1977; Klein & Eshel, 1973). In other words, once more we find a dual effect of heterogeneous student composition: It may form the background for a high degree of perceived problems and educational difficulties, and, at the same time, it can serve as a catalyst for pedagogical innovations. These phenomena may well be complementary.

Role-Behavior Variables

It seems that the clear definition of roles and differentiation in teachers' roles as a result of professionalization, academization, and school size is related to an achievement orientation, at the expense of social integration. Specifically there are some findings about the changing function and relative weight of four specific roles in the process of integration—the principal, the homeroom teacher, the subject-matter special teacher, and the guidance counselor. We examine each of these in turn.

In contrast to the view that prevailed for many years that the school principal is a part of the staff, and that the nature of the educational process is affected, first and foremost, by the teaching staff, it appears that the principal may serve more as the focal source of motivation for momentum and dynamism in the educational process, especially in periods of transition and change (Amir, Rich, & Ben–Ari, 1978; Ascher, 1981; Boyd & Crowson, 1981:311–373; Resh, Adler, & Inbar, 1980). In other words, there is evidence to indicate a trend in which the principal serves as a catalyst in shaping the pedagogical climate of the school. Schools that are similar in their structural components may differ in their pedagogical climate due to the principal's actions. The importance of the principal (or the school administration) emerges first of all through the role of explicitly defining the school's educational policy. A principal's leadership style, his authority vis a vis his staff, and his commitment to implementing policy— especially policy of school integration—are critical in creating a school climate conducive to integration. It is necessary that heterogeneous classes be carefully maintained, that the roles of teachers who deal with the problems resulting from this heterogeneity be clearly defined, that a consistent message be transmitted to the teachers about their pedagogical responsibility for the entire student population, so that neglect of the slower students be prevented. The principal must initiate and encourage the development of curricula, teaching methods, and social activities appropriate to a heterogeneous student population (Resh, Adler, & Inbar, 1980; Inbar, Adler, & Resh, 1977).

The homeroom teacher and the subject-matter teacher were found to represent opposing approaches to social integration. The homeroom teacher tends to have a stronger social orientation, thus promoting integration, whereas the subject-matter teacher tends to place much greater emphasis on academic achievement (Chen, Lewy, & Adler, 1978; Zak, 1981). The complexity of the school, the process of professionalization, and introduction of ability grouping, increase the relative weight of the subject-matter teachers and reduce the number of hours that the homeroom teacher spends with his class. These developments are also related to a growing achievement orientation at the expense of the promotion of social integration.

From this point of view, one of the negative results of the school Reform is a significant reduction in the number of hours that the homeroom teacher spends with the class (Chen, Lewy, & Adler, 1978). Teachers consider the homeroom classes the most significant educational setting for implementing integration, but steps such as ability grouping, and the reduced presence of the homeroom teacher in his class, operate in the opposite direction. Moreover, teachers in the junior high schools, whereas expressing satisfaction with the process of specialization and academization, also claimed that they could not devote sufficient time and attention to individual tutoring and treatment of the students (Chen, Lewy, &

Adler, 1978). Again, a particular educational practice exerts conflicting effects. The academization of teachers and professional specialization is being considered as a condition for improved achievement of students. But at the same time, greater exposure of students to specialized teachers reduces the importance of the homeroom teacher and thus decreases the chances for successful implementation of school integration.

Such duality is also found in the position of the educational counselor. This is a position that has much developed over recent years, performing special roles in heterogeneous schools in general and in schools established by the school Reform in particular. On the one hand, the educational counselor is the professional vested with the treatment of social problems related to integration. In many cases the guidance counselor serves as a resource person for the rest of the staff regarding the development and application of educational strategies to enhance the smooth operation of the school with a heterogenous student population. Needless to say, transferring the responsibility for the implementation of one of the main proclaimed goals of the educational system from homeroom teachers to ''professional experts'' detracts from the salience of the related policies.

Again we discern two contradictory trends in the area of teachers' roles: The emergence of large and heterogeneous schools as a consequence of the policy of school desegregation called for the introduction of professionals other than the homeroom teacher, particularly the guidance counselor. On the other hand, the presence of such professionals may have contributed to the attenuation of teachers' sense of responsibility and accountability for the integration process in their school.

Affective Variables

There is little doubt as to the importance of teachers' feelings about their work for the successful achievement of educational goals. Studies exploring the teaching process often focused on variables such as teachers' sense of autonomy, self-fulfillment, self-expression, and their evaluations of their work (Chen, Lewy, & Adler, 1978; Gat, 1972; Zak, 1981). However, no causal connection was documented between teachers' job satisfaction and pupils' academic achievement or school desegregation. Nor does the complexity of the relationship between teachers' job satisfaction and particular educational outcomes allow for a simple cause and effect explanation. We surmise that there is a relationship between teacher job satisfaction and an entire network of variables, including the ethnic composition of the student body in a given school, the background variables of the teaching staff, such as teacher's ethnic background, education, and teaching experience, and the school's social-organizational climate. It was found, for example, that the ratio of ethnic representation in the student body was related to the ethnic composition of the teaching staff. These latter variables were also found to be related to school climate and to teacher job satisfaction (Zak, 1981).

Successful coping with the educational complexities of integrated classrooms may certainly lend teachers a sense of satisfaction, whereas greater job satisfaction might provide teachers with the psychological resources needed to implement ethnic integration successfully, to the advantage of the minority students (Resh, Adler, & Inbar, 1980).

Findings about teacher job satisfaction are still inconclusive. In general, the level of satisfaction among teachers involved in school desegregation is relatively high (Chen, Lewy, & Adler, 1978), and not significantly different from that in nondesegregated schools (Minkovich, Davis, & Bashi, 1977). On the one hand, there is a link between the level of teachers' perceived problems (which is higher in desegregated schools) and their level of satisfaction in different domains: the higher the level of perceived problems, the lower the level of satisfaction (Resh, Adler, Inbar, 1982). On the other hand, it was found that teachers in desegregated schools expressed a greater sense of "mission."

It is interesting to note that there are findings that indicate clear between-school differences in levels of teacher satisfaction that cannot be accounted for by the combined effects of structural factors (composition, size, location of schools, etc.) and teacher-background factors. Clearly, teacher satisfaction is a major component of school climate, above and beyond personal and organizational differences.

The teachers' judgment of the chances for successful school integration along a continuum of pessimism–optimism can be assigned to this category of affective variables. The teachers' view is important in that it provides a picture both of the present situation and of future chances. In general, the teachers express considerable optimism about the chances for successful integration, although it should be noted that they are less optimistic about improving social relations than about improving the academic achievement level of disadvantaged students. Moreover, the different ratios of Middle Eastern students in different schools was found to affect the attitudes of teachers. The level of optimism is lowest in heterogeneous schools and highest in homogeneous schools (Chen, Lewy, & Adler, 1978). Teachers' optimism and their belief in the need for desegregation may be limited by the practical difficulty of teaching a heterogeneous class. In the study of Israel's elementary schools (Minkovich, Davis, & Bashi, 1977), more than half the teachers agreed that integration was likely to fail because of their inability to adapt instruction to a heterogeneous class, although it is worth noting that this idea was less prevalent in heterogeneous schools.

Goals and Values

The assumption behind the attempt to identify, describe, and analyze the value system of organizations is that it determines normative patterns of expectations as well as controls mechanisms aimed at realizing such expectations. Three complementary research strategies may be applied to identify a value system.

The first strategy analyzes the goals and behavioral norms of the organization on the basis of its plans, its regulations, and other written material. The second strategy studies the behavior of the organization's decision makers and administrators, the decision-making process, the nature of the decisions, and the extent to which they express the declared aims of the organization. The third strategy studies the population's perception of the nature of the value system. In the case of schools, the value perceptions of the principal and teachers, or, alternatively, the perceptions and images of the students or parents are examined. Most of the studies of desegregation conducted in Israel were based on this latter approach.

From the findings and trends revealed in the Israel desegregation research, we can conclude that teachers have a positive attitude toward the process of integration, but they feel that changes are necessary in order to realize it (Amir, Rich, & Ben–Ari, 1978; Chen, Lewy, & Adler, 1978; Gat, 1972; Minkovich, Davis, & Bashi, 1977). For many teachers, school integration is an end in itself, reflecting the demographic composition of society, and an expression of its egalitarian values. A decisive majority of teachers throughout the entire educational system favor integration and see it as an important instrument for promoting the disadvantaged groups, improving both their relative achievement standards and interethnic relations. Again, a difference is found between schools, both in the perceived methods to be used to achieve integration and in the teachers' order of priorities in realizing the goals of integration. Teachers' value preferences differentiate between schools with stronger achievement orientation and schools with a more social-integrative orientation. It is interesting to note the relationship between this value preference and mechanisms of selection and classification: Schools where teachers are more achievement oriented are also more selective. Moreover, teachers' values, as reflected in their expressed preference for achievement over integration, were also related to their preferred pedagogical methods. A positive correlation was found between an achievement orientation and a conservative educational approach, whereas an integrative orientation was found to be related to a more progressive pedagogical approach. In other words, a relationship exists between the value orientation of the schools, its operational policy, and preferred teaching methods.

School Climate

Studies of educational effectiveness received great impetus in the 1960s and 1970s. Although the study of the effectiveness of a school as a function of specific school variables is continuing, this trend is now changing. Investigators no longer study specific school variables but combine them into one complex or aggregate variable, called an atmosphere or climate, which may have greater significance than the sum total of the specific variables. Although single variables have on occasion been used to characterize school climate, the assumption is that such single variables, when combined, characterize the "climate of the school.'' The growing importance of the concept of school climate as a variable in the educational process can be seen in the emphasis placed on this concept in recent theory and research (Brookover, Schweitzer, Schneider, & Beady, 1978; Coleman, 1959; Hall & Schneider, 1973; Halpin, 1963; Inbar, 1980; Johnson, 1970; McDill, Meyers, & Rigsby, 1969; McDill & Rigsby, 1973; Zak, 1981).

In the repeatedly mentioned school Reform study a similar pattern was followed. Two distinct sets of teachers' attitudes were found—the "Conservative-Achievement-Oriented Set" and the "Progressive-Integration-Oriented Set." Additional analyses revealed that other school variables were found to group around either of those two sets, so that in fact two types of "school climate" emerged (Inbar, Adler, & Resh, 1977).

The Conservative-Achievement-Oriented Set. This set is characterized by an emphasis on achievement, advocating policies of high selectivity, limited emphasis on social concerns as being part of the teacher's role, and low emphasis on an orientation toward the individual student. This orientation also includes emphasis on order and discipline as an educational value, limited readiness for change on the part of teachers, an underestimation of the degree of actual change involved in the Reform, placing responsibility for the implementation of the school Reform on others, and a rejection of the notion that the school Reform involves meaningful educational change. Similarly, attitudes related to the teachers' job are also included: lower job satisfaction and a relatively higher degree of perceived problems in the desegregated school, which they do not see as realizing the central goals of the educational Reform.

The Progressive-Integration-Oriented Set. This set is characterized by educational approaches that stress attention to the individual student, do emphasize social concerns as being part of the teachers' role, and attach low importance to order and discipline. It includes a preference for integration and a policy of limited selection procedures. This set is also characterized by a high level of satisfaction, a low level of perceived problems in the integrated school, and a view of the school as moving toward the implementation of the goals of the educational Reform, which, in turn, is viewed as calling for changes in teaching methods. This set includes teachers' readiness for change and their consideration that the success of the Reform is their own responsibility.

These two sets were deduced primarily from teachers' attitudes, as mentioned before. However, a number of student variables also clustered around those two sets, thus moving us toward two distinct "climates." A higher level of anxiety among students, an essentially negative attitude toward the school, and a greater sense of discrimination by the teachers were found to correlate with the "conservative-achievement"-oriented set. Opposite attitudes were found to correlate with the "progressive-integrative" set. Whereas students' locus of control was more internal in the "progressive-integration"-oriented set, it was more external

᾿ in the "conservative-achievement"-oriented set. Achievement too was found to correlate with the sets. Indeed the progressive-integration-oriented climate correlates with high levels of achievements, the conservative-achievement-oriented climate with low levels of achievement.

Given the current stage of research in this field, we cannot yet point to the causes for the emergence of these climates. It warrants attention, however, that the differences between schools in terms of the sociocultural composition of the student body concur with the climates. Thus the teachers in schools with lower level of achievement and a higher percentage of Middle Eastern students have a more achievement-oriented approach, put greater stress on order and discipline, and do not profess an educational approach of individual attention to students. In other words, the low-achieving schools display a "conservative-achievement"-oriented climate. Whether the emergence of such a climate is the consequence of the situation in certain schools or rather one of the causes for the development of such a situation cannot be determined.

There is a broad consensus that desegregation and structural change, which brings students of different backgrounds and social classes under the same roof, are only one step, albeit a very necessary one, toward integration that yields educational results (mainly improvement of scholastic achievements of the disadvantaged children and/or improved interethnic relations). Comprehensive reviews of studies on desegregation stress the importance of local differences in learning circumstances and environmental conditions as variables in desegregation programs (Lewin & Hawley, 1978; St. John, 1975). However, virtually no studies have been conducted that take variables of school climate into consideration when examining differences in the success of integration. Moreover, very little has been done to develop a theoretical framework within which to understand the transition from desegregation as a formal step to integration in its full educational sense, using school climate as a mediating concept.

Discussion

Two basic approaches can be distinguished in the analysis of organizational variables: The first is structural, the second phenomenological. The first approach deals with the objective aspects of a phenomenon. It deals with the effort to identify and to analyze school variables as an objective quantity. In the present discussion, this means that the structural variables themselves—such as class composition, school size, the teachers' educational level, division of roles, or extracurricular activities—are analyzed as independent variables, which serve to explain the dependent variable of integration. Many apparently objective structural elements are undoubtedly a function of school policy and reflect the opinions and attitudes of the principal and the teaching staff. For example, ability grouping or streaming is a structural variable, but it may also be a result of school policy and teachers' attitudes toward integration.

In the second, subjective approach, variables are not dealt with as objective indicators, but rather as the subjective attitudes of the relevant parties to the studied phenomena, and their conceptions of them are measured. Size, for example, is not determined quantitatively but from the participants' perception of school size. Similarly, teachers' perception of problems is conceived to be an indicator of the overall level of school problems. The theoretical basis for this approach is derived from the assumption that people's behavior stems more from their perception of reality and from their respective image of the roles they perform than of reality itself (Boulding, 1956). According to this approach there is no place to assume a direct causal relationship between the dependent and the independent variable; rather, one must speak of reciprocal effects.

The study of school variables and integration is very complex and embraces a very great number of variables. Some remarks about future work seem to be in place. The intensity and manner of the encounter between students and the various educational processes aimed at achieving the goals of integration determine to a considerable extent the anticipated outputs, and it is these that mark the difference between one school and another. They are related to the school's educational policy, to the attitudes of the principal and teachers, to teaching strategies, and to the type of social activity in the school—in other words, to both the school "climate" and the educational process taking place in it. It may well be that the relatively disappointing findings pertaining to the relationship between school input variables and integration are the result of "input–output" studies that did not concentrate sufficiently on the *process* taking place within the school. It is, therefore, most important that educational research focus on these processes.

REFERENCES

Amir, Y. The effects of interpersonal relationships on the reduction of ethnic prejudices. *Megamot,* 1968, *16,* 5–25. (Hebrew)

Amir, Y. Ethnic interactions and intergroup attitudes and relations: A review and reevaluation. *Megamot,* 1977, *23,* 41–78. (Hebrew)

Amir, Y., Rich, Y., & Ben–Ari, R. Problems of social integration in the junior high school, gain and loss to pupils, and proposed solutions. *Studies in Education,* 1978, *18,* 15–36. (Hebrew)

Arzi, Y., & Amir, Y. Personal adjustments and scholastic gains of culturally deprived children in homogeneous and heterogeneous classrooms. *Megamot,* 1976, *22,* 279–287. (Hebrew)

Ascher, C. How to make school desegregation work—some advice from research. ERIC/Cue Fact Sheet No. 5, 1981.

Bashi, J. Effects of ethnic class composition on self-concept. *Megamot,* 1977, *23,* 124–133. (Hebrew)

Boulding, E. *The image.* Ann–Arbor: The University of Michigan Press, 1956.

Boyd, W. L., & Crowson, R. L. The changing conception and practice of public schools administration. In D. Berliner (Ed.), *Review of research in education* (Vol. 9) American Educational Research Association, 1981.

Brookover, W.,Schweitzer, H., Schneider, M., & Beady, E. Elementary school climate and school achievement. *American Educational Research Journal*, 1978, *15*, 301–318.

Chen, M., Kfir, D., & Lewy, A. Coping with a heterogeneous school population in the junior high school. *Megamot*, 1976, *22*, 379–396.

Chen, M., & Kfir, D. The students who meet the counselor in the junior high school. *Israeli Journal of Psychology and Counseling in Education*, 1979, *10*, 24–29. (Hebrew)

Chen, M., Lewy, A., & Adler, C. *Process and outcome in education: Evaluating the contribution of the Middle School to the educational system*. Israel: Schools of Education, Tel–Aviv University and Hebrew University, Jerusalem, 1978. (Hebrew)

Chen, M., Lewy, A., & Kfir, D. The possibilities of interethnic group contact in the junior high schools: Implementation and results. *Megamot*, 1977, *23*, 134–145. (Hebrew)

Coleman, J. S. *Social structures and social climates in high schools*. Washington, D. C.: U. S. Office of Education, September 1959.

Dar, Y. Educational consideration and social context factors determining teacher attitudes toward homogeneous grouping. *Megamot*, 1977, *23*, 248–260. (Hebrew)

Eshel, Y., & Klein, Z. The effects of integration and open education on mathematics achievement in the early primary grades. *American Educational Research Journal*, 1978, *15*, 319–323.

Eshel, Y., & Klein, Z. School integration, academic self-image and achievement of lower-class elementary school pupils. *Megamot*, 1977, *23*, 134–145. (Hebrew)

Gat, A. *Teachers' attitudes toward the educational reform and its implementation*. Unpublished M.A. Thesis. Haifa: Technion Institute, 1972. (Hebrew)

Gutman, I. , Gur, A., Kaniel, S., & Wall, D. *The influence of grouping on achievements and psycho-social development*. Jerusalem: The Henrietta Szold Institute (Research Report No. 150), 1972. (Hebrew)

Hall, D. T., & Schneider, B. *Organizational climates and careers*. Academic Press, 1973.

Halpin, A. W., & Croft, D. B. *Organizational climate of schools*. Chicago: Midwest Administration Center, University of Chicago, 1963.

Inbar, D. Structural aspects and trends in the operation of the reform in the Hebrew education. *Megamot*, 1975, *21*, 295–305. (Hebrew)

Inbar, D. Organizational climates: Success–failure configurations in educational leadership. *Journal of Educational Administration*, 1980, *18*(2), 232–244.

Inbar, D. The paradox of feasible planning: The case of Israel. *Comparative Education Review*, 1981.

Inbar, D., Adler, C., & Resh, N. Ethnic composition, integration, achievement and school climate. *Megamot*, 1977, *23*, 230–237. (Hebrew)

Johnson, W. D. *The social psychology of education*. New York, San Francisco: Holt, Rinehart, & Winston, 1970.

Klein, Z., & Eshel, Y. The Nachlaot project: The 'Open' class in an integrated school. Jerusalem: Israel Ministry of Education and Culture, *Trends in "Open" Education*, 1973, 119–133. (Hebrew)

Klein, Z., & Eshel, Y. *Integrating Jerusalem schools*. New York: Academic Press, 1980.

Levin, J., & Chen, M. Sociometric choices in ethnically heterogeneous classes. *Megamot*, 1977, *23*, 189–208. (Hebrew)

Lewin, B., & Hawley, W. D. School desegregation: Lessons of the first 25 years. *Law and Contemporary Problems*, 1978, *42*(3,4) (the whole issue).

McDill, L. E., & Rigsby, C. L. *Structure and process in secondary schools*. Baltimore: John Hopkins University Press, 1973.

McDill, E. L., Meyers, E. D., & Rigsby, L. C. Educational climates of high schools: Their effects and sources. *The American Journal of Sociology*, 1969, *74*, 567–86

Minkovich, A., Davis, D., & Bashi, Y. *An evaluation study of educational achievement in Israeli elementary school*. Jerusalem: School of Education, The Hebrew University, 1977. (Hebrew)

Resh, N., Adler, C., Chen, M., & Inbar, D. Teacher and educational policy in junior high schools. *Studies in Education,* 1979, *23,* 39–52. (Hebrew)

Resh, N., Adler, C., & Inbar, D. Teachers' attitudes toward ethnic integration and educational goals in junior high schools. *Megamot,* 1977, *23,* 221–229. (Hebrew)

Resh, N., Adler, C., & Inbar, D. *Initiatives and innovations in coping with heterogeneous student population in junior high schools.* Jerusalem: Center for Innovation in Education, Hebrew University, 1980. (Hebrew)

Resh, N., Adler, C., & Inbar, D. Teachers' perceptions of problems in junior high schools. *Studies in Educational Administration,* 1982, *10,* 69–84. (Hebrew)

Rosenstein, E., & Gat, E. Teachers' orientation to the educational reform and its implementation. *Megamot,* 1975, *21,* 202–218. (Hebrew)

Smilansky, S., & Shephatiah, L. Socio-cultural integration and other classroom variables as related to achievement in grades one and two: *Megamot,* 1977, *23,* 79–87. (Hebrew)

Stahl, A., Agmon, T., & Mar–Haim, M. Teacher attitudes toward the cultural disadvantaged. *Studies in Education,* 1976, *11,* 45–58. (Hebrew)

St. John, H. N. *School desegregation: Outcomes for children.* New York: Wiley, 1975.

Zak. I. The evaluation of school organization climate. In A. Lewy & D. Nevo (Eds.), *Evaluation roles in education.* Gordon & Breach, 1981.

7 School Desegregation and Achievement

Yohanan Eshel
Zev Klein

The issue of integration and achievement has been dealt with in a large number of review articles. The common denominator among all these is an attempt to reach some form of definitive statement about the effects of desegregation on achievement that fairly summarizes all the available material. Unfortunately, different reviewers, utilizing almost identical data, often reach quite different conclusions.

In attempting to reconcile these differences, we decided to discuss the issue in the form of a question and answer dialogue between "A" and "B". Hopefully, this dialogue will point to alternative and perhaps more useful ways of both defining issues and developing solutions.

A: It seems that from the moment school desegregation became a public, political issue, the promise that the academic achievement of the desegregated minority would improve was assumed.[1] I find this causal linkage problematic. It is not only a question of whether or not there is a theoretical basis for the assumption—something I address shortly—but also, why the imperative? Whether the issue is building a better, more cohesive society, or doing away with prejudice and mistrust, or providing a more equitable distribution of status and privileges, we do not need to justify them through an attempt to raise IQ scores or school grades.[2] In fact, if these are the goals, one could make a case that one of the least effective ways for attaining them is through the schools. Certainly, enough has been written and said about the bureaucracy and conservatism of the public

---

[1]Brown vs. Board of Education, 1954; Chen, Lewy, & Adler, 1978.
[2]Jencks, Smith, Acland, Bane, Lohen, Gintis, Hyens, & Michelson, 1972; Kleinberger, 1973; Lamm, 1974.

school, about its rather passive reflection of the society around it, to make one more than a little skeptical about the promise of any major social change coming from the education system.[3] And yet, tying desegregation and achievement together seems to promise just that—it is precisely the school that has to bear the responsibility for social change. What is more, it is an expectation of both social *and* personal change of a magnitude that I find hard to believe can be meant seriously by those who propose it.[4]

B: I think you are right in choosing the word "imperative" to describe the connection between the two terms. There is something pressing and powerful in the way the early supporters of this idea presented their case, in the ways researchers assumed that achievement effects were there to be found, and particularly in the way reviewers go back again and again to sift through and recombine the available data, looking for a more clear-cut answer.[5]

Something of this feeling is obviously connected to an aura of crisis that usually surrounds the integration issue. But this "crisis consciousness" does not explain a great deal unless placed in the context of classic liberal and democratic ideas of how social change should come about, and what the features of such a process should be.[6]

I think that when the issue of integration is raised publicly it may pose both a warning and a threat. The warning is that certain groups have not been assimilated into the general society, the new awareness of this being an occasion for guilt, remorse, disappointment, or a sense of failure. It is an interesting question why and when these perceptions occur historically, but that would take us too far afield. The threat is the other side of the warning, that these unassimilated groups are somehow a danger to social order, stability, and progress.[7] The fact that these groups are unassimilated, however, is not understood as something basically or radically wrong with the society, in spite of the rhetoric occasionally heard at such times. Instead, the prevailing feeling is one of unfinished business, of a problem that has, unfortunately, been neglected or handled in an inappropriate, even irrational way.[8]

To be a fully functioning and participant member of societies such as ours is to be an autonomous individual, responsible for oneself and one's actions, committed to free and equal interchange with others, and making the best of one's abilities and opportunities. Here, I think, is at least part of the reason why integration and achievement are so often raised together.[9] Including people into

---

[3]Jencks et al., 1972; Sarason, 1971.

[4]Gerard & Miller, 1975.

[5]Bradley & Bradley, 1977, Cook, 1979; Crain & Mahard, 1978; O'Reilley, 1970; Stephan, 1978; St. John, 1975; Weinberg, 1975.

[6]Cohen & Garet, 1975; Sarason, 1971.

[7]Ogbu, 1978.

[8]We believe that this approach is quite characteristic of the official Israeli policy on integration and assimilation of groups, varying in cultural and social characteristics. (Adiel, 1970.)

[9]Jencks et al., 1972.

society is important, but not just any kind of inclusion. Not only must it take the form of an orderly presentation of carrying out a social ideal, but it must also provide for and encourage more personal transformations.[10] One should not just be made a member, but a *certain kind* of member that seems summed up in the word "achievement."

A: I am not quite sure what you mean by the term *inclusion*, or what inclusion you have in mind.

B: I admit that that may have sounded a bit vague. In fact, there is little agreement in the literature about the appropriate definition of *inclusion*. Some investigators believe that inclusion of minority members will be achieved only when they have full share in the responsibility for their education.[11] Others claim that the necessary condition is no less than rehabilitation of the minority's modes of thinking.[12] The least common denominator of agreement is that the outsider must be led to change as he is included—thus, the neatness and imperativeness of a mechanism like school integration that seems to deal simultaneously with both social and personal change.[13] I call it a mechanism because it appears to be a rather simple and technical solution that, once put into motion, should almost take care of itself. The simpler and more technical, of course, the greater the sense of controlling the fear, anger, and threat that are never very far from awareness.

A: What your analysis suggests is that one major impediment to including these unassimilated groups is something that they themselves are missing—some type of talent, ability, or knowledge that is a criterion for social membership, or at least for taking full advantage of what society can offer its members.[14] If this is the case, then one might say that this mechanism is a way of "getting society off the hook." Something automatic taking place in a relatively safe setting like schools seems a rather benign way of handling an issue that is potentially explosive and could, from another point of view, demand much more radical forms of change.[15]

Your analysis, however, might be acceptable if there were really a type of automatic mechanism involved. Anyone reading the relevant literature of the last 10 or 15 years must come away confused if looking for a single answer. At the very beginning of research on desegregation, it looked as though if there were one factor that accounted for improved minority-group achievement, desegregation was the one.[16] But I can recall at least two major longitudinal studies of the

---

[10]Frankenstein, 1976; Kleinberger, 1964, 1973; St. John, 1975.
[11]St. John, 1975.
[12]Frankenstein, 1976.
[13]Schmuck, 1978.
[14]Bernstein, 1961; Deutsch, 1960; Frankenstein, 1972, Ginsburg, 1972; Jensen, 1969.
[15]Jencks et al; 1972.
[16]Coleman, Campbell, Hobson, McPartland, Mood, Wernfield, & York, 1966; Levine & Bane, 1975; O'Reilley, 1970.

past few years that indicate no effect of school integration when no additional educational intervention was offered.[17]

B: Analysis of the many studies done on school integration programs has become much more sophisticated. In the social sciences, however, a major result of increased technical sophistication is usually making the issues more, not less, complicated.[18] It is true that the reviews that have been written range from finding no conclusive evidence for the effect of desegregation on achievement, all the way to isolating a certain percentage of "successful" cases. The authors of such reviews all have their own ways of defining what studies should or should not be included in the overall analysis, which makes comparison all the more difficult.[19]

You have raised at least two additional issues that are of prime importance in the study of integration. The wide gap in scholastic performance between privileged and underprivileged pupils has led to a host of assumptions and speculations concerning the nature of the deprived child. His failure in school has been attributed to biological factors,[20] to social and cultural deprivations,[21] to weakness and inadequacy of thought processes,[22] as well as to lack of linguistic skills[23] or motivation.[24] Whereas all these explanations maintain that something is wrong with the child himself, other students of the field feel that the accusing finger should rather be pointed at the school, its conservatism, and its lack of sensitivity to the child's needs.[25] It seems fair to say, therefore, that the available data provide us with no clear-cut answer to what, in fact, (if anything) is basically wrong with either Israeli or American disadvantaged pupils.

Your second point is social rather than educational. It is quite clear that political or economic gaps between various segments of society could be neither accounted for nor abolished by educational means. Other social institutions should have been involved if a serious attempt to solve these problems was to be made.[26] On the other hand, the school system is a convenient entry point for any

---

[17]Klein & Eshel, 1980; Gerard & Miller, 1975.

[18]Cohen & Weiss, 1977.

[19]Using wide selections of current studies on integration, review articles were unable to agree whether, on the whole, school integration improved academic performance (Wilson, 1967). Pettigrew (1969) as well as Crain and Mahard (1978) conclude that integration contributed to scholastic achievement, whereas St. John (1975), Bradley and Bradley (1977), Howley (1978), and Wilson (1979) regard the results as inconclusive. No major review indicates negative effects of desegregation on academic achievement of either the majority or the minority. An interesting exception to this rule can be found in the Patchen et al. (1980) study, reporting decreased academic performance of Negro pupils under specific social conditions.

[20]Herrnstein, 1973; Jensen, 1969.

[21]Deutsch, 1960; Klaus & Gray, 1968.

[22]Frankenstein, 1976; Minkovich, 1969.

[23]Bernstein, 1961.

[24]Gerard & Miller, 1975; Katz, 1968.

[25]Ginsburg, 1972; Kohl, 1967.

[26]Jencks et al., 1972.

attempt to start a change process. It can be further argued that no matter how small an effect schooling has on adult life, educators are not free to refrain from trying to generate this change. Moreover, recent studies on effects of schooling seem to suggest that its importance for future social standing was considerably underestimated in former analyses.

To return to the main point, however, here in Israel the results have tended to be fairly consistent: There is hardly any study that has shown desegregation as such to be significantly related to improved minority achievement.[27] Of course, not so many studies have been carried out, and practically none has considered the long-range impact of integrated education. There is always the possibility of some type of "sleeper" effect. Moreover, the fact that some American and Israeli studies have identified positive effects in some instances means that the question still remains open.

A: But what is the question being asked? The complexity of the results you've described means that either there is no automatic mechanism involved, or, if there is, that it operates quite differently under various conditions. Isn't there a body of theory, or some type of model, that might help predict results more accurately, or provide a more scientific justification than the feeling that something should happen simply because it must? How much of this research has been based on theoretical premises?

B: As it turns out, very little. One could point to the fact of so many pressures involved in both getting programs under way and in demonstrating as rapidly as possible that they either were or were not accomplishing something. Many researchers had little time or opportunity to set up well-thought-out designs that could test one hypothesis against another. The list of design deficiencies that almost every reviewer has come up with in existing studies is staggering.[28] But I do not think this means that the field is characterized by poor researchers or mediocre research. It is only a further reflection of the conditions under which questions are being asked in field studies, and the concern of social scientists to provide some sort of answer, however tentative.

This, however, does not fully explain the lack of a good theory. Instead, many studies appear to have *assumed* that there was a body of theory upon which the overall enterprise rested. This is no less an interesting thing: the assumption that the implied automatic mechanism was actually a derivative of some well-developed social science ideas that could suggest a connection between social integration and cognitive functioning. This assumption seems to have been so strong that only very rarely did the persons doing the studies spell out these ideas

---

[27]Three major recent Israeli studies have found no relationship between Eastern–Western, or lower class–higher class classroom percentage and academic achievement (Minkovich, Davis, Bashi, 1977; Chen, et al., 1978; Klein & Eshel, 1980). However, some positive results were reported in several smaller research projects (Arzi & Amir, 1976; Egozi, 1980; Smilansky & Shephatiah, 1977).

[28]Bradley & Bradley, 1977; Stephan, 1978; St. John, 1975.

in detail.[29] It is only recently that some of them have been clarified in such a way as to put their various components to specific test.

A: For example . . . .

B: Two areas in this context often mentioned in the literature were the psychology of motivation and self-esteem, on the one hand, and the social psychology of group formation and group dynamics, on the other. A great deal of the first was already implicit in the 1954 U.S. Supreme Court decision to desegregate schools. The main idea is that prejudice against minorities, particularly as institutionalized in segregated schools, leads to lowered self-esteem and motivation to succeed.[30] One of the behavioral outcomes of this is lowered achievement, which depresses the chances for more equal social participation.[31] It then follows that changing the conditions of prejudice, such as desegregating schools, could start a process in which improved self-esteem leads to enhanced motivation and consequently to higher scholastic performance.[32]

It is important to note that this version of the model is by no means the only one in the literature, nor is it the one supported by the majority of more recent studies. On the contrary: There is reason to believe that self-esteem is more often than not the result of academic success or failure, rather than the reverse. There have been a number of variations on this model, but they all revolve around a central theme: A significant part of the behavior involved in academic success is a function of how one feels about oneself, and the conceptions one has about the ability to compete, to achieve, to control one's life, and to belong and be accepted by others. These feelings and conceptions can be modified by altering the conditions of interaction with others, particularly those ''others'' who are seen as the source of power, and negative evaluations of oneself. Prove to the minority members that they can successfully compete, show them that they can belong and be wanted, demonstrate that they can be as good or better than the powerful ''others'' without retribution and with continued acceptance—do these things in a desegregated setting, and changes in self-conception and motivation should follow.[33]

A: You also mentioned a second model.

B: Yes—the literature on group formation and group dynamics. Here there are several levels of complexity or emphasis. Probably the least complicated is the idea of a ''lateral transmission of values.''[34] A majority group is held to repre-

---

[29]For development of after-the-fact models of school integration and critical evaluation of these theoretical efforts, see Coleman et al., 1966; Gerard & Miller, 1975; Katz, 1967, 1968; Maruyama & Miller, 1979; Schmuck, 1978; St. John, 1975.

[30]Ausubel & Ausubel, 1963; Clark, 1963; Deutsch, 1960; Gergen & Marececk, 1976.

[31]Irwin, 1967; Katz, 1967; Minkovich, 1969; Purkey, 1970; Schmuck, 1978; Seginer, 1980; Wilson, 1979.

[32]Stephan, 1978.

[33]Epps, 1975, 1978; Gerard & Miller, 1975; Klein & Eshel, 1980.

[34]Coleman et al., 1966; St. John, 1971.

sent and enact certain values that, say, are important to social success. Minority members who, for whatever reason, are lacking these values and the behaviors linked to them are brought into the group. The desire to belong, the power of the majority, and the elimination of barriers to membership can result in the minority adopting those behaviors and values held by the majority. If we assume that some of these are involved in wanting to do well academically, the minority members, in becoming more like the majority, will improve academically.[35]

Another way of looking at this is through reference group theory,[36] that is, that in the desegregated setting, the minority members want to belong to what they perceive as a powerful and desirable majority. It is this desire not only to be accepted, but to become like the majority and thus adopt their values as one's own, that is critical in order for change to take place. This idea can be further complicated by adding a more dynamic psychological formulation. In the integrated situation, minority members are constantly comparing themselves with the behavior of the majority. It is these comparisons, and an appreciation of the payoff of one type of activity as compared to another, that are seen as the key to change.[37] But in all these variations, as well, there is a central theme: A minority group wants to belong to a majority who not only represents what is most socially rewarded but also exemplifies the values, attitudes, and behaviors that lead to reward. It is in imitation of, or identification with, the majority group that the minority members, seeing a chance for acceptance, may change both socially and academically.[38]

A: Both kinds of models you've described relate some kind of internal change in the minority members to certain forms of external influence that are all part of the integrated situation. Changes in achievement should then be an outcome of these internal changes.

B: That is correct, although it is important to note a basic assumption of these models. Inneither is there any specific mention of the actual cognitive ability of the persons involved. In fact, one could argue that these models require minority-group members whose cognitive abilities are not drastically different from anyone else's, and whose lowered achievement is, therefore, mostly a matter of

---

[35]Alexander, Fennessey, McDill, & D'Amico, 1979; Clark, 1963; Lewis & St. John, 1974; Werts & Watley, 1969.

[36]Kelley, 1952; Hyman, 1942.

[37]Bany & Johnson, 1975; Crain & Mahard, 1978; Drury, 1980; Falk, 1978; Gerard & Miller, 1975; Richter, 1976.

[38]This analysis indicates that integration may have ameliorative effects through these processes only as far as the minority group wishes to belong to or to assimilate in the majority, and the majority group is willing to offer some degree of real or token acceptance (Klein & Eshel, 1980, see also Murayama & Miller, 1979). There is a difference in this respect between the American and Israeli experience. The Israeli "minority" (amounting to about half of the population) tends to accept the majority as a positive reference group, whereas there are many signs of ambivalence or antagonism toward the majority in many sectors of American minority groups.

motivational and other personality factors that could be open to environmental manipulation.[39] For both political and humane reasons, this may be an important assumption to make. However, this places the burden of proof on interventions and internal changes that are only indirectly related to the outcome of major interest. The teacher, the school, instruction, learning—all these things seem to be assigned a position of almost secondary importance.[40]

A: You seem to be describing a kind of reaction to the compensatory education approach to disadvantaged minorities. That was a model that did stress deficiencies in the learner and did emphasize instructional and cognitive variables.[41] Perhaps it is something of the general disappointment with this approach[42] that helps account for the enthusiams over integration, with its implication that the learner is in fact "intact."[43] But I do not understand why this alternative conceptualization should bother you. What you have described are models that allow for testing some very specific hypotheses about the effects of desegregated settings on achievement. If there is any value to these hypotheses, then one should be able to set up research designs to test alternatives, and then perhaps begin to understand why some projects fail and others succeed. When you first began to describe the research situation, you implied that there was little chance of asking such detailed questions. Now you outline several models that could help clarify matters considerably.

B: Remember that I said that many researchers assumed that these models were implicit in the studies they undertook. This meant that the fact that schools were integrated was taken as an indication that conditions called for by the models were, in effect, being implemented. On this assumption, one could then measure outcomes as if a real test of a theoretical hypothesis were being made. Studies of integrated education have utilized a wide variety of outcome measures. Very few, however, have clearly specified, much less manipulated, input variables that might be dictated by one type or another.

A: Your meaning there is not very clear to me.

B: Both types of approaches I mentioned rely very heavily on some form of "elbow-rubbing"—a great deal of physical proximity and interpersonal contact between majority and minority. This is a key feature of contact theory as stated by Allport many years ago.[44] But Allport went beyond the mere fact of "elbow-rubbing." His criteria for conditions leading to effective group performance when combining majority with minority included the need for creating the perception of equal status among the members, the setting of common goals to

---

[39]Clark, (1963); Gerard & Miller, 1975; Katz, 1968.

[40]Coleman et al., 1966; Jencks et al., 1972.

[41]Bernstein, 1961; Deutsch, 1960; Frankenstein, 1972; Klaus & Gray, 1968.

[42]Averch, Carroll, Donaldson, Kiesling, & Pincus, 1975; Jensen, 1969.

[43]See, for instance, Jencks's et al. (1972) discussion of the contribution of integration, as compared to the effects of other school variables, to enhanced scholastic performance.

[44]Allport, 1954.

which all might subscribe, and the provision of opportunities for extensive, warm, and meaningful contact among the group members.[45] I don't know of any of the major American studies of integrated education that have asked or clarified whether these conditions have been met even minimally before going on to assess achievement. Yet by not making these kinds of specifications before assessment takes place, it is almost impossible to say that ineffective programs can be explained by the absence of such conditions.[46]

Furthermore, reanalysis of the aforementioned conditions indicates that, in spite of their importance for group cohesion in the integrated classroom, none of them seems to be a necessary or sufficient condition for improved academic performance. Most of the existing evidence on this issue is negative in nature: It is difficult to maintain a learning atmosphere when social tensions are very high.[47] Very little is known about the influence of the contact hypothesis conditions in more relaxed social environments.

Several investigators claim that group learning is more conducive to improved learning, implying that group processes should have a major role in any planning of learning environments.[48] However, this refers only to assignments that are built to be carried out in team work, and the specific variables involved have not been either isolated or very clearly defined.

The problem is even greater when looking at self-esteem or motivational models. Measuring self-esteem, as well as motivational variables before and after, is no substitute for determining whether or not specific attempts were made in the integrated setting to introduce changes designed to have impact on these variables. After all, if there is one thing that social scientists do know after many years of research, it is that influencing or modifying internal variables like self-esteem and motivation requires a great deal of concentrated effort, and, at best, only modest results can be expected. By not setting up studies where conditions specified by theory were being carried out, by looking for changes after 1 or 2 years when probably much more time is needed for effects to be noticed, and by utilizing mostly cross-sectional designs that lump together all kinds of classrooms and contexts indiscriminately, researchers were asking a different, and what may turn out to be, relatively unimportant question. One recent review expressed it very well: "The common error of this research can be stated in six words: Desegregation is not an educational treatment."[49] In other words, it is probably a safe bet to say that in spite of political and ideological wishes, there is

---

[45]Amir, 1969, 1976; Gerard & Miller, 1975.

[46]There is reason to believe that integrated groups can survive and even succeed under conditions that are less than optimal according to the demands of the contact hypothesis. A further refinement of the model seems warranted delineating which of its components can be reduced and to what degree, without injuring group activity beyond repair. (See, for instance, Klein & Eshel, 1977.)

[47]Gerard & Miller, 1975; Katz, 1968.

[48]Freire, 1973; Sharan, 1980.

[49]Crain & Mahard, 1978.

no automatic mechanism, no simple and easily employed connection between moving school children around and raising achievement levels.[50] This is probably the real meaning of the fact that no consistent link between school integration and achievement has been established. And if this is so, then repeated attempts to reanalyze existing data in the search for some kind of lawfulness in such things as, for example, the effect of different percentages of majority and minority children in a classroom, continue to place the burden of change not on any revision of the educational process, but on the children themselves.[51]

A: You make a convincing case that in most studies conditions are not controlled, inputs are not specified, the processes that are supposed to take place are either unclear or not at all specified, and the questions that can be asked as a result of all this are probably not even the most relevant. One logical conclusion, it seems to me, would be seriously to consider disregarding the bulk of past research and starting again in a more meaningful way.

B: Your summary of the criticism is fine, but the conclusion does not necessarily follow. My point is not to convince you one way or another. What I would like to do, as long as there is space and time to do it in, is to try and set out the complexity of a situation that has been created when "imperatives," as we have called them, of a political and social nature are mixed with questions of theory, design, instrumentation, and all the rest. These things are fine to talk about in the abstract, but political realities do not wait on all the refinements one would like to have under ideal conditions.[52]

I think that the accumulated data do give a rough indication of some general findings and trends that are both worth remembering and indicate directions and issues to be investigated further. For example, in spite of all the variations involved, and in spite of all the limitations we have spelled out, there is no real indication that the general application of desegregated schooling has had a negative effect on the achievement of either minority or majority members. With few exceptions, this is very clear in the Israeli research,[53] and American reviewers seem to have reached the same conclusion.[54] As far as one of the major fears about integration programs is concerned—that majority children will suffer or be held back in their own academic functioning—there is barely any basis for it.

A: But one can take this finding, important as it may be in helping one part of the population feel better about the whole thing, and interpret it differently—

---

[50]Falk, 1978; Maruyama & Miller, 1979; Miller & Gerard, 1976; Schofield, 1978; St. John, 1975.

[51]Several critics have pointed out that findings relating school integration and achievement often fail to account for differences in academic base level of pupils in classrooms of various SES or ethnic compositions. Both positive and negative results are difficult to interpret under these conditions (Campbell & Boruch, 1975).

[52]Cohen & Weiss, 1977; Rossell, 1978; Wooch, 1977.

[53]Chen, et al., 1978; Minkovich et al., 1977.

[54]Alexander et al., 1979.

exactly as you have been talking about it until now. Merely placing children of different levels and backgrounds together in the same classroom is not an effective enough educational intervention to affect the achievement of the minority. And if this is the case, why bother continuing the way we do? As long as change in academic achievement is a goal, all that has been said is that we have no way of really knowing that desegregation is in any way related to this goal—nor, by the way, have we ruled out alternative, nonintegrated approaches of reaching the same goal.[55]

In fact, the more it is discussed, the more it seems that this issue of linking desegregation and achievement has been dominated by something like an apocalyptic vision. By shaking up the system—and to many, integrating the schools must seem like a radical upheaval—the assumption is that a time of immense change is approaching, so immense that all improvements must follow immediately.[56] But what you have detailed up to now is that what seems like radical change is not very radical at all, and, therefore, there is no real reason to expect significant effects on outcomes.

B: Generally speaking, I think you are right, although for the sake of caution, some possible exceptions should be mentioned. It still may be that the simple act of desegregating classrooms may have effects other than on achievement.[57] Perhaps the models we have been talking about are not exactly correct in closely linking changes in motivation, self-concept, and the sense of belonging to academic achievement.[58] Perhaps these two areas of human behavior are somewhat more independent than we would like to think, or at least interact differently from the ways specified in the models.[59] Perhaps the long-term effects of desegregation in schools may be in areas other than academic achievement, and this bears close watching and follow-up.

On the other hand, what the research until now has demonstrated fairly clearly is that desegregation does not have the status of a causal variable for effecting change in academic achievement. This does not, however, rule out the possibility that it might be a contributory factor when combined with appropriate interventions and carried out in certain contexts.[60] Knowing, as we do, that the

---

[55]Abinun, 1979; Frankenstein, 1976; Lamm, 1974.

[56]It is interesting to note that scarcity of theoretical models and clear-cut positive results did not hinder a vast majority of students of integration from believing that educational improvements are inherent in the integrated setting.

[57]The plausibility of this assumption in various fields is examined in several chapters in this book.

[58]A recent review of the literature indicates that correlations between measures of self-image and scholastic performance are indeed no larger than .20 to .30 in most of the studies available (Seginer, 1980).

[59]Several studies using more sophisticated statistical methods tend to suggest that improved self-concept is more typically the effect of higher achievements than their cause (Calsyn & Kenny, 1977; Scheirer & Kraut, 1979; Spencer, 1976).

[60]Klein & Eshel, 1980.

integrated classroom as such does not have any drastic effects on either the achievement or the personality of majority or minority members means that this setting could be seen mainly as a starting point for change.

A: So, in a way, we have now come full circle. The linking of desegregation and achievement has its roots in a political conception of combining social and personal change through rational action. There is no one theory that accurately reflects this conception, although there are bits and pieces of ideas that might fit here and there. Researchers begin looking at the process, hoping to find at least some empirical justification for it, and discover that the most they can say is that it neither helps nor hinders, and much more research is needed to help turn this rather neutral state of affairs into something more effective. I have looked at some of these studies, and they say more or less what you are now suggesting: Where we are now is where we really should *begin* to look into issues of teaching, curriculum, classroom organization, and a potential host of other factors.

The general impression, from all that we have said, is that researchers are caught up in what is mainly a political argument, or end up reaffirming the conviction with which they began.[61] But what you have not said is whether interventions of any kind have been attempted and successfully combined with integration programs.

B: To even begin to answer this point, I think the first and most important thing to do is to translate the issue of integration from political into educational terms. From the educational point of view, an integrated classroom is, first of all, a heterogeneous classroom. The problem facing the teacher of such a classroom is how effectively to reach every child in such a way as to preserve the integrity of the total unit, in spite of a wide range of abilities and interests.[62] I emphasize the word "integrity," because I exclude, at least for now, all solutions that would redivide and resegregate.[63]

Having defined the problem in this way, it seems clear that some form of individualization is called for that in turn will require changes in teaching methods and classroom structure. An obvious structural change is the utilization of small, heterogeneous study groups in the classroom setting. One can view this approach, as was originally done in the United States, as a miniature social relations model intended to implement group processes toward actualizing the social goals of integration.[64] Carrying out these models in the classroom, however, necessitated the introduction of learning tasks as an integral part of group activity. Interestingly enough, some investigators found that such small-group

---

[61]Porter, 1976.

[62]Gerard & Miller, 1975; Klein & Eshel, 1980; St. John, 1975.

[63]Solutions of this kind have been suggested by many proponents of compensatory education assuming them to be in the best interest of the child (Frankenstein, 1976; Jensen, 1973).

[64]Sharan, 1980.

activity around cognitive tasks could also have a positive effect on the achievement of minority children in these groups.[65] Those who conducted the studies tended to look at these results as a confirmation of the benefits of group- over individual learning, although this seems to be a rather superficial and premature description of the findings.[66]

In Israel, the small-group approach was introduced specifically with cognitive goals in mind, whereas the social-unit aspect of the work groups was of secondary importance.[67] Israeli educators seemed to have been less concerned than their American counterparts with possible problems of intergroup prejudice, competition, loss of self-esteem, and unequal status.[68] The major point was structuring the learning process so that children of different abilities could interact positively around a cognitive task and benefit as much as possible from the interaction. In both the American and Israeli experience, however, learning assignments had to be restructured in order to maximize participation of all group members. It is interesting to note that this can be done in at least two different ways. One aims at either equating the status of all learners by dividing learning resources in a way that calls for cooperation and interdependence, or even by inflating the status of the minority learners through providing them with some proficiency needed to complete a learning task but not possessed by the majority members.[69] Another method is based on recognizing the different ability levels in the group and planning group assignments in which all members can participate. The summary group effort then reflects the performance of all the children in the group, whether slow or advanced. Majority-group children are encouraged to help and act as tutors in carrying out assignments, whereas enough variation is introduced so that each child can acquire a sense of proficiency. The latter approach typified a major experiment in the integration of Israeli elementary schools, with quite positive results for the minority children, particularly in the area of mathematics achievement. Moreover, although most of the American data are based on short-term studies of relatively brief duration, the Israeli findings reflect a sustained improvement in achievement over several grade levels and over several years,[70] although in one study a small-group program

---

[65]Aronson & Bridgeman, 1979; Aronson, Bridgeman, & Geffner, 1978; Sharan, Ackerman, & Hertz–Lazarowitz, 1980; Slavin, 1977.

[66]In most of the available studies, it is almost impossible to decide whether the innovative methods of learning or their being carried out in group settings account for the reported results.

[67]An interesting exception is a project conducted by Sharan and Hertz–Lazarowitz (1978) and Hertz–Lazarowitz, Sharan, and Steizberg (1982). See also Chapter 10.

[68]This relative lack of concern has been maintained in spite of the ongoing disput on these issues among social scientists and regardless of extensive current research efforts (Arzi & Amir, 1976; Amir, Rich, & Ben–Ari, 1978; Amir, Sharan, Bizman, Rivner, & Ben Ari, 1978.

[69]Aronson et al., 1975, Cohen, Lockheed, & Lohman, 1976; Cohen & Elchanani, 1977; De-Vries, Edwards, & Slavin, 1980; Slavin, 1980.

[70]Eshel & Klein, 1978; Klein & Eshel, 1977; Harrison, Strauss, & Glaubman, 1980.

carried out in classrooms of only minority children had little or no effect on achievement.[71]

A: That would suggest that perhaps there is something to the ''elbow-rubbing'' models you spoke of before. Perhaps what was missing was a structure like the small group that could intensify effects, rather than expecting more spontaneous progress.

B: That might be acceptable as long as one takes into account the fact that the intensification you speak of is a function of changes in curriculum, materials, learning tasks, the goals set for individual and group performance, and the nature of the interactions between teacher and pupils. It would be a terrible mistake to expect small-group learning to arrive at another kind of ''automatic mechanism.'' The small group, as implemented in many Israeli schools, might be seen as a compromise between absolute individualization on the one hand, and the disregarding of differences on the other.[72] But it is that kind of compromise that can bring children with a variety of abilities into close interaction and then allow for the posing of questions about the kinds of learning that can take place in such interaction. There is, for example, a suggestion in the studies I have mentioned that the minority-children's achievement in the small groups is not affected in some simple, additive way. Under certain conditions, at least, the changes that are noted are in high-level, more abstract forms of cognitive functioning, rather than in simpler, rote-learning functions.[73] There is more than a hint in these findings that there are certain learning processes that can be enhanced in the integrated classroom, if appropriate conditions are met.[74] We now need to know much more about what these conditions are.

A: Do you have any leads as to what they might be?

B: Well, one major source is the people who are now doing work on small-group learning and their attempts to describe the parameters of such activity, and differential outputs associated with different forms of group organization and task presentation. This work does not always relate directly to the integrated classroom, but it does combine most of the elements of pupils, teacher, task, curriculum, and forms of cooperative interaction that are important to know.[75]

Other conditions are more general. Most reviewers, for example, now agree that the earlier integration begins for the minority child, the ''better''—that is, the greater the impact on achievement.[76] There seems to be a great deal of obvious

---

[71]Klein & Eshel, 1980.

[72]This is, of course, only one way of looking at study groups. It is mentioned mainly because attempts to handle integrated classrooms in Israel have been characterized mostly by individualistic ideology and small-group practice.

[73]Freire, 1973; Sharan et al., 1980.

[74]Eshel, 1980.

[75]Klein & Eshel, 1980; Sharan, 1980.

[76]Crain & Mahard, 1978.

sense in this finding, although one wonders if this is due to the integration process itself, or merely to longer exposure to what may be better schooling.[77] There are some kinds of conditions, however, which cut across all types of school interventions, and which probably have even greater significance where a complex program like school integration is concerned. Researchers seem to be more aware than ever that programs that do have impact are most often to be found in schools with strong leadership, where sufficient time is provided to plan suitable strategies and teaching approaches, where the teachers themselves develop programs and methods, and where programs are specifically tailored to the needs of the school. In other words, the promise of impact is greatest in those school settings where the staff are themselves responsible for the problem and can handle it competently.[78] I think we often forget how threatened—on a personal and professional level—teachers must feel who are thrust into integration programs and faced with a challenge to their competence for which few around them seem to have any answer. This very threat may be a powerful factor in explaining teachers' attitudes toward an integrated classroom—more so than endless exploration of whether they "like" or "dislike" minority children.[79]

It is interesting to note, by the way, that the conditions for successful impact I have mentioned overlap considerably with what the literature has to say about the positive effect on achievement of some of the small-group methods. In both cases, tailoring programs to specific needs, knowing clearly what one's aims are, believing that one has the method to achieve them, and seeing the results as both a personal and mutual endeavor on the part of all participants—all these elements stand out in importance.

A: If I may again summarize what you have said, it is that the possibility of linking desegregation and achievement in any specific setting has to do with something like creating an atmosphere of exploration and experimentation in that setting—an atmosphere in which all feel and take a personal part in examining the possibilities for learning and are not afraid to discard and change when necessary.[80] Furthermore, this kind of exploration in integrated classrooms may begin to open up some new viewpoints on the interactive and interpersonal side of cognitive functioning that have often been neglected in the classical learning theories.[81]

With all this positive and highly commendable thinking, however, I still cannot get over the feeling that much of what you say is a way of trying very hard

---

[77]Jencks et al., 1972.

[78]Tucker, 1977.

[79]For detailed description of threat to professional competence and integrity caused by school integration, see Sherf (1973) and Minkovich et al. (1977).

[80]Sharan & Hertz–Lazarowitz, 1978.

[81]Alternative ways for discussing learning processes were suggested by social comparison models, as well as by models of reference groups Bandura & Walters, 1963; Gerard & Miller, 1975; Kelley, 1952; Schachter & Singer, 1962.

to rescue what is primarily a political and social program by searching high and low for some kind of empirical justification. Again, is it really worth it? If the aim is achievement, are there not more efficient, or at least less problematic, ways of going about it? Suppose we agree for the moment that integrated education was at least partially offered as an alternative to more segregated, compensatory approaches that were generally taken to have failed or disappointed. Very little in what you have told me, however, outside of some suggestive leads and programs, indicates that it is as yet a proven alternative.

B: You are really asking two questions—one, as to whether all the effort can be justified, and two, if there is any way of choosing between different approaches to attempting to influence the achievement of minority children. As far as the second question is concerned, there is probably no decisive evidence for preferring integrated over compensatory (segregated) approaches, if the measure in question is a significant increase in test scores, and if no additional intervention is offered. We can all remember that chilling statement of several years ago—"Compensatory education has failed"—and the furor it touched off, the mass of articles, reanalyses, and stepped-up programs, most of which did very little to change the original estimate. What we learned from that episode and all that activity is very similar to the issues raised in our present discussion—that creating impact on achievement is not a simple and automatic proposition, that methods that are specifically directed at cognitive gain can have a meaningful effect if carefully designed and responsibly implemented, and that programs are often carried out more on faith than with actual technical and professional competence.

But what we also learned is that no matter how well thought out, compensatory education is still the more difficult and problematic to implement. Homogeneous schools do not seem to benefit from teacher quality, programs, material inputs, and leadership the way that integrated schools do. Nor do teachers and pupils in homogeneous settings have sufficient access to sources of feedback and interaction that could help and support the learning effort, rather than placing almost the entire burden on the teacher alone.[82] Perhaps with the state of our knowledge today, there is no absolute way of choosing between compensatory and integrated approaches—but there are enough suggestions in the literature to indicate that many of the conditions necessary for effecting achievement are more feasible in an integrated setting, if the possibilities of such settings are taken seriously.[83] As you said a moment ago, the real question is, how much effort will be devoted to the serious exploration and investigation of the integrated classroom as a context in which improved learning can, as we know, take place?

---

[82]Klein & Eshel, 1980.

[83]According to recent Israeli studies, relevant resources are unequally distributed schools, so that homogeneous lower class pupils may, on the whole, enjoy less than their share of learning conditions that are conducive to higher academic performance (Minkovich, et al., 1977; Razel, 1978).

Is it worth it? Neither you nor I can answer that question in any satisfactory way, because, as we both agreed from the outset, the way to organize schools and what kind of visions to impose on them are questions not answerable by statistics or cost-benefit analyses. What the research and technical discussions can contribute is a certain amount of realism and level-headedness in the way the debate over whether it is "worth it" is carried out. What we have learned from all the studies is that schools neither create miracles nor destroy populations. Schools are greatly limited in what they can accomplish, but even within these limitations they can exceed expectations when given the time, responsibility, and help to do so. The brief history of the attempts to link integration and achievement should teach us something about the need not to become seduced by our own rhetoric, and how apocalyptic visions, as you called them, can blind us to the everyday but important changes that can be made, even in our less-than-perfect world.

REFERENCES

Abinun, J. Disadvantaged, equality and integration in education. *Studies in Education,* 1979, *24,* 51–60. (Hebrew)

Adiel, S. (Ed.). *Ten years of compensatory education.* Jerusalem: Ministry of Education and Culture, 1970. (Hebrew)

Alexander, K. L., Fennessey, G., McDill, E. L., & D'Amico, R. J. School SES influences— composition or context? *Sociology of Education,* 1979, *52,* 222–237.

Allport, G. W. *The nature of prejudice.* Cambridge, Mass.: Addison–Wesley, 1954.

Amir, Y. Contact hypothesis in ethnic relations. *Psychological Bulletin,* 1969, *71,* 319–342.

Amir, Y. The role of intergroup contact in change of prejudice and ethnic relations. In P. A. Katz (Ed.), *Towards the elimination of racism.* New York: Pergamon Press, 1976.

Amir, Y., Rich, Y., & Ben–Ari, R. Problems of social integration in junior high school, gain and loss to pupils, and proposed solutions. *Studies in Education,* 1978, *18,* 15–36. (Hebrew)

Amir, Y., Sharan, S., Bizman, A., Rivner, M., & Ben–Ari, R. Attitude change in desegregated Israeli high schools. *Journal of Educational Psychology,* 1978, *70*(2), 129–136.

Arzi, Y., & Amir, Y. Intellectual and scholastic achievements and adjustment of underprivileged pupils in homogeneous and heterogeneous classrooms. *Megamot,* 1976, *22.* (Hebrew)

Aronson, E., Blaney, N., Sikes, J., Stephan, C., & Snapp, M. Busing and racial tension, the jigsaw route to learning and liking. *Psychology Today,* 1975, *8,* 43–50.

Aronson, E., & Bridgeman, B. Jigsaw groups and the desegregated classroom: In pursuit of common goals. *Personality and Social Psychology Bulletin,* 1979, *5,* 438–446.

Aronson, E., Bridgeman, B., & Geffner, R. The effects of cooperative classroom structure on student behavior and attitudes. In D. Bar–Tal & L. Saxe (Eds.), *Social psychology of education.* New York: Hemisphere, 1978.

Ausubel, D. P., & Ausubel, P. Ego development among segregated Negro children. In H. A. Passow (Ed.), *Education in depressed areas.* New York: Bureau of Publications, Teachers College, Columbia University, 1963.

Averch, H. A., Carroll, S. J., Donaldson, T. S., Kiesling, H. J., & Pincus, J. How effective is schooling? A critical synthesis and review of research findings. In D. M. Levine & M. J. Bane (Eds.), *The inequality controversy: Schooling and distributive justice.* New York: Basic Books, 1975.

Bandura, A., & Walters, R. H. *Social learning and personality development.* New York: Holt, Rinehart, & Winston, 1963.

Bany, M. A., & Johnson, L. V. *Educational social psychology.* New York: Macmillan, 1975.

Bernstein, B. Social class and linguistic development: A theory of social learning. In A. H. Halsey, J. Floud, & C. A. Anderson (Eds.), *Education, economy and society.* New York: Free Press, 1961.

Bradley, L. A., & Bradley, G. W. The academic achievement of black students in desegregated schools: A critical review. *Review of Educational Research,* 1977, *47,* 399–449.

Calsyn, R. J., & Kenny, D. A. Self-concept of ability and perceived evaluation of others: Cause or effect of academic achievement? *Journal of Educational Psychology,* 1977, *69,* 136–145.

Campbell, D. T., & Boruch, R. F. Making the case for randomized assignment to treatments by considering the alternatives: Six ways in which quasi-experimental evaluations in compensatory education tend to underestimate effects. In C. A. Bennet (Ed.), *Evaluation and experiment: Some critical issues in assessing social programs.* New York: Academic Press, 1975.

Chen, M., Lewy, A., & Adler, C. *Educational process and outcome: Evaluation of the junior high school reform.* Jerusalem: Ministry of Education, 1978. (Hebrew)

Clark, K. B. Educational stimulation of racially disadvantaged children. In H. A. Passow (Ed.), *Education in depressed areas.* New York: Teachers College Press, Columbia University, 1963.

Cohen, D. K., & Garet, M. Reforming educational policy with applied research. *Harvard Educational Review,* 1975, *45,* 17–43.

Cohen, D. K., & Weiss, J. A. Social science and social policy: Schools and race. *The Educational Forum,* 1977 (May), 394–413.

Cohen, E. G., Lockheed, M. E., & Lohman, M. R. The center for interracial cooperation: A field experiment. *Sociology of Education,* 1976, *49,* 47–58.

Coleman, J. S., Campbell, E. R., Hobson, C. J., McPartland, J., Mood, A. M., Wernfield, F. D., & York, R. L. *Equality of educational opportunities.* Washington, D. C.: U. S. Government Printing Office, 1966.

Cook, S. W. Social science and school desegregation: Did we mislead the Supreme Court? *Personality and Social Psychology Bulletin,* 1979, *5,* 420–437.

Crain, R. L., & Mahard, R. E. Desegregation and black achievement: A review of the research. *Law and Contemporary Problems,* 1978, *42,* 17–56.

Deutsch, M. *Minority group and class status as related to social and personality factors in scholastic achievement.* Ithaca, N. Y.: Cornell University Press, 1960.

DeVries, D. L., Edwards, K. J., & Slavin, R. C. Biracial teams and race relations in the classroom: Four field experiments using teams–games–tournament. *Journal of Educational Psychology,* 1978, *70,* 356–362.

Drury, D. W. Black self-esteem and desegregated schools. *Sociology of Education,* 1980, *57,* 88–103.

Egozi, M. *Classroom social structure and academic achievement of pupils of higher and lower social classes,* 1980. (Mimeograph) (Hebrew)

Epps, E. G. Impact of school desegregation on aspiration, self-concepts and other aspects of personality. *Law and Contemporary Problems,* 1975, *39,* 300–313.

Epps, E. G. The impact of school segregation on the self-evaluation and achievement orientation of minority children. *Law and Contemporary Problems,* 1978, *42*(3), 57–76.

Eshel, Y. *Team instruction and academic performance of lower class and middle-class elementary school children.* Unpublished paper, 1980.

Eshel, Y., & Klein, Z. The effects of integration and open education on mathematics achievement in the early primary grades in Israel. *American Educational Research Journal,* 1978, *15,* 319–323.

Falk, W. W. School desegregation and the educational attainment process: Some results from rural Texas schools. *Sociology of Education,* 1978, *51,* 282–288.

Frankenstein, C. *They think again.* Jerusalem: Hebrew University Press, 1972.

Frankenstein, C. The complexity of the concept of integration. In C. Frankenstein (Ed.), *Teaching as a social challenge*. Jerusalem: Sivan Press, 1976.

Freire, P. *Education for critical consciousness*. New York: The Seabury Press, 1973.

Gerard, H. B., & Miller, N. *School desegregation*. New York: Plenum, 1975.

Gergen, K. J., & Marecek, J. *Psychology of self-esteem*. Morristown, N. J.: General Learning Press, 1976.

Ginsburg, H. *The myth of the deprived child*. Englewood Cliffs, N. J.: Prentice–Hall, 1972.

Harrison, J.,Strauss, H., & Glaubman, R. *The activity classroom: A follow-up*. Ramat–Gan: Bar–Ilan University, 1980.

Herrnstein, R. J. *I.Q. in the meritocracy*. Boston: Atlantic–Little, 1973.

Hertz–Lazarowitz, R., Sharen, S., & Steinberg, R. Classroom learning style and cooperative behavior of elementary school children. *Journal of Educational Psychology*, 1982, 72, 97–104.

Howley, W. D. The new mythology of school desegregation. *Law and Contemporary Problems*, 1978, 42(4), 214–233.

Hyman, H. H. The psychology of status. *Archives of Psychology*, 1942, 269, 269–284.

Irwin, F. S. Sentence completion responses and scholastic success or failure. *Journal of Consulting Psychology*, 1967, 14, 269–271.

Jencks, C., Smith, M., Acland, H., Bane, M. G., Lohen, D., Gintis, H., Hyens, B., & Michelson, S. *Inequality: A reassessment of the effect of family and schooling in America*. New York: Harper & Row, 1972.

Jensen, A. R. How much can we boost I.Q. and scholastic achievement? *Harvard Educational Review*, 1969, 1–123.

Jensen, A. R. *Educability and group differences*. New York: Harper, 1973.

Katz, I. Socialization of academic motivation. In D. Levine (Ed.), *Nebraska Symposium on Motivation*. Lincoln: University of Nebraska Press, 1967.

Katz, I. Factors influencing performance in the desegregated school. In M. Deutsch, I. Katz, & A. Jensen (Eds.), *Social class, race and psychological development*. New York: Holt, Rinehart, & Winston, 1968.

Kelley, H. H. Two functions of reference groups. In G. E. Swanson, T. M. Newcomb, & E. L. Hartley (Eds.), *Readings in social psychology*. New York: Holt & Rinehart, 1952.

Klaus, R., & Gray, S. The early training project for disadvantaged children: A report after five years. *Monographs of the Society for Research in Child Development*, 1968, 33, (220).

Klein, Z., & Eshel, Y. Towards a psycho-social definition of school integration. *Megamot*, 1977, 23, 17–40. (Hebrew)

Klein, Z., & Eshel, Y. *Integrating Jerusalem schools*. New York: Academic Press, 1980.

Kleinberger, A. Reflections on equality in education. *Megamot*, 1964, 13, 257–288. (Hebrew)

Kleinberger, A. Social integration as a main purpose and justification of the educational policy in Israel. *Beminhal Hachinuch*, 1973, 3, 11–24. (Hebrew)

Kohl, H. *36 children*. New York: New American Library, 1967.

Lamm, Z. Social integration and educational policy. *Molad*, 1974, 25, 589–596. (Hebrew)

Levine, D. M., & Bane, M. J. (Eds.). *The inequality controversy: Schooling and distributive justice*. New York: Harper & Row, 1975.

Lewis, R., & St. John, N. H. Contribution of cross-racial friendship to minority group achievement in desegregated classrooms. *Sociometry*, 1974, 37, 79–91.

Maruyama, G., & Miller, N. Reexamination of normative influence processes in desegregated classrooms. *American Educational Research Journal*, 1979, 16(3), 273–283.

Miller, N., & Gerard, H. B. How busing failed in Riverside. *Psychology Today*, 1976, June, 66–100.

Minkovich, A. *The disadvantaged pupil*. Jerusalem: Hebrew University, School of Education, 1969. (Hebrew)

Minkovich, A., Davis, D., & Bashi, J. *An evaluation study of Israeli elementary schools*. Jerusalem: Hebrew University, 1977.

Ogbu, G. *Minority education and caste, the American system in cross-cultural perspective*. New York: Academic Press, 1978.

O'Reilley, R. P. (Ed.). *Racial and social class isolation in the schools*. New York: Praeger, 1970.

Patchen, M., Hoffmann, G., & Brown, W. R. Academic performance of black high school students under different conditions of contact with white peers. *Sociology of Education*, 1980, *53*, 33–51.

Pettigrew, T. F. The Negro and education—problems and proposals. In I. Katz & P. Gurin (Eds.), *Race and the social sciences*. New York: Basic Books, 1969.

Porter, R. J. School desegregation: Outcomes for children by Nancy St. John (book review). *Harvard Educational Review*, 1976, *46*, 127–131.

Purkey, N. W. *Self-concept and school achievement*. Englewood Cliffs, N. J.: Prentice–Hall, 1970.

Richer, S. Reference group theory and ability grouping: A convergence of sociological theory and educational research. *Sociology of Education*, 1976, *49*, 65–71.

Razel, O. *Compensation and welfare to whom? A reanalysis of resources allocation in elementary education*. Jerusalem: Ministry of Education and Culture, 1978. (Hebrew)

Rossell, C. R. School desegregation and community social change. *Law and Contemporary Problems*, 1978, *42*(3), 133–183.

Sarason, S. B. *The culture of the school and the problem of change*. Boston: Allyn & Bacon, 1971.

Schachter, S., & Singer, J. E. Cognitive, social and physiological determinants of emotional state. *Psychological Review*, 1962, *69*, 379–399.

Scheirer, M. A., & Kraut, R. E. Increasing educational achievement via self-concept change. *Review of Educational Research*, 1979, *49*, 131–150.

Schmuck, R. Applications of social psychology to the classroom life. In D. Bar–Tal & L. Saxe (Eds.), *Social psychology of education: Theory and research*. Washington, D. C.: Hemisphere, 1978.

Schofield, J. School desegregation and intergroup relations. In D. Bar–Tal & L. Saxe (Eds.), *Social psychology of education: Theory and research*. Washington, D. C.: Hemisphere, 1978.

Seginer, R. Relationships among social status, self-esteem and academic achievement: A review. *Megamot*, 1980, *25*, 305–321. (Hebrew)

Sharan, S. Cooperative learning in small groups: Methods and effects on achievement, attitudes and ethnic relations. *Review of Educational Research*, 1980, *50*, 241–271.

Sharan, S., Ackerman, Z., & Hertz–Lazarowitz, R. Academic achievement of elementary school children in small group versus whole class instruction. *The Journal of Experimental Education*, 1980, *48*(2), 125–129.

Sharan, S., Cohen, E., & Elchanani, D. Modifying status relations in Israel youth through expectation training. *Megamot*, 1977, *23*, 146–160. (Hebrew)

Sharan, S., & Hertz–Lazarowitz, R. *Cooperation and communication in schools*. Tel–Aviv: Schocken, 1978. (Hebrew)

Sherf, T. *Stabilization and change of teacher expectations from first-grade pupils in the process of planned change in the school system*. Unpublished M.A. thesis, Hebrew University, Jerusalem, 1973. (Hebrew)

Slavin, R. E. *Student team-learning techniques: Narrowing the achievement gap between the races*. Baltimore, Md.: Johns Hopkins University, 1977.

Slavin, R. E. Cooperative learning. *Review of Educational Research*, 1980, *50*, 315–342.

Smilansky, S., & Shephatiah, L. Relationships between integration, other classroom variables and achievement in the first grade and the second grade. *Megamot*, 1977, *23*, 79–87. (Hebrew)

Spencer, M. E. B. *The social-cognitive and personality development of the black preschool child: An exploratory study of developmental process*. Unpublished doctoral dissertation, University of Chicago, 1976.

Stephan, W. G. School desegregation: An evaluation of predictions made in Brown vs. Board of Education. *Psychological Bulletin*, 1978, *85*, 217–238.

St. John, N. H. The elementary classroom as a frog-pond: Self-concept, sense of control and social context. *Social Forces*, 1971, *49*, 581–595.

St. John, N. H. *School desegregation outcomes for children.* New York: Wiley, 1975.

Tucker, *A research perspective on educational improvement.* Harvard University, 1977. (Mimeograph)

U. S. Supreme Court. Brown vs. Board of Education. 347, U. S. 483, 494, 1954.

Weinberg, M. The relationship between school desegregation and academic achievement: A review of the research. *Law and Contemporary Problems,* 1975, *39,* 241–270.

Werts, C. E., & Watley, D. J. A student dilemma: Big fish–little pond or little fish–big pond. *Journal of Counseling Psychology,* 1969, *16,* 14–19.

Wilson, A. B. Educational consequences of segregation in a California community. U. S. Commission on Civil Rights. *Racial isolation in the public schools* (Vol. II). Washington, D. C.: 1967, pp. 165–206.

Wilson, K. L. The effects of integration and class on black educational attainment. *Sociology of Education,* 1979, *52,* 84–98.

Woock, R. R. Social perspective on desegregation policy and research. *Education and Urban Society,* 1977, *9,* 385–394.

8 Integration and Attitudes

Aharon Bizman
Yehuda Amir

One of the central goals of the educational Reform program in Israeli education was to increase social integration between children from different ethnic and socioeconomic backgrounds. The assumption of this program was that direct contact in the school between pupils from different ethnic groups will reduce prejudice and improve intergroup relations. It is worth noting that in Israel, unlike the United States, there has never been school segregation by law or by public consensus. Even before the implementation of the school reform, many children from the different ethnic groups studied together in the same schools. Therefore, the reform in Israel was not designed to abolish segregation but to increase interethnic contact, in the belief that this would lead to better overall interethnic relations. This belief does not apply exclusively to intergroup contact in the schools but to contact in any sector and is based on the hypothesis that greater opportunity for intergroup acquaintance tends to increase mutual understanding (Watson, 1947; Williams, 1947). The advantage of the school setting is that it allows for continuous, daily contact over a number of years among participants who are young and whose social attitudes are not yet fully formed.

These factors mean that schools have a potential advantage over other settings in influencing the attitudes of the participants. However, as Allport (1954) noted, unless certain conditions are present, ethnic contact does not necessarily result in a positive attitudinal change. Cook (1969), in light of his review of the literature on interethnic contact, noted the following conditions that help improve interethnic relations:

1. Equal status between participants of different groups
2. A situation requiring cooperation to achieve a common goal

155

3. A social climate or norm that approves closer ethnic relations
4. The presence among the minority group members of traits that differ from the stereotypes attributed to them by the majority group
5. A contact situation that encourages intimate relations between members of both groups.

These conditions, however, are formulated in general terms and could be related to any contact situation, as Schofield (1978) noted, and it is not yet clear how they should be applied in practice in the schools.

In light of these constraints, it is not surprising that reviews summarizing the studies conducted in the United States on this subject indicate that the attitudinal changes resulting from integration are sometimes positive and sometimes negative: In general, the changes found were either insignificant or ambivalent (Carithers, 1970; St. John, 1975; Stephan, 1978).

This chapter deals with the effect of desegregation in Israeli schools on changes in interethnic relations among those participating in the process. First, we present general data on interethnic attitudes among the various groups in Israeli society that may be considered the background against which desegregation occurs. The following sections focus on the effects of integration as a function of situational factors relevant to interethnic contact: the relative status of the interacting groups, intimate versus casual contact, interdependence and mutual cooperation, and the ethnic composition of the classroom. Subsequent sections focus on the effects of integration as a function of subject-related factors: the subject's status, sex, personality variables, the intensity of initial attitudes, and prior contact. Each section begins with a short presentation of the theoretical basis and the existing research data on the topic from studies outside Israel, followed by a review of the relevant research in Israel. The concluding section in this chapter examines the major findings of Israeli research and compares them with those reported in the general literature, which are primarily based on interethnic research in the United States.

INTERETHNIC ATTITUDES IN ISRAEL

Interethnic contact serves as a means to alter existing intergroup attitudes and perceptions and to improve the relations between the interacting groups. But what are the initial attitudes that we want to change? Are they the attitudes of the minority toward the majority, or those of the majority group toward the minority? Furthermore, are these two similar or different from each other? Perhaps each group's self-image is also significant; if so, what is it? In light of all this, what is the expected effect of contact between the two groups? Before we present the attitudinal changes effected through contact, we try to answer these questions.

Interethnic contact may be either symmetrical or asymmetrical. It is symmetrical when one ethnic group perceives itself and the other ethnic group in a way that coincides with the view of the second ethnic group. For example: *Both* groups have a similar positive evaluation of themselves and of the other group; or both groups have a positive view of themselves and a negative view of the other group. One generally refers to intergroup attitudes as asymmetric when members of one group see themselves positively and the other group negatively, whereas members of the other group view themselves negatively and the other group positively.

Brand, Ruiz, and Padilla (1974), who reviewed American research on this subject, reported that the higher status group tends to prefer itself viewing the lower status group as inferior, whereas the lower status group prefers the other group, perceiving it as higher in status than itself. The study conducted by Clark and Clark (1952), though criticized by Brand et al., still can serve as a classic example of this phenomenon. When children were asked which of the different dolls (black and white) presented to them was prettier and which they would like to play with, both white and black children preferred the white doll. When asked which of the dolls was bad, the children of both groups chose the black doll. A different situation exists in Great Britain among West Indian, Asian, and white ethnic groups; there, each group's self-evaluation is higher than its evaluation of the other groups (Bagley, Verma, Mallick, & Young, 1979). It should be noted that a number of recent studies in the United States indicate a change among blacks, demonstrating a more positive view of themselves than in the past (Hraba & Grant, 1970; Stephan & Rosenfield, 1978; Williams, 1966).

Studies carried out in Israel indicate asymmetry in the perceptions of the Middle Eastern and Western groups. Peres (1968, 1976) found that members of both groups evaluate the Western group more positively on a number of traits, such as diligence, sociability, pleasantness, weakness, intelligence, and progressiveness. Furthermore both groups exhibit more social acceptance toward Westerners than toward Middle Easterners. Peres (1968) found that 58% of 17-year-old high school students of Western background expressed reservations about marriage with Middle Easterners, whereas only 17% of the Middle Eastern subjects expressed reservations on marriage with Westerners. Another study (Levy & Guttman, 1974) conducted at a later period among 15–18-year-old high school students found indications of asymmetric attitudes: Students of Western origin expressed greater reservations about interethnic marriages than did those of Middle Eastern origin, though the difference was smaller than that found by Peres.

Asymmetry in ethnic perception was also found among younger children. Rim (1968) presented second- through sixth-grade pupils with photographs of men of Western and Middle Eastern origin and asked them to indicate if the men were Israeli and how much they liked them. Results showed that Western features were perceived to be more Israeli and aroused greater affection than Middle Eastern features, among children of both Western and Middle Eastern origin.

Further evidence of asymmetry in ethnic perception can be found in the study by Amir, Sharan, Ben–Ari, Bizman, and Rivner (1978a), which included 1033 ninth-grade students from a broad spectrum of high schools in Israel. The students responded to a multiscale questionnaire aimed at examining various aspects of ethnic attitudes. Asymmetry was found in all scales: Members of both ethnic groups gave a more positive evaluation of the Western group than of the Middle Eastern group on a series of personal characteristics; both groups revealed a greater willingness to participate in various social activities with Western students than with Middle Eastern students; members of both ethnic groups preferred Western to Middle Eastern students.

Further analyses of these data revealed that the asymmetry in the evaluation of personal characteristics of the groups was more salient among low-academic achievers of both groups than among higher achievers. In other words, low-achieving Western students expressed greater preference for their own ethnic group than did high-achieving Western students, and low-achieving Middle Eastern students perceived their ethnic group less favorably than did the higher achieving Middle Eastern students. These results seem to indicate that the asymmetry found in this and other studies reflects attitudes prevalent among certain subgroups within a given ethnic group, particularly those with low status, rather than characterizing the ethnic group as a whole.

Support for this hypothesis can be found in the study by Schwarzwald and Yinon (1977). This study examined the attitudes of eleventh-grade students in vocational schools. The schools included in the sample consisted of students with an above-average record of achievement thus representing a higher socio-economic and academic level than the subjects in the study by Amir et al. In this study, responses to an Osgood-like semantic differential scale revealed symmetrical ethnic attitudes; that is, pupils preferred their own ethnic group to the other one. The absence of asymmetry among high achievers of both groups was found on the evaluative measures, which were the only indices examined in this study. As noted previously, the study by Amir et al, revealed a similar phenomenon, namely, asymmetry was weaker on the evaluative measures, among high achievers than among low achievers. On the other hand, on the sociometric indices asymmetry was particularly great among the high achievers.

The difference between the findings on the evaluative and the sociometric dimensions has been explained by the fact that there is a larger number of high achievers among students of Western origin and a larger number of low achievers of Middle Eastern origin. The varying frequency of high- and low-achieving students in the two ethnic groups led the higher achievers of both groups to prefer primarily Western students (who are similar to them) in their sociometric choice, whereas the lower achievers of both groups chose the Middle Eastern students, with whom they see a similarity in level of achievement. Thus the low-achieving

Western students tend to interact more with their Middle Eastern peers. At the same time, they have a more negative evaluation of the latter's ethnic group. This negative evaluation can be assumed to have an effect on the nature of their interaction and on the power relations that develop between the two groups. It is reasonable to assume that the choice of friends of the low-achieving Western students from among the Middle Eastern students rather than within their own group does not stem from factors of attraction. Rather, it is a reaction to a situation in which they have no alternative—they are not accepted by the high achievers of their own ethnic group.

In a study on a representative sample of junior high school students, Schwarzwald (1980) found that intergroup perception depends on the content of the perceptual dimension measured: The Western Israeli is perceived as more successful and advanced than the Middle Eastern Israeli; on the other hand, the latter is perceived more positively than the former on traits related to human relations.

Asymmetry in interethnic relations and perceptions was found not only among youth but among adults as well. Shuval (1962), for example, found that North African immigrants adopted a negative self-concept, corresponding to the negative stereotyped image of this group prevalent within Israeli society at large. In accordance with this stereotype, qualities of aggressiveness, uncleanliness, and lack of culture were attributed to the North African immigrants. On the basis of data collected in 1959, Shuval also found evidence of asymmetry in social distance: Subjects in four development towns were asked to indicate the ethnic group they felt was least desirable as neighbors. More than half the Westerners rejected Jews of African and Asian origin as neighbors, whereas among the Middle Eastern group only 11% displayed parallel feelings of rejection toward the Western group.

The asymmetry in interethnic perception of Westerners and Middle Easterners is compatible with the findings on their perceptions and attitudes toward their own group. It is apparent that the question of ethnic affiliation concerns Middle Easterners more than Westerners. The former also feel greater solidarity (both positive and negative) with members of their ethnic group than do the latter. On the other hand, their sense of satisfaction with their ethnic identity is lower than that of the Westerners (Peres, 1968). This finding (of low satisfaction) among Middle Easterners agrees with findings on their lower evaluation of their own group and is perhaps a result of this evaluation.

In Israel, as in other countries, academic achievement and ethnic origin are correlated: High-achieving students are mostly of Western origin, and low-achieving students mostly of Middle Eastern origin. Does the asymmetry that has been found in the preceding studies stem from ethnicity per se or from difference in academic achievement between the groups? Schwarzwald and Cohen (1982) found that the degree of social acceptance that junior high school students exhibited toward their classmates was based primarily on the target student's academic level, regardless of his/her ethnic origin. However, their study did not cover areas of high intimacy in social relations. Additional studies are needed to determine whether similar results will be obtained for more intimate levels of interpersonal relations, as well as for other dimensions of intergroup perceptions.

In conclusion, it seems that the attitudes of members of the two ethnic groups in Israel are generally asymmetrical. This asymmetry exists in the various aspects of these attitudes—perceptual, evaluative, and behavioral—and seems to be mainly related to the gap in achievement that exists between the Western and Middle Eastern groups. Given these initial attitudes, what optimal changes can we expect from interethnic contact? Westerners' evaluation of their own group is positive and of the Middle Eastern group negative. The Middle Eastern group, on the other hand, evaluates the members of the Western group positively and itself negatively. Thus the optimal change for the Western group would be a more positive attitude toward and willingness to interact with the *other group*, whereas the optimal change for the Middle Eastern group would be a more positive attitude toward its *own group*.

SITUATIONAL FACTORS

The Relative Status of the Interacting Groups

There is a general consensus that in order to achieve positive changes in attitude the ethnic groups in a contact situation should be equal in status (Allport, 1954; Amir, 1969, 1976; Cook, 1969). A favorable change will also occur when the members of the minority group participating in the contact situation have a higher status than that of the majority group. After reviewing the empirical evidence on this subject Amir (1976), concluded that equal status may be a positive factor in attitudinal change, but it is not always a necessary condition: "What may be important is the gap between what is expected from the other group and what is actually perceived and experienced in the contact situation [p. 267]." In fact, this argument shifts the emphasis from equal status to another condition cited by Cook (1969), namely that a positive change will take place when the traits of the members of the minority group in the contact situation are different from and more positive than the stereotyped traits attributed to them by the majority group, though it is not necessary that these traits be of a level equal to those of the majority group (i.e., equal status).

Despite the widespread use of status in the literature on interethnic relations, this concept has been variously defined by the different psychologists. For example, several studies refer to the economic, social, or educational status of the individual as determined *outside* the contact situation. However, Kramer's (1950) argument that the status of the individual *within* the contact situation is more important for attitudinal change than his socioeconomic status is widely accepted today. The implication of this argument is that the personal characteristics of the student, such as his popularity and/or academic achievement, may be more important in a school setting than the socioeconomic status of his family or even the status determined by his ethnic origin. Even within the contact situation, a distinction can be made between two types of status: the personal status of the individual and the general status of his ethnic group. We present here the studies conducted in Israel on the subject of status and examine to what extent the results of these studies correspond to the conclusions reached and reported in the literature, which are, as noted, primarily based on research and data from the United States.[1]

An extensive study in Israel examined the variable of status, (Amir, Sharan, Rivner, Ben–Ari, & Bizman, 1979). Evaluations were obtained from, ninth-grade students of Western and Middle Eastern origin from 30 classes in seven high schools in Israel, representing the different types of schools throughout the country. Two variables were used to evaluate the student's status in the class— first, academic achievement, as determined by his score on a standard test administered to all graduates of the eighth grade in Israel; and second, popularity, as reflected in a sociometric questionnaire distributed to the students toward the end of the school year. The 30 classes participating in the study were divided into four groups according to the relative status of Western and Middle Eastern students in each class: (1) classes in which the average status of the Western students was much higher than the average status of the Middle Eastern students; (2) classes in which the average status of the Western students was higher than that of the Middle Eastern students, but less so than in the first group; (3) classes in which the status of the two groups was similar; (4) classes in which the status of the Western students was lower than that of the Middle Eastern students. (There were no classes in which the average status of the Middle Eastern students was found to be much higher than that of the Western students.)

Attitudinal changes were examined by means of a questionnaire administered during the third week and in the last month of the school year. The questionnaire contained several scales examining various aspects of social perception and preference, such as social and popularity preferences, willingness to participate in interethnic activity, ethnic perceptions and interethnic differences, and ethnic identification.

The analysis of the attitudinal changes found in each of the four different types of classes revealed the following pattern. The optimal class composition for positive attitudinal changes among Middle Eastern students was that in which the status of their group was higher than that of their Western peers. This composition led to a greater social preference of the Middle Eastern students for

---

[1]This section deals with findings on the relative overall status of students of a particular ethnic group in the class; in the next section that deals with personal factors, we focus on findings relevant to the student's personal status.

their own group, and a positive change in their evaluation of the Western students. On the other hand, a class composition in which the status of the Middle Eastern students was equal to that of the Western students resulted in a negative change in their evaluation of both groups. When the status of the Western students was somewhat higher than that of their Middle Eastern peers, no consistent changes were found in the attitudes of the Middle Eastern students. However, when the status of the Westerners was much higher than that of the Middle Eastern students, there was a marked change among the latter in the direction of a more positive evaluation of and greater preference for their own group. This last finding was attributed to self-enclosure among the Middle Eastern students when faced with rejection by their Western peers. The rise in their self-evaluation was thought to be a defensive reaction. This is elaborated on later.

With regard to the Western students, the optimal composition occurred when the status of both groups in the class was equal. In such a situation, they chose a relatively larger number of Middle Eastern students as friends and leaders at the end of the year than at the beginning. In classes in which their status was slightly lower than that of the Middle Eastern group similar changes were found, but to a lesser extent. When the Western group was of a much higher status than the Middle Eastern group, they were less likely to choose Middle Eastern students as leaders; when the Western students had a slightly higher status than the Middle Eastern group, no changes were found.

Taking both groups into account, the authors concluded that a class in which the Middle Eastern students surpass the Western students has the most positive effect on interethnic relations, whereas one in which the Western students greatly surpass the Middle Eastern students has the most negative effect. Class composition in which the Westerners enjoy a slightly higher status than the Middle Easterners has no special effect, whereas in the case of equal status there is a positive change among the Western students toward their Middle Eastern peers, but a somewhat negative change among the Middle Eastern students.

The results of this study again indicate the importance of the status variable in determining the outcome of interethnic contact. Nevertheless, several points should be stressed: (1) Although different status compositions were found to affect certain aspects of ethnic attitudinal change, they did not affect *all* aspects. In all status compositions, the willingness of both groups to interact increased equally. Nor was the students' perception of the similarity between the different ethnic groups affected by different status compositions. In all groups the Western students' perception of similarity increased, and that of the Middle Eastern group remained unchanged. These results indicate that, at least with regard to certain aspects of attitude, equal status is not a necessary condition for positive change; (2) the different status compositions had different effects on members of the two groups. Among the Middle Eastern students different status compositions affected both their evaluation of the various ethnic groups and their social preferences. On the other hand, among Western students only social preferences were affected by class composition, whereas, regardless of class composition, their evaluation of the Middle Eastern group improved and the positive evaluation of their own group declined somewhat.

This finding indicates that certain aspects of interethnic attitudes are not affected by the relative status of the different groups, but rather by other features of the contact situation. In addition, these features may bring about positive change within only one of the participating groups—in the present case, the majority group. The last finding, combined with the finding that the same status composition may produce opposite reactions among the two groups, leads us to conclude that a class composition that is optimal for attitudinal change in one group is not necessarily optimal for the other.

The previous study was the only one to examine a range of relative status compositions, in a broad spectrum of schools. The following studies examined a particular composition of relative status, generally in a single school. We first discuss those studies in which the status of the ethnic groups was similar.

Smilansky and Nevo (1979) examined social acceptance between ethnic groups in a special type of boarding school in Israel. These boarding schools, a special project initiated by the Israeli Ministry of Education, place economically underprivileged students of relatively high-scholastic potential together with students from middle-class homes, housing the former in a special dormitory throughout their high school studies. The present study examined one of these schools. It is important to note that the socioeconomic background of the boarders was very low and most were of Middle Eastern origin, whereas the regular students came mostly from families of middle- and upper-middle socioeconomic status, mostly of Western origin. However, the academic potential of the boarders as measured by general intelligence tests was equal to that of the day students. Both groups were above the average level of intelligence in Israel, parallel to that of students in selective academic high schools. In short the two groups differed in socioeconomic background and ethnic origin but obtained equal scores on tests of intellectual academic potential.

The study focused on the degree of acceptance of ninth-grade boarders in the school. This acceptance was measured by a sociometric questionnaire to which the students were asked to respond. In it, all ninth-grade students were asked to indicate the names of the students whom they wanted as friends, and the names of those whom they did not want as friends. In general the findings of the study showed that the boarders were distributed equally among all levels of acceptance in the class. There was a high correlation between the boarder's social acceptance among his fellow boarders from the Middle Eastern group and his level of acceptance by the middle-class day students. At the same time, within both groups there was a tendency to prefer intragroup social relationships. This tendency was particularly striking among the boarders, who also indicated more ''rejects'' among their fellow boarders than among the day students, whereas the latter indicated an equal number of "rejects" among both themselves and the boarders.

The fact that the popularity of the boarders, as determined by all students, was not less than their popularity within their own group indicates that under conditions of equal status intragroup preference is prevented and mutual acceptance develops. Moreover, such results were obtained despite the fact that the two groups differed widely in economic and cultural status. This fact confirms the notion that equal status within the contact situation is probably more important than equality on general status factors, such as economic status. The tendency of both groups to develop intragroup friendships is to be expected, considering the fact that the boarders and regular students meet only during school hours, whereas the boarders remain together after school hours as well. The extensive social activity within the dormitory, including parties, clubs, and evening activities, ensure that the boarders need seek no social contact after school hours with the regular students who live relatively far away from the dormitory.

This study examined only the social acceptance of those students who took part in the interaction. We do not know whether any changes occurred in the overall attitude of the students toward the other ethnic group as a whole, or if their overall willingness to come into contact with that group increased. In a study conducted in a summer camp, 12–13-year-old girls spend 12 days together. The 100 girls who took art in the study, 78 of Western and 22 of Middle Eastern origin, functioned within 10 subgroups. The organizers of the camp formed ethnically heterogeneous groups, seeing to it that the girls in each group were not previously acquainted. The camp itself was organized by Israel's largest bus company for employees' children. All the girls, of both ethnic groups, were of middle-class background and thus of similar economic status, and the treatment and attitude of the camp personnel toward the girls of both groups was uniform (Amir & Garti, 1977).

On the second and eleventh days of their stay at camp, a questionnaire was distributed to the girls similar to the multiscale questionnaire used in the Amir et al. study described earlier. It included a scale of "participation in activities" that examined the girls' readiness to be involved in social activities both related and unrelated to camp life, both with girls whose families had immigrated to Israel from countries represented in the camp (e.g., Iraq) and from countries not represented in the camp (e.g., Iran and India). In addition, in the semantic differential questionnaire, the girls were asked to evaluate others originating from countries represented in the camp and from countries not represented.

A comparison of the data obtained at the end of the study with those obtained at the beginning revealed the following picture: Among the Western girls, there was a positive change in attitude toward the Middle Eastern group, although their initial attitudes toward this group were quite positive. These positive changes occurred both with regard to the specific girls in the camp and also toward girls, in general, from Middle Eastern countries represented in the camp—both in regard to camp-related activities and to replies on the semantic differential questionnaire. The positive change was even generalized to a willingness to participate in noncamp-related activities with children from Middle Eastern countries represented in the camp or in camp-related activities with children from Middle Eastern countries not represented in the camp. The change did not reach the highest level of generalization—that is, to noncamp-related activities with children of Middle Eastern countries not represented in the camp.

Among the Middle Eastern girls, no significant change was found in their attitudes toward the Western group, although in all indices the direction of the change was positive. This nonsignificant result may have been due to the relatively small number of Middle Eastern subjects in the sample.

The positive results obtained in these studies match those obtained in similar studies conducted in the United States on the effect of contact in summer camps (Yarrow, Campbell, & Yarrow, 1958). However, one should be hesitant about arriving at generalizations about schools based on these studies; conditions in camps and boarding schools are not identical to those in a regular school. Whereas contact in a regular school is principally academic-achievement oriented, contact in camp is based on social activities in which the individual competitive-achievement element is not salient. In the boarding school too, social elements are more important than in the regular school. The studies conducted show that if equal status is achieved in dimensions important to the students, there may be positive changes in the attitude of the majority toward the minority students—not only to the specific participants in the contact situation, but to members of that ethnic group in general—with regard to activities and behavior in the contact situation, and to other behavior. However, the determinants of status may vary in different settings.

In the studies following, there were wide gaps in the status of the participating groups. The study conducted by Ambar (1976) examined the effect of integration in three seventh-grade classes in a junior high school located in an upper-middle-class neighborhood. There were 105 students in these classes, of whom 78 lived in the neighborhood of the school and 27 lived in a lower socioeconomic neighborhood. The latter students were bused every day from their homes to the school. In addition to the socioeconomic gaps between the two groups, academic-intellectual gaps were also evident. All the students of the low socioeconomic class were Middle Eastern. Of the students of the higher socioeconomic class, 59 were of Western and 19 of Middle Eastern origin. At the beginning and the end of the school year, a questionnaire similar to the multiscale questionnaire of Amir et al. was administered to all students.

The results obtained produced the following picture. The students of the low socioeconomic class showed an overall positive change in their evaluation of the Western group, in their willingness to participate in activities with them, and in their social preferences for members of that group. The Western students of the high socioeconomic class showed a positive change only in their willingness to participate in activities with Middle Eastern students, whereas on the other indices no change could be detectable. Thus, it seems that, whereas the students of the low socioeconomic class try to establish closer relations with students of the high socioeconomic class, the latter merely assert their willingness to participate in joint activities (in other words, they reconcile themselves to the situation of mutual contact), but there is no genuine change in their tendency to make friends with the other students or in their evaluation of them. These last results show that even when the status of the minority group is relatively low, contact with them may increase the majority-group's willingness to interact with them—but no more than this.

There was some improvement in the attitudes of the Middle Eastern students from a high-level socioeconomic status toward their Western peers. However, this improvement appeared only in evaluations of the Western students' overall characteristics. It should be recalled that these students live in the same neigbborhood as the Western students and attended the same school prior to entering junior high school. Still, the additional contact over a period of a year raised their evaluation of the Western students. This may be attributed to the gap in socioeconomic and academic levels between the Western students and the Middle Eastern students bused to the school that highlighted the higher standing, and therefore the prestige, of the Western group.

In the same junior high school, and with the same general type of population, Schwartz (1975) conducted another study that focused primarily on the effect of contact on the ethnic identification of the Middle Eastern students from low socioeconomic background. Three aspects of ethnic identification were examined (Peres, 1968): (1) *centrality*—the part ethnicity plays in the consciousness of the individual, and to what extent he considers that it affects his daily actions; (2) *solidarity*—the extent of the individual's sensitivity to praise or insult directed toward members of his ethnic group and the degree of affinity he feels with them; (3) *attractiveness*—the extent to which the individual is satisfied with his ethnic affiliation.

The results of the study showed that in the course of the year there was a significant increase among Middle Eastern students in the first two components of ethnic identification, and a decline in the third. The increase in the centrality and solidarity components has important psychological significance. It means that, as a result of the Middle Eastern students' daily contact with Western students of appreciably higher socioeconomic status and intellectual ability, the former tended to view and to interpret social events in the classroom from an "ethnic looking-glass" perspective. Consequently they became more sensitive to any offense directed against a member of their group. At the same time the individual tended to underrate his own group and choose the dominant group as his reference group. It seems therefore that this sense of solidarity is defensive rather than constructive in nature. This conclusion agrees with the findings of the previous study by Ambar conducted in the same school: Following intergroup contact, the Middle Eastern students expressed a higher evaluation of the Western students and chose a larger number of them as friends. The interpretation in terms of defensiveness is consistent with the explanation offered by Amir et al. (1979) about the finding that showed that there is an increase in the self-esteem and in the intraethnic preferences of Middle Eastern students when they occupy a much lower status in the classroom than their Western peers.

Evidence about the limited effect of contact when there are wide gaps in status between the groups can also be found in the study conducted by Feitelson, Weintraub, and Michaeli (1972) with 3-year olds in preschool. Because this study is unique in that it was carried out as a field experiment, we describe it in detail. Ninety-six children took part in the experiment, half of them from very low socioeconomic classes (hereafter "disadvantaged") and half of them of middle-class background (hereafter "advantaged"). Four preschools, each with 24 children, were set up as part of the experiment. Three of the schools were heterogeneous, with 16 advantaged and 8 disadvantaged children in each. The fourth was homogenous, composed solely of disadvantaged children. The study lasted 2 years, during which time-controlled observations of the behavior of the children in the schools were carried out.

In the course of the 2 years, the disadvantaged children in the homogeneous preschool and the advantaged children in the heterogeneous preschools increased their contacts with their peers and decreased contacts with their teachers; on the other hand, among the disadvantaged children in the heterogeneous preschools, the number of contacts with the adults did not decline, although there was some increase in cooperation with their peers. This finding is consistent with other results showing that at both the beginning and the end of the year the advantaged children came into contact mainly with other advantaged children and ignored the disadvantaged children. The authors conclude that the sensitivity of 3-year-olds to the gaps between the two groups and their tendency toward intragroup association derived, not from their awareness of ethnic differences as such, but primarily from cultural differences and the lack of shared experiences between the two groups.

Observations of the children supported this hypothesis. These observations showed that, during the early period in the preschool, the advantaged children tended at first to associate and cooperate with all the other children, disadvantaged and advantaged alike. Only later did they develop a tendency to associate with children of their own socioeconomic class, with whom they had a basis for joint activity. For example, during free play, they used experiences learned at home, such as ordering groceries by phone and instructing the cleaning woman. These activities were not familiar to the disadvantaged children, in whose homes there was no telephone and no cleaning woman. In the course of time, this lack of shared experiences led to alienation from each other and greater dependence on the adults in the preschool. Apparently the principle of equal status and similarity between the groups in the contact situation is already operative at age

3. Nevertheless, it is important to stress that this finding refers to the behavioral aspect of interethnic relations.

Summary of Studies on the Relative Status of the Groups. The results of these studies indicate that the notion that contact leads to positive attitudinal change only when it takes place under conditions of equal status between the groups, or when the minority group enjoys a higher status than the majority group, seems too simplistic. The effect of the relative status of the groups in a contact situation varies with the different dimensions of attitude examined. The effect may also be different for the minority and majority groups.

It seems that in Israeli schools the very fact of integration creates greater willingness on the part of both groups to live together and maintain various kinds of interaction, and that this willingness is barely affected by the relative status of the two groups. The fact that there are almost no major clashes between the two groups, irrespective of their relative status, or symptoms of escape mechanisms such as the attempt to transfer from the integrated school to a different one, supports this conclusion and indicates that such willingness is not merely verbal. Why is this willingness not sensitive to relative status? One reason may be what Aronson (1980) called the psychology of inevitability, which basically implies that sooner or later a person will accept something he cannot avoid. Secondly, students of both groups may have learned that even when there are gaps in academic status, it is still possible to share and enjoy other activities.

In contrast to this attitude, friendship patterns—as reflected in the answers to the question, "who are your *best* friends in the class"—are greatly affected by the relative status of the groups as determined by academic achievement. However, it should be noted that all the studies reporting on social preferences used a sociometric questionnaire including the question, "who are your best friends?". This question does not reflect the different levels of mutual attraction that people can feel toward one another. Between indifference or dislike on the one hand, and the selection of a best friend on the other, there are many degrees of attraction or rejection. Changes may have occurred as a result of contact within these extremes, but their identification requires more refined tools than those used in past studies (Cohen, 1975; Schofield, 1978; Schwarzwald & Cohen, 1982).

The question of relative status becomes even more complex when we examine its effect on each of the groups separately. The Westerners, who constitute the higher social-status group, revealed a positive change in their attitude toward Middle Easterners when the status of the Middle Easterners in the contact situation was equal to or higher than their own status. In situations where the Middle Easterners had lower status than the Westerners, there was no change in the latter's attitudes. When the gap between the two groups was very great, Western intraethnic social preference increased.

As for the Middle Easterners, in situations where their status was higher than that of the Western group, they revealed a positive attitudinal change both to their own group and to members of the Western group. The positive change in their attitude toward the Western group, despite its lower status, apparently stems from the Western students' positive attitude toward them and willingness to make friends with them. In this situation positive reciprocal attitudes are established in both groups.

Situations in which the status of the Middle Easterners is lower than that of the Westerners can be divided according to extent of the difference in status between the groups. Where the gap is not extreme, no changes occur in their attitudes. When there is a particularly large gap, contradictory reactions are found: On the one hand, the higher status Western group continues to serve as the reference group that the Middle Easterners seek to imitate; on the other hand, because of their inferior position, the latter develop defensive responses that are expressed in higher self-esteem and social withdrawal into their own group. The conditions under which each of these opposite reactions will prevail still needs to be studied.

And what of the Middle Easterners in an equal-status situation? The equal-status hypothesis suggests an improvement in the attitudes of the Middle Easterners toward the Westerners. Indeed, two studies support this approach (Amir & Garti, 1977; Smilansky & Nevo, 1979). However, they did not focus on typical school conditions but rather on conditions in a summer camp and in a boarding school for gifted students, respectively. A comprehensive study on a sample of regular schools (Amir et al., 1979) found a negative change among Middle Eastern students as a result of interethnic contact under conditions of equal status in school. In this study status was determined by means of the student's academic and intellectual achievements. But even under conditions of equality on these criteria, Western students still preferred their own group (though to a lesser degree than under conditions of unequal status). It seems that equality in achievement, if not followed up by equality in social acceptance, may result in frustration and even alienation, and this may explain the negative results obtained for the Middle Eastern group.

Intimate as Opposed to Casual Contact

Interethnic contact can take on various forms: It can be superficial and casual, or more intimate, involving positive emotional relationships with members of the opposite group. Superficial relations, even when frequent, do not necessarily result in positive attitudinal change, and frequency of such contact may even reinforce prejudices (Jordan, 1973). On the other hand, positive experiences encourage positive interethnic relations. This kind of contact may develop when intimate relations are established with a member of another ethnic group. Attraction to a particular person and the enjoyment and satisfaction accompanying such a relationship lead to positive change through their extension to other members of the same group (Ashmore, 1970). In this regard, Cook (1962) proposed that a distinction be made between contact situations with potential for intimate mutual acquaintance, and those in which such potential is limited.

Evidence of the effect of intimate contact as compared to superficial contact can be found in the study by Hofman and Zak (1969), which examined the experience of American Jewish youths who stayed together with Israeli youths in a summer camp. Ninety American boys and girls aged from 14½ to 17½ spent 6 weeks in an agricultural boarding school in Israel, during which time they lived together with Israeli students of that school, taking part in a variety of social activities, trips, sports, and various activity groups. On two occasions—before their arrival in the camp and toward the end of their stay—the Americans were given a questionnaire that examined their attitude toward Israel and Jews. The Americans were divided into two groups: those who had had close contact with the Israelis, and those who had not. The findings of the study showed that, whereas prior to camp there were no differences in the attitudes of these two groups, afterwards the group that had had close contact with Israelis showed a positive change in attitudes toward Israel and toward Jews. Further evidence that such positive change can be attributed to intimate and enjoyable contact with the Israelis can be seen in the views expressed by those children who had close contact with the Israelis. What most affected their impressions of Israel were their social relations with Israelis. On the other hand, the participants who did not have close contact with the Israelis indicated factors outside of social experiences, such as the landscape and nature. Another relevant finding was that the members of the older group revealed a greater tendency to develop social relationships and as a result experienced greater attitudinal change. The older Americans, it should be recalled, worked together with the Israelis during the morning hours and thus had greater opportunity to form intimate relations with them. Because of their age they were also more open to relations with the opposite sex.

Another study (Chen, Shapira, & Hausdorf, 1970) examined the attitudes of foreign students in an Israeli university toward Israel and Zionism over the course of a year. A positive—albeit weak—link was found between attitude and association with Israelis. Those students who reported intimate contact with Israelis expressed a more positive attitude toward Israel and Zionism. They also tended to view Israel as their "homeland."

A study mentioned earlier (Amir & Garti, 1977) found positive changes in interethnic attitudes among members of the two groups that came into contact in a summer camp. These changes were attributed primarily to the equal status of the participants. In addition, the authors considered that the atmosphere in the camp also contributed to these changes. The many social activities that took place in camp provided the potential for mutual acquaintance between the two groups. These activities helped to create a positive atmosphere and added to the enjoyment experienced by the participants. It is interesting to note that the children who expressed a change in attitude were those who enjoyed their stay at camp, whereas those whose attitudes were unchanged reported less enjoyment.

This result raises the question of whether intimacy is a precondition for positive change. The intimacy variable, as referred to in the literature, includes two components. One refers to the degree of acquaintance and the mutual exposure of the participants, and the second to the degree of enjoyment derived from the encounter. Usually, the very fact of acquaintance and mutual exposure gives rise to enjoyment and satisfaction, for otherwise the participants would sever relations (Altman & Taylor, 1973). However, there may be sources of enjoyment that are not derived from intimacy. In the study by Amir and Garti, the contact situation itself (summer camp with the variety of attractive activities it entails) was enjoyable. Given a certain level of intimacy, can a positive change be produced by raising the level of enjoyment of the contact situation? Such a conclusion would be of practical significance, because even while the level of intimacy is largely controlled by the participants themselves, the element of enjoyment derived from the ethnic contact situation can be planned by the school.

To sum up this subject, it seems that the relevant studies conducted in Israel on children and youth support the general conclusion of the literature on the subject, namely that intimate contact is a powerful variable that can contribute to a positive attitudinal change, whereas superficial contact alone will not reduce prejudice and may even strengthen it (Amir, 1976).

Interdependence and Cooperation

Contact situations are likely to differ in the number of cooperative and competitive factors they entail. Joint aims and activities, and emphasis on elements shared by the different groups, increases interdependence and cooperation. On the other hand, contradictory aims and differing objectives increase competition between the groups. Many theoreticians (Allport, 1954; Ashmore, 1970; Williams, 1947) viewed these factors as being of primary importance in determining the results of interethnic contact. Amir and Ben–Ari (1981) hypothesized that the satisfaction of interpersonal needs (Schutz, 1966) within the framework of the classroom would increase interdependence and cooperation between the students, and that this would consequently lead to an improvement in interethnic attitudes and relations. The study was conducted in 20 seventh-grade classrooms in 3 integrated junior high schools, through a special program designed to increase the satisfaction derived from the intergroup activities. These activities were varied in nature and included role playing, social games, and discussions specifically aimed at satisfying certain interpersonal needs. The effect of these activities on intergroup relations among the students as well as on their ethnic stereotypes was measured. The results showed positive changes among the children in the experimental groups as expressed in a greater number of interethnic sociometric choices, including friendship and evaluation, but not in more general aspects of the interethnic attitude, such as ethnic prejudice.

In Bizman's (1978) study, Jewish and Arab students met in a situation that resembled group dynamics activities. The meetings centered around personal and social subjects common to the members of both groups. The group leader directed the discussions in such a way as to avoid controversial and political issues related to the Jewish–Arab conflict. Following these meetings, the Jewish students displayed certain positive changes in their attitude toward Arabs.

These findings agree with the results obtained following the implementation of cooperative teaching methods in school instead of the traditional method of frontal teaching. It seems that the increased interdependence and cooperation between the participants raises the level of ethnic integration. Such interaction is both enjoyable and satisfying, as it leads the participants toward the achievement of their social goals and satisfies various personal needs. Also, each individual's contribution to the achievement of the group's aims promotes feelings of equality (See Sharan, 1980 and Chapter 9).

Ethnic Class Composition

This subject is of great concern to the public at large and the educational system in Israel. However, scientific knowledge in this area is very limited. Several scholars argue that there is an optimal ratio of ethnic representation in the class and the school that facilitates ethnic integration. Pettigrew and Pajonas (1964) proposed an optimal ratio of 20–45% blacks in integrated schools. The argument that a larger percentage of majority students must be maintained in integrated classes is based on the claim that the numerical majority of this group will lead to the adoption of their norms by the minority students who come into contact with them. As for the effect of class composition on interethnic attitudes, it has been argued (Mercer, Iadicola, & Moore, 1980) that the numerical ratio is seen as a psychological reflection of the balance of power between the two groups in the school, and hence a 50–50% ethnic ratio that reflects parity will increase the chances for equal status. This ratio also increases the chances of minority students' being given prestigious roles in the school (committees, varsity teams, etc.), which also contribute indirectly to the equalization of status within the school system and may well have a positive effect on attitudes.

In two Israeli studies that directly examined this aspect, no link was found between the ratio of ethnic representation in the class and attitudinal change. The study by Amir, Sharan, Bizman, Rivner, and Ben–Ari (1978b), in which the 30 classes participating were classified by level of ethnic integration, from almost nonrepresentation of Western students to 90% Western students, found no link between the numerical ratio of the two ethnic groups and change in attitude and ethnic preferences. Kalinsky (1975) compared the interethnic attitudes of eighth-grade students in three schools. The schools were similar in the socioeconomic background and intelligence level of their students but differed in the percentage of Middle Eastern students in their classes (29%, 52%, 87%). No distinctions were found between the schools with regard to interethnic attitudes. The findings of Lewy (1977) and Bashi (1977) also indicate that ethnic composition is relatively unimportant in changing the academic achievement and self-concept of students.

Although a ratio of 50–50% seems optimal for opportunities for interethnic contact, such a ratio does not in fact ensure that these opportunities will be realized. Contacts and friendships may be intraethnic regardless of the numerical ratio in the class or school, and the nature, rather than the quantity, of the contact remains the most important issue (as discussed earlier). A given numerical ratio in itself does not ensure the formation of significant relationships between the two groups. Thus, on the whole, the significance hitherto attached to the effect of ethnic composition on the results of integration seems to be greater than is justified by research results.

SUBJECT FACTORS

The Status of the Interacting Subject

Research findings in the United States show that, following integration, children with a higher level of academic achievement undergo a more positive change in their interethnic attitudes than children with low academic achievement (St. John, 1975). Let us examine the research results on this in Israel.

The study by Amir et al. (1978b) found that students with relatively high levels of achievement in both ethnic groups displayed greater attitudinal changes than the low achievers; this was expressed by a narrowing in the perceived gap between the two groups. Among Western students, this narrowing was expressed in a less-positive evaluation of their own group, whereas among Middle Eastern students it was expressed in a more positive attitude toward their own group and a less-positive evaluation of the Western group, as well as a perception of greater similarity between the two groups at the end of the first year in the integrated class. On the other hand, among low-achieving students of both groups, no change occurred in their initial asymmetrical perception of the superiority of the Western group.

A similar picture was found in a study that examined the interethnic attitudes of seventh-grade students in an integrated school. T. Amir (1976) found that the high-achieving Middle Eastern students expressed a greater preference for making friends with the Western students in their class than did the low-achieving students. Similarly, those Middle Eastern students whose academic achievement declined after their transfer to the integrated school showed a lesser tendency to make friends with Western students than those whose academic status did not decline. Findings with regard to Western students were parallel: Those with low academic achievement revealed a greater tendency to reject the Middle Eastern students in their class than those with high achievement. Both this finding and the previous one indicate that desegregation leads to positive attitudinal changes among high-status students of both groups, whereas among low-status students of both groups no change occurred; on the contrary, the latter may even display seclusion within their own group and rejection of the other group.

The study by Schwartz (1975) reported earlier found that in the course of an academic year, high-achieving Middle Eastern students were socially accepted in their class by both Middle Eastern and Western students, more than low-achieving Middle Eastern students. They also revealed a greater preference for the company of the Western students in their class as compared with low-achieving Middle Easterners.

In the last two studies, a link was found between the academic achievement of the Middle Eastern students and the social preferences of the Western group. This social preference could be seen as an indication of the internalization of the achievement norms of the Western group by the Middle Eastern students that contributed to their academic achievement (Mercer et al., 1980). However, the fact that the high-achieving Middle Eastern students expressed a decline in their evaluation of the Western group and an improved evaluation of their own group indicates a different causal process. The high achievers among the Middle Eastern students are attracted to and accepted by Western students of similar achievement level. This process is accompanied by a narrowing of the gap in their evaluation of the two ethnic groups. This interpretation concurs with conclusions reached by Maruyama and Miller (1979) that achievement appears to exert causal influence on popularity, but popularity does not influence achievement. A similar process was not found among the low achievers of both groups. The unwillingness of low-achieving Western students to make friends with the Middle Eastern students of similar achievement level perhaps suggests an attempt by them—with no academic foundation—to stress their social superiority within the class.

The effect of integration on low-status Middle Eastern students can be seen in the study by Erez (1973). This study examined the effect of integration on the ethnic identification of the students. The school where the study was conducted comprised nine classes of homogeneous intellectual levels: The higher level students studied prestigious subjects (such as academic studies or electronics) and the lower level students studied less-prestigious subjects (such as mechanics or clerical work). The "lower" classes were composed primarily (at a ratio of about 80–20) of students of Middle Eastern origin, whereas the "higher" classes were composed primarily (about the same ratio) of students of Western origin. In the course of the year, the students in the lower classes experienced increased satisfaction with their ethnic affiliation, so that by the end of the year their satisfaction exceeded that of the students in the higher classes. This high satisfaction with ethnic affiliation among the students in the lower classes seems to run counter to the overall findings in this area. It is, however, difficult to draw definite conclusions about these findings because no differentiation has been made—either in the lower or in the higher classes—between Western or Middle Eastern students. Thus, the observed changes cannot be definitely attributed to a certain group.

Cohen (1974) found that students in special classes for slow learners composed primarily of Middle Eastern students increased their sense of deprivation and ethnic discrimination. The reason for this response among Middle Eastern students apparently lies in their negative self-image and their tendency to interpret events on the basis of interethnic relations. It seems that the students in the class for slow learners attributed the presence of a Middle Eastern majority in their class to the desire of the school administration to separate them from the higher achieving Western students in order to permit the latter more rapid advancement. They did not see their special class as a means for their own advancement. In their study of a sample of Israeli schools, Chen, Lewy, and Kfir (1977) also found that the lower the percentage of Western students in the class, the stronger the feeling of ethnic discrimination and conspicuousness.

In the last few sections, we dealt with two aspects of status—the relative status of the groups in the contact situation, and the personal status of the individual. Which aspect is more important in determining attitudinal change? A possible answer can be found in the study by Amir et al. (1979), which compared these two aspects. Although this study revealed changes in interethnic attitudes and perceptions as a product of the individual's personal status, these were small in comparison to changes in attitudes and perceptions as a result of the relative status of the group. This suggests that the status of the individual is less important to changes in interethnic attitudes and perceptions than the relative status of the ethnic groups participating in the contact situation.

Because there is a correlation between academic level and ethnic origin, creating ethnically ''equal-status'' classes means that in the upper level classes the number of Western students will exceed that of the Middle Easterners; conversely, for the low-level classes. We have already reported that the ethnic ratio within the class seem to have no effect, in and of itself, on attitudinal change. Thus, from the point of view of intergroup relations these classes should be preferred to heterogeneous ones, where the preponderance of high-level types of students will typically be of Western origin. On the other hand, one should take into account that the Middle Easterners in the lower level classes may feel deprived because of being placed in such classes. There is also the possibility that the Westerners who are in the minority in these classes may experience a status loss and consequently react negatively. The issue obviously requires further study.

Sex

Several studies conducted in the United States indicate that intergroup contact affects boys and girls differently. Carithers (1970) noted that the presence of whites in integrated schools constitutes a greater threat to black girls than to black boys, so the black girls encounter greater difficulties. A similar conclusion was reached by St. John (1975).

In the study by Amir et al. (1978b), it was found that following 1 year of integrated schooling boys of both ethnic groups evidenced greater change than girls. Among Western students, differential changes in interethnic attitudes as a function of sex were found with Western boys displaying positive and Western girls negative changes. Among Middle Eastern students, the differential changes found were in the different aspects of ethnic identification: The Middle Eastern boys revealed an increased attraction to their own group than did the Middle Eastern girls. However, among Middle Eastern boys an increase was found in regard to the centrality dimension of ethnic identification (which can be regarded as a negative phenomenon), whereas a decline was recorded for this dimension among Middle Eastern girls. The study by Cohen (1974) conducted among seventh-grade students in integrated junior high schools found that the Middle Eastern girls tended equally to make friends with girls of both their own and the opposite ethnic group, whereas Middle Eastern boys preferred members of their own group.

These findings indicate that, in Israel, Middle Eastern girls have a stronger tendency than Middle Eastern boys to make friends with Western children, and that the issue of ethnicity is of less concern to Middle Eastern girls. It can be surmised that, unlike black girls in the United States, it may be easier for Middle Eastern girls in Israel to adapt to interethnic social integration than for Middle Eastern boys. However, not all findings are in the same direction. Levin and Chen (1977) examined the friendship patterns within a national sample of eighth-grade students in Israel and found that the sociometric choices were to a great extent intrasexual, and to a lesser extent intraethnic. They found no differences between boys and girls in this area.

Personality Variables

Many studies indicate a relationship among personality traits, such as authoritarianism and self-concept and prejudice (Adorno, Frenkel-Brunswick, Levinson, & Sanford, 1950; Ehrlich, 1973). Very few studies have been conducted on the question of whether the effects of interethnic contact are contingent upon the personality of the participants. Musen (1950) found that the 25% of white boys who, following a summer spent in camp together with black boys, revealed greater prejudice and also expressed greater aggressiveness and a greater need to defy authority, as compared to those white boys who expressed less prejudice toward the other group. On the other hand, in their study of summer camps in Israel, Amir and Garti (1977) did not find a link between authoritarian personality and the extent of attitudinal change toward the opposite group. Bizman (1978) examined the effect of contact between Jewish and Arab students on the attitudes of the Jews toward the Arabs. This study, too, found no link between the authoritarianism of the Jewish participants and extent of attitudinal change toward Arabs following contact. However, a link was found between authoritarianism and initial attitudes.

Another variable related to prejudice is the individual's self-concept. In the few studies conducted in Israel on this subject, no link was found between self-concept and the degree of attitudinal change following interethnic contact. T. Amir (1976) examined the self-concept of Middle Eastern and Western students in mixed seventh-grade classes at the beginning and the end of the year. No link was found between changes in self-concept over the course of the year and the student's preference in choosing friends from among the opposite ethnic group. Similar results were obtained in the study by Amir and Ben–Ari (1981). They examined the effect of a special program for increasing social satisfaction and group cohesiveness in integrated classes. No link was found between the self-concept of the students and the changes that occurred in their attitudes. The aforementioned study by Bizman (1978) also found no link between the subjects' self-concept and attitudinal change, although a link was found between self-concept and initial attitudes. This last finding agrees with the numerous studies that found a link between negative self-concept and the rejection of others, as well as between negative self-concept and antiblack attitudes (Ehrlich, 1973).

In conclusion, it seems that although there was reason to surmise that personality variables might affect the results of interethnic contact, the research evidence in Israel to date does not support this hypothesis.

Intensity of Initial Attitudes

Williams (1964) noted that interethnic contact has a positive effect primarily on people with relatively little prejudice. These people have a greater tendency to develop close ties and friendships with members of the opposite group, which in turn contribute to the lessening of prejudice. The findings of Amir and Garti (1977) support this view. Their study examined the effect of an integrated summer camp on the attitudes of the participants. The results obtained indicated a positive change in the interethnic attitudes of the participants. Whereas there were a number of factors contributing to this positive change (e.g., equal status, cooperation) and the effect of each variable could not be isolated, it should be noted that the attitudes of the girls in the camp were quite positive to begin with, and perhaps it was this that contributed to the positive change following contact.

The question is: Is there a qualitative or quantitative difference between people with little prejudice and those with greater prejudice? In other words, should the latter group, in order to change their attitudes, be exposed to a type of treatment qualitatively different from that suitable for others, or should the same variables be applied, but with greater intensity. Social-psychological research has not yet provided a clear answer to this question.

Previous Intergroup Contact

Assuming that direct contact with members of the opposite group can bring about attitudinal change—beyond that achieved by other means—it can still be conjectured that the effect of contact within the school system depends on the individual's previous intergroup contacts. The effect of interethnic contact may be greater if the participants have not experienced similar contacts in the past; if they have already had contact, a potential positive effect may already have occurred.

Two studies reported earlier examined this question. Amir and Garti (1977) found in their summer camp study that only those subjects who reported limited or nonexistent previous contact with members of the opposite group altered their ethnic attitudes positively, whereas those who reported more extensive previous contact did not change. The study by Amir et al. (1979) on ninth-grade students in Israel also measured the extent of the subjects' previous contact. In this study no link was found between previous contact and the degree of interethnic attitudinal change.

The contradictory results of these two studies may perhaps be attributed to the different measures used to evaluate the extent of previous contact. The measure used by Amir and Garti was subjective (i.e., the subjects' own evaluation of the extent of their previous interaction with members of the opposite group). The measure in the study by Amir et al., on the other hand, was objective, based on the number of members of the opposite group in the individual's previous environment (former class and school) with whom he could have interacted. As noted previously, the number of members of the opposite group in the individual's environment does not necessarily reflect the extent of actual contact between them. In view of the results obtained by Amir and Garti, it may be important for future studies on the effect of contact on attitudinal change to take into account the subjects' opportunities for interethnic contact prior to the contact situation under examination.

Another question in this area is that of the weight of contact in school as compared to other contact situations, whether prior or parallel. Does contact in school have a greater or lesser effect than, for example, contact in youth movements or in the student's neighborhood. A possible advantage of the school is that it permits continuous contact over an extended period, as opposed to—for example—a summer camp, which permits intensive but short-term contact.

CONCLUSION AND DISCUSSION

The process of improving interethnic attitudes following contact in school can be divided into two stages. The first stage involves the actual act of desegregation and its maintenance. The establishment of such a setting generally requires positive attitudes from both groups toward the idea of ethnic contact and interactions. The maintenance of desegregation is dependent on the absence of conspicuous manifestations of rejection and rivalry between members of the different groups in the contact situation. This stage does not necessarily or automatically lead to an improvement in intergroup attitudes, but the fact that the shared experience is not negative in character is a prerequisite for the second stage—a positive improvement in mutual attitudes.

In the United States, for example, desegregation of blacks and whites often sharpened existing trends of social isolation within the ethnic group and mutual hostility on an ethnic basis. In Israel, on the other hand, ethnic relations in the schools are generally characterized by an absence of hostility and alienation. The phenomenon of Western students leaving school following the implementation of integration is also rare. Three factors not directly related to school settings can explain this difference between the two countries:

1. Unlike the United States, ethnic attitudes in Israel are not markedly negative. Although there is a certain asymmetry in interethnic perceptions (namely, more positive attitudes toward Westerners), both among the majority and the minority groups, Israel, unlike American society, is not characterized by acute alienation and ethnic isolation. This can be exemplified inter alia in the steady rise in the rate of ethnic intermarriage in Israel over the years (Peres, 1976). Furthermore, Israel's schools have never been ethnically segregated. Even before the recent implementation of the integration program, many children of both groups attended the same schools. Nor is there a history of ethnic segregation in residential neighborhoods. There have always been areas where members of both groups lived side by side.

2. The State of Israel was established with the aim of uniting the Jewish people scattered throughout the diaspora into a single nation. This ideological goal of the "ingathering of the exiles" is accepted and emphasized in Israeli society (See Chapter 1).

3. The constant threat from its neighbors is a unifying factor in Israeli society, highlighting the common fate and interdependence of its citizens and minimizing ethnic differences.

The second stage in the process of ethnic integration involves the *positive* changes in attitudes, relations, and interactions. Although there are those who argue that the very fact of contact constitutes a motivating factor for both sides to seek the positive aspects of their peers (Aronson, 1980), the success of this stage is to a great extent dependent on characteristics of the contact situation itself, the characteristics of the groups in the contact situation, and the nature of their interaction.

The initial attitudes of the participants in the contact include stereotyped expectations with regard to the beliefs, attitudes, traits, and behavior of members of an outgroup. If we view the interethnic contact as a situation of relearning (Baker, 1934; Rose, 1947), direct contact with the object of the prejudice that contradicts—positively—initial attitudes, will lead to a change in these stereotypes and the acquisition of other, more positive beliefs. Thus, not every encounter between ethnic groups will lead to a positive attitudinal change. Contact with members of the minority group whose behavior and traits confirm the stereotyped traits ascribed to them will fail to bring about positive change and may even reinforce existing stereotypes.

Did the transfer to an integrated setting in Israeli schools lead to changes in interethnic attitudes, relations, and interactions? In general, our review indicates that despite the readiness, or at least the lack of objection, on the part of both groups to come into contact with each other and participate in joint activities positive changes in intergroup relations do not necessarily occur. Even in those studies where the overall results indicate a positive change, these changes are quite small or are found in special social settings (such as boarding schools and summer camps). It is possible that at present the major social contribution of desegregation in Israel is in preventing a possible deterioration of interethnic attitudes that might otherwise have developed (Amir & Ben–Ari, 1981).

In the following sections, we deal with the effect of the characteristics of the contact situation including those of the participating groups, and the nature of the interaction on the results of integration. Finally, we discuss possible ways of achieving its optimal implementation in the schools.

The Characteristics of the Groups in the Contact Situation

Most studies in Israel and throughout the world have dealt with those characteristics that determine the relative status of the groups coming into contact with each other. This seems justified, because equal status between the groups signifies contact with members of the minority group who have traits different from the existing stereotypes, thus facilitating the process of relearning. In most of the studies that we reviewed, the status of the student in the class is measured by his achievement in the academic-intellectual sphere. The use of this measure is derived from the fact that Israeli schools, like many schools elsewhere, emphasize academic achievement; hence, this measure can indeed be assumed to determine the student's status among his fellow classmates.

Findings in Israel confirm to some extent those reported in U.S. studies, namely: The attitude of the minority group changes positively when they occupy a higher status than their majority peers; under equal academic status conditions some negative changes were found. Positive changes in attitude of the majority group occur under equal-status conditions or when the minority group exceeds the majority students in academic achievement. When the intergroup-status differences in the classroom were similar to those found in society at large, no major changes in attitude were found in both groups. However, even when there are gaps in status, there are certain aspects in which positive changes occur (e.g., willingness to participate in joint activities, the perception of the similarity of the ethnic groups). How can these findings be explained? We have already noted that in most of the studies, the status of the interacting groups is measured by their academic-intellectual achievements. Yet, despite the importance of these achievements, it may be that, in the course of the encounter, the members of both groups discover other significant aspects in which they resemble one another, and it is this that creates the positive change. In any case, there is a need for further research to identify those attitudinal areas in which changes are possible even when academic status is unequal, as well as areas in which equal academic status is a prerequisite for positive change.

A further distinction with regard to status should be stressed. When two ethnic groups come into contact in the classroom, we can refer to two different aspects of status: the relative status of the groups in the contact situation as determined by group achievement (e.g., in their studies), and the personal status of the individuals within the group. The findings cited here suggest that, at least in Israel, the status of the *individual* is less important to changes in interethnic relations and attitudes than the relative status of the *groups* in the class. It seems that the student's evaluations of the different ethnic groups in his class are determined by the comparisons he makes between the overall (or average) abilities and traits of the two groups. Personal ability has less effect on his evaluation of members of the different ethnic groups. This conclusion cannot be evaluated against other research, because we know of no other study that examined and compared the effect of these two aspects of status.

The Nature of the Interaction

Three characteristics of the contact situation encourage rapprochement between the different groups: (1) Intimate contact permits the discovery of unique aspects of one's counterpart in the other group. As a result people relate to each other as individuals, not as representatives of groups; (2) a social atmosphere or norms that encourage interpersonal and intergroup contact can facilitate rapprochement and greater understanding between members of different ethnic groups; (3) situations that foster interdependence between participants lead to reciprocal rapprochement. We deal now with the first two characteristics and their effect within the school framework. The third characteristic of interdependence and its implementation in the schools is discussed in Chapter 9.

Those studies that examined the outcome of nonacademic contact situations generally found positive attitudinal changes (Amir & Garti, 1977; Chen, Shapiro, & Hausdorf, 1970; Hofman & Zak, 1969). The findings coincide with those of Yarrow, Campbell, and Yarrow (1958) on the effect of contact between white and black youth in a summer camp setting. The changes found were attributed to the opportunities for mutual acquaintance inherent in these encounters, where social and emotional aspects were emphasized. Moreover, it may be that the enjoyment derived from the contact situations also contributed to a positive attitudinal change. This possibility raises the question of whether, within a school setting, the satisfaction experienced by the student has an effect on interethnic relations. For example, can positive experiences that derive from more attractive methods of instruction, or from enjoyable activities in school, encourage and increase mutual attraction between the participants?

Another factor that should be taken into consideration in explaining the findings of the preceding studies relates to the fact that interethnic contact took place in a nonacademic environment. In such situations, it may be possible that other, nonintellectual traits (e.g., sociability, sports) determine the status of the participants. Because with regard to nonintellectual traits there are no noticeable gaps between the different ethnic groups in Israel, it is hard to distinguish between the contribution of equal status and that of other factors (social, emotional) in producing the positive attitudinal changes found.

The second characteristic of the interaction that affects the results of integration is that of social atmosphere and norms. As noted earlier, the issue of integration in Israel gained the backing of various social institutions outside the schools. However, what directly affects the environment in the school are the administration and teaching staff. Resh, Inbar, and Adler (1977) found that there is no consensus among teachers in Israel on the question of integration. Although many support it, some believe that integration will adversely affect the academic achievements of the students, and they therefore have a less-favorable attitude toward integration. We can assume that the students are sensitive to their teachers' attitudes and will to some degree be affected by them. Moreover, policy decisions regarding class structure, academic tracking, special classes for slow learners that may effect the results of integration are subject to the sole control of the administration and teaching staff. Their basic attitudes toward integration affect their decisions in these areas (Inbar, Adler, & Resh, 1977).

From the previous discussion, it seems that three types of factors affect the results of integration: (1) the attitudes, norms, and ideology prevalent in the society in which integration is implemented; (2) the individual traits of the members of the groups among whom integration is applied; (3) the specific situation and nature of intergroup interaction in the school. Because of the attitudes, norms, and ideology in Israeli society, the implementation of integration did not encounter special difficulties. Members of both groups generally display a positive attitude toward the maintenance of integrated settings, and their willingness to live together is even increasing. However, with regard to the other two factors, our review indicates that conditions and results in Israel are no different from the conditions and results found in other parts of the world. It seems that two basic conditions in the schools, as they are at present, hinder the improvement of interethnic relations in Israel, and elsewhere in the world: These are the disparity in the relative status of the two groups, and the relative lack of social interaction outside the academic environment.

What steps can be taken to lead to a breaking down of ethnic barriers through daily contact between students. In Israel, academic achievement of Western students generally exceeds that of Middle Eastern students. It is therefore hard to find—or set up—classes in which the Middle Eastern group has a higher status than the Western group. A similar situation also exists in other countries where the academic abilities of the minority students are lower than those of the majority students. Considering the significance of the status variable, this may explain the limited findings on positive attitudinal change following integration in the schools. How then, under existing conditions, can we narrow the gap in status and thus bring about positive changes in interethnic attitudes and relations? Israeli schools, like those in many other countries, emphasize academic-intellectual achievements. The status of the student is to a great extent determined by his academic achievements. Abilities in other areas, such as social, behavioral and personal traits, and athletic and creative abilities, are less emphasized by the school administration and teaching staff. Because they are the principal socializing agents in the school, the importance of these other abilities is also reduced in the eyes of the students. The small significance given to such achievements also prevents more intimate acquaintance between students of different ethnic origin, because the primary contact between them remains in the classroom, where emphasis is on academic achievement, in a frontal teaching situation, under competitive conditions. This in fact narrows interaction and cooperation between the students. On the other hand, if a broad range of learning activities would be employed, the gap in status between the different groups would be narrowed. In these areas the Middle Eastern students are not surpassed by the Western students. Teaching methods that stress the interpersonal interaction and interdependence of the students would facilitate such a change.

In Israel there is an extensive system of boarding schools that comprise about one quarter of the high school student body. These schools usually do not emphasize academic studies only but also specialize in other fields in accordance with the type of school (e.g., agriculture, technical training). The students in these schools live together 24 hours a day, which raises the significance of their social and personal traits as factors in determining status. Moreover, in a large number of the schools, students are encouraged to manage their own lives. The student body thus becomes a relatively independent society determining its own social life and dealing with problems of cooperation, independence, and work ethics. By their very nature, these conditions help foster intimate acquaintances and greater cooperation among the students. It can be expected that contact in boarding schools will therefore result in greater changes in interethnic attitudes than contact in regular schools (Smilansky & Nevo, 1979). To date, almost no research has been carried out on the effect of boarding schools on attitudinal change, in Israel or elsewhere. Nevertheless, reports from the teachers and observations in the schools strengthen the notion advanced here that emphasizing additional aspects of human behavior and learning may produce positive changes in intergroup attitudes and acceptance.

Finally, it should be noted that studies conducted in Israel, like the studies in the United States, examined only the effects of integration on life in school and over short periods of time (generally 1 year). Few studies have examined the results of integration outside of school, (Amir & Garti, 1977) and over longer periods of time (Klein & Eshel, 1980). Amir, Bizman, and Rivner (1973) also found a preference for intragroup friendships within a combat platoon in the Israeli army. It would be interesting to examine whether this phenomenon is weaker among soldiers who attended integrated schools prior to their army service. Would the fact that they studied together with students of different ethnic backgrounds make it easier for them to be in close contact with people of different ethnic origin and relate to them more positively at a later stage in life? Israel, as a small country in which information about students is carefully documented and stored, may be an ideal place to conduct such a follow-up study.

REFERENCES

Adorno, T. W., Frenkel-Brunswick, W., Levinson, P. J., & Sanford, R. H. *The authoritarian personality.* New York: Harper, 1950.

Allport, G. W. *The nature of prejudice.* Reading, Mass.: Addison–Wesley, 1954.

Altman, I., & Taylor, D. A. *Social penetration: The development of interpersonal relationship.* New York: Holt, Rinehart, & Winston, 1973.

Ambar, B. *The influence of integration in junior high school on changes in attitude of parents and children.* M.A. Thesis, Bar–Ilan University, 1976. (Hebrew)

Amir, T. *Influence of intergroup contact on ethnic attitudes, self-image, sociometric status and school achievement.* M.A. Thesis, Bar–Ilan University, 1976. (Hebrew)

Amir, Y. Contact hypothesis in ethnic relations. *Psychological Bulletin,* 1969, *71,* 319–342.

Amir, Y. The role of intergroup contact in change of prejudice and ethnic relations. In P. A. Katz (Ed.), *Towards the elimination of racism.* New York: Pergamon Press, 1976.

Amir, Y., & Ben–Ari, R. *Satisfaction of interpersonal needs in ethnic contact situations and improvement of intergroup relations in junior high schools: A research report.* Jerusalem: Ministry of Education and Culture, 1981. (Hebrew)

Amir, Y., Bizman, A., & Rivner, M. Effects of intergroup contact on friendship choices in the military. *Journal of Cross-Cultural Psychology,* 1973, *4,* 361–373.

Amir, Y., & Garti, C. Situational and personal influence on attitude change following ethnic contact. *International Journal of Intercultural Relations,* 1977, *1,* 58–75.

Amir, Y., Sharan, S., Ben–Ari, R., Bizman, A., & Rivner, M. Asymmetry, academic status and differentiation in the ethnic perception and preference of Israel youth. *Human Relations,* 1978, *31,* 99–116. (a)

Amir, Y., Sharan, S., Bizman, A., Rivner, M., & Ben–Ari, R. Attitude change in desegregated Israeli high schools. *Journal of Educational Psychology*, 1978, *70*, 129–136. (b)

Amir, Y., Sharan, S., Rivner, M., Ben–Ari, R., & Bizman, A. Group status and attitude change in desegregated classrooms. *International Journal of Intercultural Relations*, 1979, *3*, 137–152.

Aronson, E. *The social animal* (3rd ed.). San Francisco: W. H. Freeman, 1980.

Ashmore, R. D. Solving the problem of prejudice. In B. E. Collins (Ed.), *Social psychology: Social influence, attitude change, group processes and prejudice*. Reading, Mass.: Addison–Wesley, 1970.

Bagley, G., Verma, G. K., Mallick, K., & Young, L. *Personality, self-esteem and prejudice*. Farnborough: Saxon House, 1979.

Baker, P. E. *Negro–White adjustment*. New York: Association Press, 1934.

Bashi, J. Effects of ethnic class composition on self-concept. *Megamot*, 1977, *23*, 124–133. (Hebrew)

Bizman, A. *Status similarity, status level and the reduction of prejudice following contact between national groups*. Unpublished doctoral dissertation, Bar–Ilan University, 1978. (Hebrew)

Brand, E. S., Ruiz, R. A., & Padilla, A. M. Ethnic identification and preference: A review. *Psychological Bulletin*, 1974, *81*, 860–890.

Carithers, M. W. School desegregation and racial cleavage, 1954–1970: A review of the literature. *Journal of Social Issues*, 1970, *26*, 25–47.

Chen, M., Lewy, A., & Kfir, D. The possibilities of interethnic group contact in the junior high school: Implementation and results. *Megamot*, 1977, *23*, 101–123. (Hebrew)

Chen, M., Shapira, R., & Hausdorf, H. Acquaintance with Israelis and attitude change among foreign students in an Israeli university. *Megamot*, 1970, *17*, 158–165. (Hebrew)

Clark, K. B., & Clark, M. P. Racial identification and preference in Negro children. In T. M. Newcomb & E. L. Hartley (Eds.), *Readings in social psychology* (Rev. ed.). New York: Holt, 1952.

Cohen, E. The effects of desegregation on race relations. *Law and Contemporary Problems*, 1975, *39*, 171–299.

Cohen, U. *Social integration at Hadassim Junior High school* (during the first year). M.A. Thesis, Tel–Aviv University, 1974. (Hebrew)

Cook, S. W. The systematic analysis of social significant events: A strategy for social research. *Journal of Social Issues*, 1962, *18*, 66–84.

Cook, S. W. Motives in a conceptual analysis of attitude-related behavior. In W. J. Arnold & D. Levine (Eds.), *Nebraska Symposium on Motivation* (Vol. 17). Lincoln: University of Nebraska Press, 1969.

Ehrlich, H. J. *The social psychology of prejudice*. New York: Wiley, 1973.

Erez, T. *Ethnic identification of high school pupils and their status in class and in the school*. M.A. Thesis, Tel–Aviv University, 1973. (Hebrew)

Feitelson, D., Weintraub, S., & Michaeli, O. Social interactions in heterogeneous preschools in Israel. *Child Development*, 1972, *43*, 1249–1259.

Hofman, J. E., & Zak, I. Interpersonal contact and attitude change in a cross-cultural situation. *Journal of Social Psychology*, 1969, *78*, 165–171.

Hraba, J., & Grant, G. Black is beautiful: A reexamination of racial preference and identification. *Journal of Personality and Social Psychology*, 1970, *16* 398–402.

Inbar, D., Adler, C., & Resh, N. Ethnic composition, integration, achievement, school climate. *Megamot*, 1977, *23*(3–4), 230–237. (Hebrew)

Jordan, J. E. Caste–ethnicity race–tribalism (CERT): Object specificity, situation specificity, object generalizability, cultural specificity, and cross-cultural invariance. *Symposium presented at the 81st Convention of the American Psychological Association*, Montreal, 1973.

Kalinsky, T. *The effect of ethnic group interaction in schools upon prejudice and self-esteem*. M.A. Thesis, Bar–Ilan University, 1975. (Hebrew)

Klein, Z., & Eshel, Y. *Integrating Jerusalem Schools*. New York: Academic Press, 1980.

Kramer, B. M. *Residential contact as a determinant of attitudes towards Negroes*. Unpublished doctoral dissertation, Harvard University, 1950.

Levin, J., & Chen, M. Sociometric choices in ethnically heterogenous classes. *Megamot*, 1977, *23*, 189–205. (Hebrew)

Levy, S., & Guttman, L. *Values and attitudes of high school youth in Israel*. Publication No. 438, Jerusalem: Israel Institute of Applied Social Research, 1974. (Hebrew)

Lewy, A. Class composition and school progress. *Megamot*, 1977, *23*, 88–97. (Hebrew)

Maruyama, G., & Miller, N. Reexamination of normative influence processes in desegregated classrooms. *American Educational Research Journal*, 1979, *16*, 273–283.

Mercer, J. R., Iadicola, P., & Moore, H. Building effective multiethnic schools: Evolving models and paradigms. In W. G. Stephan & J. R. Feagin (Eds.), *School desegregation: Past, present and future*. New York: Plenum Press, 1980.

Mussen, P. H. Some personality and social factors related to changes in children's attitudes towards Negroes. *Journal of Abnormal and Social Psychology*, 1950, *45*, 423–441.

Peres, Y. *Ethnic identity and ethnic relations*. Unpublished doctoral dissertation, Hebrew University, 1968. (Hebrew)

Peres, Y. *Ethnic relations in Israel*. Tel–Aviv: Hapoalim Press, 1976. (Hebrew)

Pettigrew, T. F., & Pajonas, P. J. *Social psychological considerations of racially-balanced schools*. Unpublished working paper prepared for the New York State Commissioner of Education, 1964.

Resh, N., Inbar, D., & Adler, C. Teachers attitudes towards educational aims and social integration. *Megamot*, 1977, *23*, 221–229. (Hebrew)

Rim, Y. National stereotypes in children. *Megamot*, 1968, *16*, 4–51. (Hebrew)

Rose, A. *Studies in reduction of prejudice*. Chicago: American Council on Race Relations, 1947.

Schofield, J. W. School desegregation and intergroup relations. In D. Bar–Tal & L. Saxe (Eds.), *Social psychology of education: Theory and research*. Washington: Hemisphere, 1978.

Schutz, W. C. *The interpersonal underworld*. Palo Alto, Calif.: Science and Behavioral Books, 1966.

Schwartz, Z. *Ethnic identity and interethnic contact*. M.A. Thesis, Bar–Ilan University, 1975. (Hebrew)

Schwarzwald, J. Relatedness of ethnic origin to the stereotypes of the Israeli in the eyes of junior high school students. *Megamot*, 1980, *25*, 322–340. (Hebrew)

Schwarzwald, J., & Cohen, S. The relationship between academic tracking and the degree of interethnic acceptance. *Journal of Educational Psychology*, 1982, *74*, 588–597.

Schwarzwald, J., & Yinon, Y. Symmetrical and asymmetrical interethnic perception in Israel. *International Journal of Intercultural Relations*, 1977, *1*, 40–47.

Sharan, S. Cooperative learning in small groups: Recent methods and effects in achievement, attitudes, and ethnic relations. *Review of Educational Research*, 1980, *50*, 241–271.

Shuval, J. T. The micro-neighborhood: An approach to ecological patterns of ethnic groups. *Social Problems*, 1962, *9*, 272–280.

Smilansky, M., & Nevo, D. *The gifted disadvantaged*. New York: Gordon & Breach, 1979.

Stephan, W. C. School desegregation: An evolution of predictions made in Brown vs. Board of Education. *Psychological Bulletin*, 1978, *85*, 217–238.

Stephan, W. G., & Rosenfield, D. Effect of desegregation on race relations and self-esteem. *Journal of Educational Psychology*, 1978, *70*, 670–679.

St. John, N. H. *School desegregation: Outcomes for children*. New York: Wiley, 1975.

Watson, C. *Action for unity*. New York: Harper, 1947.

Williams, R. M., Jr. *The reduction of intergroup tensions*. New York: Social Sciences Research Council, 1947, Bulletin 57.

Williams, R. M., Jr. *Strangers next door*. Englewood Cliffs, N. J.: Prentice–Hall, 1964.

Williams, J. E. Connotations of racial concepts and color names. *Journal of Personality and Social Psychology,* 1966, *3,* 531–540.

Yarrow, M. R., Campbell, J. P., & Yarrow, L. J. Acquisition of new norms: A study of racial desegregation. *Journal of Social Issues,* 1958, *14,* 8–28.

9 Field Experiments on Ethnic Integration in Israeli Schools

Shlomo Sharan
Yisrael Rich

This chapter describes several recent field studies conducted in Israel that evaluated classroom interventions intended to improve educational outcomes for pupils studying in ethnically and socially desegregated settings. Some comments on the shortcomings of earlier desegregation research appear at the beginning of this chapter, whereas the final section discusses the implications of the Israeli studies for designing more adequate educational environments for the desegregated class.

Israeli investigators interested in school integration have examined its impact on various cognitive, social, and affective variables associated primarily with the pupil (*Megamot,* 1977). However, as in the United States, virtually all this research, until very recently, has concentrated on structural aspects of the desegregated school and has either ignored or bypassed the teaching–learning process within the classroom. The impression gained from this research is that many investigators have assumed that the organizational act of desegregation would inevitably cause school personnel to bring about significant changes in the classroom resulting in increased achievement for minority pupils, improved interethnic relations and other benefits, or that the structural act of desegregation is in itself a sufficiently powerful manipulation to achieve these goals even without engendering changes in classroom process.

Virtually all summative evaluations of desegregation, whether in Israel (Chen, Levy, & Adler, 1978) or in the United States (Gerard & Miller, 1975), lead to the conclusion that this is a false assumption, at least at the "microlevel" of analysis (see Chapter 1), and that desegregation in itself yields little, if any, positive psychological, social, or academic results for minority pupils in the few years following its implementation. Furthermore, when considering the impact of various structural variables—such as the percentage of minority pupils in the class, the busing factor, or the number of minority school personnel—on the results of desegregation, we find that they contribute little to the explained variance and do not necessarily make it easier to determine the best conditions for making integration effective. The consistency of results indicating that these structural variables, without accompanying changes in the classroom, do not have major or even moderate psychosocial effects on pupils argues against technical explanations of this phenomenon, such as the inadequate measurement of the complex variables associated with desegregation.

A more reasonable explanation for such results is that desegregation is a political, legal, and social act that, although providing the framework for educational change that will benefit minority-pupils' achievement and improve interethnic relations, does not ensure that the requisite change will in fact occur. As Slavin (1981) notes: " desegregation is an opportunity, not a cure [p. 225]." Because the classroom is the primary social and academic school setting where all pupils spend most of the school day, where status issues are most salient, and where the teacher has relatively high control of resources and processes, it seems clear that positive effects are more likely to be achieved when desegregation is accompanied by educational adaptations within the classroom, which aim to improve both minority-pupils' achievement and interethnic relations. Without discounting the importance of structural variables, it is clear that the quality and quantity of teacher–pupil and pupil–pupil interactions are of paramount importance to childrens' social and emotional development. Whether a teacher encourages or depresses a child's ability, whether a minority pupil has the opportunity to display competence in different areas of school life—these are just two of a long list of classroom-related variables with a major bearing on desirable outcomes of desegregation, such as self-esteem and motivation. Furthermore, the manner of teaching and studying have strong implications for academic progress and the quality of interethnic relations in the classroom (Sharan, 1980; Slavin, 1980).

Unfortunately, the little research available that focuses on desegregated classroom processes in the United States (Schofield, 1978) and in Israel (Rich, Amir, & Ben-Ari, 1981) suggests that the opportunity has not been well exploited, and the same teaching–learning conditions characterizing the ethnically and socially homogeneous class have been transplanted to the mixed class with only nominal alterations. These conditions simply do not allow for the effective treatment of the two major problems plaguing the desegregated class—the low social status and poor academic achievement of many minority pupils. Because advantaged pupils generally dominate the classroom scene, and the disadvantaged are more passive (Cohen & Sharan, 1980; Rich & Plato, 1981) adverse conditions for effective integration may be created. Thus, not only do the opportunities provided by desegregation remain unexploited, but there is even a real danger that minority pupils may suffer in a variety of ways. It is no wonder then, that most research on desegregation leads to the conclusion that the quality of schooling and its outcomes was not enhanced despite the initial potential.

One could legitimately ask if the social science research literature can provide a basis for more effective ways of exploiting the desegregation opportunity. Because research has focused on structural aspects of the school, most prescriptions for more effective school functioning must rely on a combination of educational commonsense, isolated research findings, and some loosely related theoretical principles. Perhaps the most coherent and comprehensive prescription was recently presented by Miller (1980), who concentrated on three interdependent issues—the ability of desegregated schools to provide quality education, conditions for positive interracial contact, and community acceptance of desegregation. Rather than discuss Miller's work, this chapter reviews several recently completed research projects conducted in Israel. Implications from these studies are related primarily to Miller's second category—creating conditions for positive intergroup contact—and, to a lesser extent, to the issue of quality education. It is worth noting that very little research has been conducted in Israel on community acceptance of integration (See Chapter 3).

Aside from the general goal of enhancing outcomes for pupils in desegregated schools, these projects are characterized by their focus on events that occur in the classroom either naturally or as a result of experimental manipulation. Two projects (the Nachlaot study and the Open Education study), involving variants of open education, aimed at achieving both academic and social benefits for elementary school pupils. In four other projects reviewed in this chapter, different types of cooperative small-group learning were employed among junior high school pupils. The classroom was the setting for all four treatments, but two utilized nonacademic curricular materials to improve interethnic relations, (Ben-Ari & Amir, 1981; Ben-Yitschak, Lotan, & Sharan, 1980), whereas the regular academic curriculum presented in a cooperative small-group format was used in the other projects to achieve both academic and social objectives. (We do not cite the several Israeli classroom-based projects that have no accompanying research, nor the numerous studies completed in Israel that have examined aspects of school desegregation outside of classroom events.)

Nachlaot Project

Two outstanding features characterized this study of school desegregation carried out in the Nachlaot neighborhood of Jerusalem (Klein & Eshel, 1981).

First, the investigators overcame many of the flaws in research design that typically plague educational field research, by identifying appropriate school settings with variation in instructional style and student population needed for constructing a complex factorial structure. Their study encompassed eight groups of subjects varied for SES, ethnicity, classroom instructional method, and level of desegregation. Thus, there were middle-class pupils (primarily from Western ethnic backgrounds) and lower class pupils (from Middle Eastern background). These two groups of children studied in ethnically desegregated or segregated classrooms that were either taught by conventional methods or conducted as activity classrooms.

The second outstanding characteristic of the study is its longitudinal dimension. Measure of academic achievement for reading and arithmetic and academic self-concept (pupils' own estimates of their grades in reading and arithmetic at the end of the school year) were administered once a year for 4 consecutive years and covered the full 6-year range of elementary school grades.

Desegregation in the four "experimental" open schools was gradual, beginning with the first grade, and a new desegregated first grade was added annually until all six grades were included. In this way, the long-term effects of each of the independent variables and their possible interactions could be studied.

The "activity classroom" which constituted the primary "treatment" in the Nachlaot study, emerged gradually in the schools as teachers learned from their own experience. In general, this educational approach was intended to incorporate elements of the open classroom as developed in England. The guiding notion of this approach was that the formal structure of the conventional classroom should be altered so that pupils can engage in a variety of study projects using a range of instructional materials. Uniform, whole-class instruction should be diminished to allow for the emergence of direct pupil contact with learning materials, and for informal task-oriented groups not based on homogeneity of ability or ethnic background. In the Nachlaot project a second half-time teacher was allocated to each activity classroom. The activity classroom did not stem from any previously formulated model of classroom organization and instructional process. Hence, the investigators could not determine if the practices actually implemented succeeded in incorporating the critical features of the model. They did state the abstract principles guiding practitioners and, at the end of the study, collected data describing what transpired at a given time in the various classrooms.

The Nachlaot investigators gathered pupils' sociometric choices and conducted systematic observations of classroom instruction only during the final year of the project. The sociometric data derived from two questions about pupils' classmates with whom they wanted to study and with whom they wanted to play. Classroom observations were made on the basis of a structured observation schedule of 80 items composed by the investigators. These items were concrete descriptions of behavior requiring a minimum of observer inference and covered a wide variety of domains, such as characteristics of the conventional versus the open classrooms, and physical conditions in the classroom. Forty-six classes equally divided between the conventional and the open systems were observed at the 1st-, 2nd-, and 3rd-grade levels. They constituted about half the classrooms involved in the whole research project.

The authors concluded that desegregation in the conventionally taught classrooms brought about no consistently discernible changes in the reading or mathematics achievement of the lower class, Middle Eastern children. Though academic self-image of all children declined over their years in elementary school, this decline was greater among lower class Middle Eastern children than among their Western peers. Neither instructional method nor the ethnic composition of the classroom had any consistent effects on this measure. Similar findings have been reported in other Israeli studies (Hertz-Lazarowitz & Sharan, 1979).

Lower class Middle Eastern pupils in desegregated classrooms with activity-oriented instruction consistently achieved higher scores on the arithmetic achievement test than did their ethnic peers in the segregated classroom where the activity method was employed. The difference reached almost a full standard deviation at all grade levels, although it tended to diminish in size with years in school. Clearly, the combined effect of desegregation with activity-oriented instruction produced significant gains in arithmetic achievement for the lower-class Middle-Eastern pupils. Indeed, the children studying in desegregated activity classrooms reached a level of mathematics achievement comparable to that of middle-class Middle-Eastern children in conventional classrooms. It is noteworthy that parallel results were also found for the middle-class Western children. In arithmetic achievement, middle-class Western children who studied in the desegregated activity classrooms performed better than their middle-class Western peers who studied in the segregated activity classrooms. Thus, desegregation combined with activity-oriented instruction was beneficial for the middle-class pupils as well.

Why should the desegregated classroom produce better academic results than a segregated classroom with comparable middle-class children and the same instructional methods? One answer might be that middle-class Western pupils had greater opportunity to tutor lower class Middle Eastern pupils in the desegregated classroom than they did in the middle-class segregated classes. Peer tutoring has been shown in a series of recent field experiments to foster higher level achievement in subjects like arithmetic, probably because it encourages pupils to review the materials taught by the teacher. Also, helping others to learn has often been demonstrated to be a powerful motivational force as well as encouraging greater attention to the material, thus leading to improved memory for the subject (Sharan, 1980; Slavin, 1980).

Extrapolating from earlier research done in Israel on the results and conditions of elementary school education (Minkovich, Davis, & Bashi, 1977), Klein and Eshel (1981) argued that lower class pupils in the desegregated activity classrooms reached better achievement scores than their peers in segregated activity classrooms, because the former group studied in middle-class schools providing superior resources, such as better teachers, higher teacher morale, and better curricular input. They also contended that teachers in lower class, segregated schools expressed low expectations regarding their pupils' potential academic achievement. This implies that the relatively inferior achievement of the lower class pupils in the segregated open classrooms can be partially explained as a function of poorer professional quality of the teachers, and of the negative effects of teachers' expectations for achievement on their lower-class pupils. These depressed expectations supposedly influence the pupils through the various behavioral manifestations associated with the self-fulfilling prophecy (Brophy & Good, 1974).

Interethnic relations in the Nachlaot classrooms were evaluated in the last year of the study by two sociometric questions administered in the desegregated classrooms only. It was learned that both lower and middle-class pupils of both ethnic groups made more friends in the desegregated activity classroom than their peers in the desegregated classrooms taught with the traditional whole-class method. Regarding the direction of the sociometric choices, lower class children selected almost evenly between members of both ethnic groups, whereas Westerners selected members of their own group more than expected by chance.

The issue of classroom instructional process and its effect on psychoeducational pupil outcomes brings us to consider the results of the classroom observation data gathered during the final year of the project. These data are crucial to understanding the results of the research. Because the investigators had little control over the implementation of the treatment variables associated with the 'activity' classroom, they could not ensure that classrooms designated as "active" did in fact incorporate the processes characteristic of that model of classroom. This was all the more problematic, because the implementation of "active" classroom methods required teachers to acquire patterns of instructional behavior different from those they had previously been accustomed to in conventional forms of instruction. Reports by the research staff convey the feeling that teachers who intended to adopt the activity classroom model were offered only sporadic assistance in making the transition from conventional to activity-classroom instruction.

Because teachers were thrown back on their own resources in their attempt to learn a new method, it is not surprising to discover from the observation data that many of the classes officially designated as activity classes did not differ essentially from conventional classrooms, and, hence, the independent variable being measured in these particular classrooms was never truly implemented. Nevertheless, there were indeed systematic differences in the degree of implementation of activity-classroom methods between segregated and desegregated classes, specifically that the latter group had a larger number of instructional features characteristic of the open classroom than the former. Classrooms with segregated lower class populations tended to retain conventional forms of teaching even when specifically designated as being activity classes. The pupils' seating arrangements may have been altered to create small clusters of children scattered throughout the room, but teachers did not relinquish their tight control over instruction, the selection of materials, and the pace at which materials were presented to children. Nor were the pupils asked to participate in selecting learning tasks or encouraged to cooperate with each other in carrying out tasks, as is typical of genuine group-centered open schooling. If this was the case in the lower three grades, it can be assumed that there was similarly little implementation of open-classroom techniques in the upper three grades, where Israeli teachers are under more pressure to "cover the material."

On the other hand, the desegregated classrooms showed more substantial change in instructional process. Subject matter was presented in a variety of modes, including small groups, rather than primarily through the verbal-presentation-and recitation method, which is standard practice in most schools. Also, a reasonable degree of pupil cooperation in small groups engaged in learning tasks was implemented. It seems that desegregated classrooms presented social conditions that seemed to the teachers to render conventional forms of teaching inappropriate. Teachers apparently felt a need to use more varied modes of instruction to cope with the wider range of pupils' educational needs, and to promote an acceptable level of cohesiveness in a classroom distinguished by diversity in ethnic background and achievement level. By contrast, teachers in segregated classes could continue to assert that cooperative learning in small groups did not allow middle-class pupils to learn quickly enough, or that lower class pupils were incapable of functioning independently in small groups without constant control and direction by the teacher. In this sense, desegregation encouraged teachers to find new ways of coping with the classroom situation.

The lack of change in sociometric selections of Middle Eastern children by their Western peers in the activity-oriented classrooms runs contrary to reports from other group-oriented learning experiments in desegregated classrooms (Sharan, 1980; Slavin, 1980). Only more extensive observations in the classroom could supply us with the answer to the question why the lower-class children did not become more accepted socially over the course of time. How was the membership of the small groups constituted? Were the children taught to cooperate with each other during the performance of the learning task? Physical proximity alone is not sufficient to have children overcome their sense of strangeness or lack of skill in helping children from other neighborhoods and cultural groups.

The Nachlaot project demonstrated that desegregation in combination with a social-interactive form of classroom instruction, yielded superior outcomes compared to segregated classes or to desegregated classes without instructional innovation. These key elements form the basis of future experimental work on integration in the schools.

Open-Education Study

The combined effects of desegregation and "open education" on pupils in the lower elementary school grades were evaluated in another study (Harrison, Strauss, & Glaubman, 1980). It should be clear from the outset that despite the investigators' choice of the term *open education* and the fact that instruction was allegedly activity oriented, many essential elements of fully implemented open-education programs were lacking. We return to this point later. Also, it is noteworthy that in the initial stages of this study the investigators planned a formative evaluation of the effects of open education on pupil development without special attention to the subject of desegregation. They became interested in the desegregated open school only when it was discovered that teachers in three of the four sample schools chose to implement variants of open schooling as a way of coping with the difficulties of teaching in ethnically mixed classes, where the range of academic ability and prior achievement varied widely. As a result, the integration variable was examined post facto rather than being part of the original experimental design.

Harrison et al. (1980) set out to examine the differential impact of "quality traditional schooling" and "grass-roots open education" on elementary school pupils' cognitive development, attitudes toward school, and self-concept. Two elementary schools (grades 1–6), one in a low socioeconomic neighborhood and the other middle class, were recommended by the district supervisor as typical of quality traditional schooling, where school children's academic development was fairly rapid and teacher dedication and morale were reportedly high. Those elementary schools (grades 1–6) that had decided at the local level on an open-education program and implemented it with no special financial support or professional guidance from the Ministry of Education were included in the grass-roots open-education population. Five such schools, all with ethnically mixed populations, were chosen for intensive observation at the beginning and end of the school year. Open education had been practiced for at least 3 years in each of the schools.

Eighteen classes comprised of 6 first, 6 third, and 6 fifth grades were selected for the study. Five boys and 5 girls from each of the 18 classes were randomly selected to respond to the various measures. The total number of participating pupils was 180, with 60 children at each grade level.

Harrison et al. (1980) used Evans' (1971) Classroom Observation Rating Scale and Teacher's Questionnaire to determine the basic characteristics and degree of openness of each class. They discovered that some of the classes labeled as "open" were scored as being more "closed" than in traditional classes. Accordingly, the sample was redivided into 2 groups of 9 more open and 9 traditional classes. Four first-, 2 third-, and 3 fifth-grade classes were classified as open and the remainder as traditional.

Despite the reclassification of classrooms, many essential elements of open schooling were not implemented more fully in the open than traditional classes. Of 23 measured characteristics of the open and traditional classes, only eight demonstrated significant differences. These were primarily in the area of authority relations and learning materials. However, in curriculum, evaluation procedures, learning styles, and levels, open classes proved to be no different than traditional classes. Furthermore, when the scores of these open classes were compared to those of open and traditional classes in the United States and

England, it became clear that the "open" classes in Israel were far less open than their counterparts abroad and, in fact, did not markedly differ from American and English traditional classes (Harrison, Strauss, & Glaubman, 1981).

Pupils were compared on four types of dependent measures. First, standardized achievement tests were administered in mathematics and reading comprehension. In addition, children's essays were analyzed for quality of expression according to criteria stipulated by the authors. Second, pupils responded to tests of verbal and figural creativity. A third type of development was assessed by an instrument developed by the authors to measure ability to solve social and intellectual problems. Finally, a homemade three-item school attitude scale was given to the pupils. A semiprojective measure of self-concept (Itskowitz & Strauss, 1980) was also included, but data from this test were not reported.

Though all classes were ethnically integrated to some extent, three classes, all with traditional instruction, had about 90% Middle Eastern population. In another three, only one of which used traditional instruction, Westerners made up about 75% of the class population. In all other classes Middle Eastern pupils comprise from 25 to 75% of the class population. Social class measures indicated that two classrooms, one with traditional instruction and one with activity-oriented instruction, were upper class, and all others were characterized as ranging from lower to upper middle class.

We concern ourselves only with those results from the Harrison et al. study that have bearing on the issue of open education as a strategy for the desegregated elementary school classroom. Turning first to the achievement measures, quality of composition scores for low-SES pupils in open classes did not differ significantly from those of low-SES children in traditional classes. This was true at all three grade levels (Harrison, personal communication). Reading comprehension scores of low-SES children were consistently higher in open than in traditional classes at the beginning and end of the year of observation. Although no major gains for low-SES open-class pupils were apparent during the year, the gap between the low- and high-SES groups increased in traditional, but not in open, classes.

Both at the beginning and end of the year, mathematics achievement scores for fifth-grade low-SES children were higher in open-class conditions than in traditional classes, whereas high-SES fifth graders received higher math scores in traditional than in open classes. This interaction was not found in the first or third grades. Once again, no major gains accrued to the low-SES open as compared to the low-SES traditional pupils during the year, and did not narrow meaningfully the gap in mathematics. It seems, therefore, that low-SES pupils benefited from the open class in the area of reading comprehension, but not in composition or math.

Low-SES pupils in open classrooms did not demonstrate significantly greater advances in figural creativity during the school year than did their counterparts in traditional classes. This was true for verbal creativity as well; however, in traditional classes the gap between low- and high-SES pupils widened, whereas it stabilized in open classes (Harrison, Glaubman, & Strauss, in press).

Analyses of the data using father's country of origin (Western, Middle Eastern, Israeli) as an independent variable revealed similar results. Reading comprehension scores of Middle Eastern first and fifth graders improved more in open than in traditional classes during the year. No differences were found at the third-grade level. The reading comprehension of both Western and Israeli children did not differ in open as compared to traditional classes at any grade. Math achievement scores of fifth-grade Middle Eastern pupils improved more in open than in traditional classes, whereas their Western classmates received higher math scores in traditional settings. No interaction effects were evident for first- or third-grade math achievement, nor for figural or verbal creativity scores at any grade level.

The third measure of cognitive development—social and intellectual problem solving—did not produce any significant differences between low-SES children learning in open or traditional settings. High-SES pupils were not significantly higher on these measures than low-SES pupils.

Overall, no major differences emerged between open and traditional pupils in attitudes to school, though low-SES open-class pupils had the most favorable attitudes. Clearly, pupils' SES was a more salient variable here than was the open-traditional issue. Consistent with other research in Israel (Hertz–Lazarowitz & Sharan, 1979; Rich & Darom, 1981), low-SES children expressed more positive attitudes toward school than high-SES children.

Unfortunately the investigators of the open education project did not confront the desegregation issue from the start of the project, and several important, relevant questions were not dealt with. For example, social relations in the desegregated open classroom were not examined. One could hypothesize that improved social relations between the two ethnic groups would be more prevelent in the open desegregated class than in the traditional class, because conditions in the open class should conform more closely to those advocated by Allport (1954). Properly implemented open classes should foster more intensive and prolonged social interaction than is possible in the traditional class. Also, more of these interactions should occur with activities that allow for equal status relations, in which the middle-class child does not set out with an advantage over the lower class one, providing the latter with greater scope to demonstrate competence and receive social recognition. Furthermore, evaluation techniques advocated in open schooling should remove the emphasis from social comparison and competition, thereby leading to increased interethnic cooperation.

Results from the Harrison et al. study (1980) lead to a guarded prognosis of the efficacy of open education as practiced in the classes sampled here, as a means of advancing creativity, problem-solving ability, or improving pupils' attitudes to school. Although there were positive results for mathematics achievement among some low-SES pupils in the integrated open class, only in the area of reading comprehension were there relatively consistent benefits to low SES pupils. Again, it should be recalled that open-education principles were only partially implemented here and differed significantly from those advocated by its proponents. Thus, our rather somber picture cannot be applied to open education in general, which theoretically remains a promising strategy for the integrated elementary school class and deserves further serious study. Researchers should focus especially on the categorization of processes in the open desegregated classroom and the measurement of relationships between these processes and pupil outcomes in the cognitive, affective, and social domains.

Cooperative Learning in Small Groups

Two studies are discussed in this section. The first was more in the nature of a pilot study carried out in three ethnically mixed junior high school classrooms (Hertz-Lazarowitz, Sapir, & Sharan, 1980). The second study was a field experiment encompassing all seventh-grade pupils from three junior high schools (Sharan, 1984), where children from Middle Eastern background constituted approximately 40% of the population and those from Western background numbered 60% of the population. In both studies the scholastic and social effects of traditional whole-class instruction were contrasted to one or more group-centered learning methods. The latter methods had pupils in ethnically mixed small groups cooperate with each other in performing learning tasks.

Study I

The two small-group methods employed in this study were the Jigsaw method (Aronson, Blaney, Stephan, Sikes, & Snapp, 1978) and the Group Investigation (G–I) method (Sharan & Hertz-Lazarowitz, 1980; Sharan & Sharan, 1976). These cooperative methods share the fundamental feature of engaging pupils in mutual assistance in small groups within the larger classroom. However, the Jigsaw method emphasizes peer tutoring of teacher-prepared materials, whereas the G–I method stresses pupil-directed inquiry in a cooperative social setting. Detailed descriptions of the two methods are available in other recent publications (Sharan, Hare, Webb & Hertz-Lazarowitz, 1980).

The same teacher taught 20 class sessions of Arabic language and culture to three eighth-grade classes. Each class used a different method—conventional whole-class teaching, Jigsaw, or the G–I method. Western (N=67) and Middle Eastern (N=32) students were divided almost equally among the three classrooms according to their mean academic achievement scores. Eight class sessions were devoted to Islamic culture, six sessions to vocabulary and grammar, and six sessions to the relationship between Islamic and Hebraic cultures. In the small-group classrooms, the subtopics were divided among the groups for investigation or peer tutoring based on materials supplied by the teacher. In the traditionally taught classroom, the teacher presented the material verbally and pupil recitation and questions and answers followed.

Systematic observations established that 95% of observed classroom time in the G–I classroom was devoted to small-group interactions and study, whereas 5% of the time was used by the teacher for direct verbal teaching or giving instructions to groups. In the traditionally taught classrooms, 40% of the time was occupied by direct verbal instruction by the teacher and 60% to two-way communication consisting of teacher and/or pupil-initiated questions and answers. Peer cooperation was greater in the G–I groups (61%) than in the Jigsaw groups (51%), whereas individual study was more pronounced in the Jigsaw groups (32%) than in the G–I groups (24%).

Findings on two sets of achievement tests administered before and after the experiment revealed no significant differences among the three classes on the tests of knowledge of Arabic culture, but there was a significant gain on a test of Arabic language and grammar in the Jigsaw classroom. Further analysis revealed that this gain was made primarily by the Middle Eastern students, whereas the increase in achievement in the scores of the Western students was very modest.

Pupils of Middle Eastern background in the G–I classroom felt that they were less vulnerable to abuse or insult by their Western classmates at the close of the experiment than they did when asked this question on the pretest. There were no changes on this item in the Jigsaw classroom and a negative trend was found in the traditional method. At the beginning of the experiment in the G–I class, after pupils had studied for one trimester with the usual whole-class method, not a single Middle Eastern students out of the eight in the class was selected as a class star. At the conclusion of the 5-week period, three Middle Eastern students out of the eight in the class was selected as a class star. At the conclusion of the 5-week period, three Middle Eastern students were chosen in the G–I class as "stars." No changes in cross-ethnic selections emerged in the Jigsaw and whole-class methods. Also, Middle Eastern pupils in the G–I class lowered their evaluations of the Western groupmates' contributions to the group's learning activities, whereas Western students expressed more positive evaluations of Middle Eastern groupmates. In the Jigsaw class, the opposite effect emerged: Middle Eastern pupils raised even further their evaluation of Western students, and the latter lowered further their evaluation of the Middle Eastern students.

On questions assessing personal and social functioning of classmates from the other ethnic group, Middle Eastern pupils in the G–I class again lowered their estimation of the Western peers, and the Westerners developed a more positive attitude to their Middle Eastern classmates than before. Thus, the social distance separating the two groups was clearly narrowed in the G–I classroom, and the social status of the minority group was improved on several measures of academic and social behavior. A different effect emerged in the Jigsaw class. Both groups of pupils lowered their evaluation of the Middle Eastern children, so that the Jigsaw method resulted in lowered cross-ethnic evaluations of all participants. The investigators suggested that the G–I class created a relaxed and cooperative social climate, whereas the Jigsaw class promoted achievement, accompanied by increased stress, because each pupil must tutor all his group-mates simultaneously on a given portion of the learning task. Because all the children depend on each other for learning the material needed to pass the test, this creates tension over one's own performance and the demand by others to perform well. Apparently, cross-ethnic relations do not benefit from this kind of stimulation.

Study II

The effects of two cooperative learning methods and traditional whole-class instruction on children in mixed ethnic classrooms (Sharan, 1984) were studied in an extensive field experiment. The two different small-group methods and traditional whole-class instruction were compared when implemented in seventh-grade classes devoted to English as a foreign language and to literature. In this study the two cooperative learning methods were the Small-Group Teaching/Group Investigation approach (Sharan & Sharan, 1976; Sharan & Hertz–Lazarowitz, 1980) and Student Teams and Academic Divisions (Slavin, 1980). These two methods both employ peer cooperation in mixed ethnic groups as an important procedural component of their design of classroom learning. However, the G–I method involves the pupils in planning study activities, carrying out these plans through mutual assistance and exchange, small-group discussions, and preparing collaborative-group products. STAD is a peer-tutoring technique where pupils tutor each other on materials taught previously by the teacher. All the small teams of pupils in the class "compete" by having their scores on individual tests graded according to a system that compares pupils of similar academic status combined into a group score and published weekly in a class-room newsletter. Further details about these methods and the differences be-tween them were published elsewhere (Sharan, 1980).

Teachers were assigned at random to methods. In some instances a teacher taught more than one class: 13 teachers taught with the G–I method, 11 teachers with STAD, and 9 teachers taught according to the traditional whole-class meth-od. Altogether over 800 pupils participated in the experiment. Implementation of this study required extensive retraining of all teachers who employed the two cooperative learning methods. Teacher training took place by conducting a series of workshops, one 2½ hour workshop per week for 5 months. A separate series of workshops was held for the teachers in each teaching method, and each series was led by its own trainer. In addition, three subject-matter consultants attended many of the meetings of each workshop series to provide assistance to the teachers in preparing curricular materials appropriate for use with the different methods. The consultants also ensured that the teachers in all three methods agreed upon a common curriculum to be taught for an identical number of classroom sessions. The experimental period, during which this curriculum was taught, extended for 16 weeks during the months of February through the beginning of June.

The effects of this experiment were evaluated in three domains: scholastic achievement in English as a foreign language, and Literature; children's cooperative behavior both within and between ethnic groups; and pupils' social relations and perceptions of classmates. Special achievement tests were constructed in collaboration with the teachers for pre- and posttest administration; a social-relations questionnaire, including seven sociometric questions on which each pupil evaluated all other classmates, was administered on a pre–post basis; and a "cooperative-behavior" experiment was conducted to observe the children's degree of cooperation with classmates in small groups as a function of their having studied in one or another of the three instructional methods.

Cooperative behavior was assessed by selecting 6-person mixed-ethnic groups of pupils at random from each classroom (3 pupils of Western and 3 of Middle Eastern ethnic background) and asking each group to construct a human figure out of pieces of Lego that were supplied to them. This "criterion task" was performed in an unoccupied room without the teacher's presence and directed by an experimenter whom the pupils did not know. Two observers made systematic recordings of the children's behavior during the ½-hour group session, of which the first 15 minutes were devoted to discussing plans for performing the task, and the second period of up to 15 minutes was devoted to constructing the figure. There were 21 groups from the G–I condition, 26 groups from the STAD classrooms, and 18 groups from the traditional classrooms. Thus, 390 pupils, selected at random, participated in this analysis with the 6-person group as the unit of analysis. This group problem-solving task was viewed as providing the investigators an opportunity to conduct controlled observations of the pupils' spontaneous ethnic interactions outside the classroom, so that peer cooperation could be studied without relying exclusively on self-reports.

A capsule statement of the results, reported in full in another publication (Sharan, 1984), is as follows: Both cooperative learning methods proved equally effective for teaching English as a second language, while the whole-class traditional approach was less effective. This finding emerged on the Listening Comprehension subtest (57 out of 91 items) and on the Total Test score. On the three other subtests, all methods produced the same amount of achievement over the course of the experiment. In the study of literature the results were generally as predicted, with pupils in the Group-Investigation method demonstrating higher scores on the High-level questions than pupils in the other two methods. High-level questions were defined by reference to the upper three categories of Bloom's cognitive taxonomy. On the Lower-level questions assessing pupils' acquisition of points of information and simple understanding, the STAD and Whole-Class methods were more effective than the Group-Investigation method. There were no findings for ethnicity in any of the analyses, so that pupils from both ethnic groups progressed at the same rate in each of the three teaching methods.

Turning to the study of the pupils' cooperative and competitive behavior, the cooperative learning methods did in fact foster more cooperation, both within and between ethnic groups, than the Whole-Class method. Predictably, the latter method fostered more competition among peers from both ethnic groups and between ethnic groups. The Group-Investigation method yielded more coopera- tion and less competition on the criterion task than did the STAD method, while the STAD method limited competition but fostered less cooperation among peers than did the Group-Investigation method. Clearly, reducing competition is not necessarily associated with promoting cooperation. Of particular interest is the finding that children from the Group-Investigation classrooms of both ethnic groups were equally cooperative with same-ethnic as with cross-ethnic peers, so that reciprocity emerged in these groups in terms of the extent of each ethnic group's response to the *other* group. On the other hand, in the groups from the STAD classrooms, the lower status Middle-Eastern pupils addressed twice as many cooperative statements and nonverbal acts to Western children as the latter addressed to pupils from Middle Eastern background in their group.

A similar pattern emerged in the data obtained about the pupils' perception of ethnic attitudes and stereotypes. No change occurred over the year in these attitudes among pupils in the Group-Investigation or STAD classrooms, but there was a significant decline in ethnic attitudes, i.e. those directed toward the other *group* as an entity, among pupils in the Whole-Class method. The decline was more marked in the scores registered by the Middle-Eastern pupils, but it was statistically significant for Western pupils as well.

Findings obtained with sociometric measures revealed that the Middle-East- ern pupils' social status improved significantly more than that of the Western pupils in all classrooms regardless of teaching method, although a positive change occured for Western pupils as well. Moreover, this positive change was found in the evaluations made by pupils of both ethnic groups. Despite this improvement, however, pupils from Middle Eastern background continued to evaluate themselves and their Western classmates much less favorably than the evaluations expressed toward both groups by pupils of Western background (in all three methods).

On the other hand, pupils' evaluations of classroom social climate declined in all classrooms over the course of the year. Thus, the two measures of friendships among peers and of classroom social relations were not affected by instructional method, and they revealed changes in opposite directions.

A full explanation for these diverse effects cannot be offered here. Moreover, each set of dependent measures employed in this experiment emerged from a different theoretical framework and, hence, employs a different set of explanato- ry concepts. In short: the superior effect of cooperative group learning on the study of English as a second language is consistent with the communicative theory of foreign language instruction; interethnic cooperation improved by co- operative learning is consistent with Allport's three point approach to the reduc- tion of intergroup prejudice; change—or no change, as the case may be—in ethnic attitudes was discussed in light of Tajfel's theory of intergroup relations. The decline in classroom climate appears to be the result of the fact that pupils were exposed to a large number of classroom sessions which were not influenced by cooperative learning, and the decline in relationships reflects the fact that classrooms seem to be perceived progressively more negatively by pupils over the course of time in traditional classes. Since only six out of more than 24 hours of weekly classes were altered by the cooperative learning methods, their effects could not be distinguished by pupils when asked to make a global evaluation of classroom-wide relationships not typical of specific classes. On the other hand, pupils generally came to like each other more over time quite independent of the style of classroom learning, which is why sociometric questions yielded improved friendship scores in all three teaching methods.

In sum, there is growing evidence that having children cooperate with each other in mixed-ethnic groups during the pursuit of learning tasks yields positive results academically and socially. It does not "close the academic gap," but neither does it result in academic losses for any subgroup. The peer-tutoring approach promotes somewhat better achievement on the acquisition of low-level information (in Literature), but the investigation–discussion approaches, allowing each child to contribute to the group with minimum emphasis on members' status, promote higher level learning for all children and superior social interaction between ethnic groups. The less than satisfactory effects of the Whole-Class method should not be overlooked. As predicted, pupils from traditionally taught classes were, in fact, more competitive with each other, both within and between ethnic groups, than were their peers who studied in the cooperative learning classes. Even more pointedly, all pupils perceived the other ethnic group, as a group, more negatively at the end of the year if they had studied in the traditional classes, whereas this deterioration of ethnic attitudes did not occur in cooperative classes. One would conjecture that the competition typical of the traditional class casts the ethnic groups in a negative light, the lower status group experiencing the situation as one which highlights their inferior status, and the higher status group probably coming to view the lower-status group even more negatively than they had before. Concurrently, the lower status group perceives the other group as less friendly and more competitive. All in all, the social comparison processes fanned by competition which many authors have identified in the traditional classroom appears to have taken its toll in terms of the ethnic attitudes assessed in this study. These findings confirm the widely held view that a failure to design the desegregated classroom to minimize status differences and to enhance mutual assistance and cooperation among the pupils can lead to distinctly undesireable consequences for some or all of the pupils participating in desegregated classes.

Expectation Training

Two studies were performed in Israel emerging from the work of Elizabeth Cohen (1972, Cohen & Roper, 1972) on Expectation Training. The first study was a laboratory experiment to test the conditions and applicability of Expectation Training in groups of children from different ethnic and social groupings (Cohen & Sharan, 1980). The second study was a field experiment conducted in several junior high schools combining Expectation Training with cooperative small-group activities.

Expectation Training is a social-educational method designed to produce more equalized interaction in task-oriented small groups with members of different social status. Group interaction is generally dominated by the higher status social groups, and their superior status is carried over into the functioning of the small group, even though there has been no previous contact between members. This prestige ordering in the small group is alleged to be a function of stereotyped expectations held by members of both the high- and low-status groups about the potential performance of the low-status group (Berger, Fisek, Norman, & Zelditch, 1972). Expectation Training seeks to change these status roles by creating a social encounter between high- and low-status groups, in which the performance of the low-status persons contradicts expectations for their incompetence. Expectation Training teaches pupils from the low-status ethnic group to perform high-prestige tasks unfamiliar to the high-status pupils.

When the training sequence is completed, they instruct their peers from the higher status group in the tasks. Following this, 4-person groups composed of 2 low-status "teachers" and 2 high-status "students" engage in problem-solving tasks that require discussion and collective decision making.

Group sessions are filmed on videotape and analyzed by judges for pupils' rates of participation in the discussion and influence on the decision adopted by the group.

Following the laboratory experiment that demonstrated the efficacy of the training experience in the role behavior of low- and high-status Israeli children, a field study (Ben-Yitschak, Lotan, & Sharan, 1980) was planned that sought to improve ethnic relations among children in desegregated junior high school classrooms. However, it was unreasonable to expect that the effects of Expectation Training could be prolonged for an entire academic year, as Expectation Training is based on the assumption of differences on one status characteristic alone, in this case that of ethnic background. The classroom with a desegregated population is a multicharacteristic status situation, as pupils are exposed daily to classmates' academic and social behavior as well as their ethnic differences (Berger, Fisek, Norman, & Zelditch, 1977). Accordingly, it was imperative that the Expectation Training method be amplified so that each child in the classroom could enjoy some degree of status in the eyes of classmates from both ethnic groups over the course of the year.

Cooperation is known to exert a positive effect on children's mutual relationships, so the investigators decided to amplify the expectation training by establishing cooperative small-group projects throughout the year. These cooperative group projects involve a division of labor within the small group, so that each child has to perform a task that contributes to the group goal but is not identical with the tasks performed by other group members. Hence, the low-status child can make an important contribution to the group's progress without his product being subjected to direct comparison with others. This allows low-status children to maintain status alongside higher status children.

Three treatment conditions formed the design of this field study: (1) Expectation Training administered in the summer followed by once-a-week extracurricular club sessions involving small-group projects. Club-session attendance was compulsory and included the entire desegregated seventh-grade class (N=229); (2) cooperative small-group club sessions were held once a week throughout the year, but the subjects did not participate in Expectation Training (N=70); (3) a no-treatment control group (N=115). All dependent measures including the criterion tasks were administered at the end of the academic year.

Club sesions focused on two general topics, "Psychology" and "Energy and Space Studies," and detailed plans for pupils' activities in small groups were prepared by the project staff. Preparation of these materials was guided by two principles: (1) The activities should have maximum interest value and be intellectually stimulating, whereas trying to avoid giving advantage to pupils with prior knowledge of the subject; (2) the structure of the task would require that it be carried out cooperatively by a small group of pupils (3 to 6), and that the end product be produced by the whole group. Finally, each small group was to present a summary report of its activities to the entire class (Sharan & Hertz–Lazarowitz, 1980).

Six classrooms in four schools participated in the study, and each of the three conditions was administered in each school so as to avoid contamination of treatment with a particular school. Measures of pupil participation and influence on the group decision-making sessions were obtained from videotapes, and posttreatment questionnaires were administered about pupils' evaluations of the club session, of competition and cooperation in the club work, of sociometric questions, and on attitude toward school. There were 16 four-member groups selected at random from each of the three treatment conditions that participated in the group sessions filmed for analysis, but all 414 participants in the study replied to the posttreatment questionnaire.

The results of the field study are complex but basically negative. Data derived from the group session showed no change in the amount of influence exerted by Middle Eastern children on the group process as a result of either treatment condition. All pupils from the experimental groups in both conditions were more active on the criterion tasks than their peers from the control group, but the relative participation of the low-status children was not increased.

However, closer analysis of the data revealed that there were positive effects on the behavior of the low-status Middle Eastern children in the criterion groups, but only under certain conditions, which were identified by the observations carried out in the club sessions three times during the course of the year. Expectation Training did not play a meaningful role. Rather, the determining characteristic of the club sessions, which discriminated between those Middle Eastern pupils whose behavior was more assertive in the criterion groups and those who registered no change, was the extent to which cooperative interaction in the small-group projects was actually implemented. The cooperative small-group clubs did have some effect on these children's interaction with their Western peers: Low-status children who worked in the clubs where there were cooperative relations behaved more assertively in the criterion groups than those whose clubs did not reveal cooperative relations. On the other hand, Middle Eastern children whose behavior in the criterion groups was less assertive than their Western peers were divided almost equally between the cooperative and non-cooperative groups.

Why did so few children who were in the experimental groups improve their performance in the criterion group? Early in the experiment it became apparent that there were several impediments to cooperative interaction among the pupils attending the club sessions. Cooperative interaction in small groups differed radically from the kind of social relationships to which the children were ac-customed in their regular classrooms, because the majority of classes in Israeli schools use the whole-class presentation-recitation method, coupled with com-petition for grades. Consequently, a club session held 1 hour per week, sand-wiched between the traditionally taught academic lessons, was inconsistent with the child's past schooling experiences. Many pupils saw the club sessions' rela-tively free, permissive atmosphere as a convenient setting for discharging ten-sions and frustrations, and many club sessions had barely a modicum of order. The fact that the club leaders were not teachers, and therefore not seen as figures of authority, only undermined further their control of the situation. In short, the cooperative small-group sessions were like a foreign body injected into an alien social system, and the discontinuity proved disrupting to the children and their group leaders.

Nevertheless, children's responses to the posttreatment questionnaire indi-cated favorable evaluation of their experiences in the small-group club sessions. Middle Eastern children preferred small-group instruction to whole-class instruc-tion, though the differences between the two groups were not large. Also, Mid-dle Eastern children in all treatment classes received more sociometric choices on a question of "who are chosen as playmates outside school" than did their counterparts in the untreated classes. Equally important is the fact that the West-ern and Middle Eastern children received an almost identical mean number of choices on this question in the treated groups, whereas there was a large dif-ference in favor of the Western pupils among children in the untreated classes. This finding is noteworthy because it may point to a generalized effect of class-room relationships beyond the confines of the school. The most straightforward explanation of the lack of behavioral effects, in contrast to the positive results on the verbal level, is the fact that the two sets of measures apply to different dependent variables. Influence on group decision-making processes in mixed-ethnic groups differs markedly from questions of interpersonal friendship and liking for one or another method of classroom interaction. Changes registered on paper-and-pencil measures of ethnic evaluations, perceptions, and attitudes may not be accompanied by changes in manifest behavioral patterns in mixed-ethnic groups. This explanation is congruent with the many reports of inconsistent results obtained on the attitudinal and behavioral levels in psychological research.

Interpersonal Need–Satisfaction Project

An educational treatment based on Schutz's (1966) three-dimensional theory of interpersonal behavior was designed by Ben-Ari and Amir (1981) to improve social relations among pupils in ethnically mixed classes. The aim of the treatment was to transform the class into a "significant" group in the eyes of the pupils by satisfying their primary interpersonal needs in the class. Ben-Ari and Amir assumed that interethnic attitudes and social relations among the children would improve as a result of satisfying pupils' needs in the classroom, which may, in turn, lead to improved academic and emotional development.

Schutz (1966) contended that all interpersonal behavior can be grouped into three categories of needs—inclusion, control, and affect—which can be satisfied only in a group setting. Inclusion refers to the need to sense that others are interested in and understand the individual. Control reflects the need to feel a source of influence on one's own behavior and on the human environment. Affect is the need to feel liked, to develop open relations with others. Satisfaction of these needs within a group setting, claims Schutz, invariably leads to members' increased attraction to the group and its members. Thus, if both the Middle Eastern and the Western pupil see their class as a significant group that satisfies interpersonal needs, positive relations will inevitably develop between the two. Furthermore, because one's self-perception is a function of the quality of one's interactions with others, it follows that positive interactions with others should contribute to more positive self-perceptions.

With this theoretical rationale the study attempted to answer three questions. First, do the mutual attitudes of children in a mixed-ethnic contact situation improve as a result of the satisfaction of interpersonal needs? Second, is there a differential contribution of the three interpersonal needs to attitudinal change? Third, does the satisfaction of interpersonal needs lead to improved perceptions of self and/or the contact situation?

Implementation of the independent variable required manipulation of the classrooms to satisfy pupils' needs for inclusion, control, and affect and thereby create a "significant" group for the youngsters. To this end, Ben-Ari and Amir developed a series of social exercises, each pretested for content, mode of presentation, and whether inclusion, control, or affect needs were satisfied. All the exercises conformed to a format composed of a small-group activity or game followed by a group discussion. The activities and games were mixed and some exercises required a great deal of group activity, whereas others needed less. All exercises were designed to assure that the previous academic achievements of the high-status group would not give them any advantage. Meetings were held once weekly over a 15-week period, for 2 hours during the regular hours of the school day.

Twenty desegregated seventh-grade classes from three junior high schools were randomly divided into experimental and control groups. Each experimental class was further divided into two groups to allow for greater contact between pupils and group leaders who received both theoretical and practical training. It was discovered in the pretest that affect could not be isolated from the inclusion or control exercises. Accordingly, three experimental subgroups were formed as follows: Some classes within each school received inclusion (10 weeks) followed by affect (5 weeks) exercises only; others received control (10 weeks) followed by affect (5 weeks) exercises only; and a final group received a combination of inclusion, control, and affect exercises (15 weeks total). All the children were tested prior to the treatment, after 10 weeks, and at the end of the project on the following dependent variables: attitudes toward classmates; attitudes toward Western and Middle Eastern ethnic groups; self-concept; and perception of class climate.

No positive changes in the experimental groups as compared to the control group were registered for self-concept, perception of class climate, or generalization of attitudes toward ethnic groups. However, significant differences between both ethnic groups were found on two quasisociometric indices of relations with classmates. Experimental children as opposed to control pupils reported more frequent visits to the homes of classmates and gave more positive evaluations of each other on a series of personality dimensions.

It is noteworthy that these two measures indicated negative changes for the control group and positive change among experimental children. This general pattern of results was repeatedly found when comparisons were made between various subgroups of children on the following variables: pupil gender, pupil ethnic group, (Middle Eastern, Western, Israeli), academic level of previous school (identical, similar, dissimilar), pupils' present academic level (identical, lower, higher), and the socioeconomic level of the pupil's home neighborhood (lower, higher). For another sociometric factor—"play with during recess" and "spend time with"—no overall gains were reported for control or experimental children, nor was there a significant difference between the two groups. This result also held for all comparisons of subgroups of children except for the breakdown into pupils' ethnic group. When Middle Eastern pupils were evaluated, a significant difference appeared between the experimental and control groups: Evaluations improved in the former, whereas they deteriorated in the latter. No significant differences between experimental and control groups were found for evaluations of Westerners or Israelis.

Finally, there were strong indications that only the inclusion treatment resulted in positive changes on all sociometric measures, whereas the control and combined treatment demonstrated gains for some variables and losses for others. However, each of the experimental groups resulted in higher overall sociometric scores than did the control group. Regarding the addition of affect exercises to the inclusion and control manipulations, no cumulative gain was evident in either case.

Ben-Ari and Amir (1981) concluded that the interpersonal need–satisfaction project positively affected pupils' evaluations of and interactions with classmates but had little effect on factors not directly related to interaction, such as self-concept or generalization of attitude change. This result is not surprising, as the primary activity of the experimental groups was pupil interaction, and there was no direct input geared to change pupils' self-perceptions or evaluations of ethnic groups outside the classroom. With the accumulation of data from field experiments in desegregated classes, it is becoming more and more clear that changes in dependent measures are very unlikely unless the intervention is uniquely tailored to impact those variables. Also, perception of classroom climate may not have changed, because, as in the previous report (Ben-Yitschak, Lotan, & Sharan, 1980), the projects' activities were merely appendaged to the usual schooling process, without concomitant changes in instructional method or in other school activities. Again, it is unlikely that major school components such as teaching methods or teacher–pupil relationships could change meaningfully as a result of a 2-hour weekly session conducted by outsiders.

Results of this study underline the need for judicious implementation of carefully designed plans to improve social relations in the desegregated classroom. The negative change characterizing the control pupils reinforces what is now axiomatic in the desegregation literature, that without intervention social relations in the desegregated class are as likely to deteriorate as to improve. Even when a particular treatment is anchored in theory and well conceptualized, the desired change does not necessarily occur in a consistent manner, as evidenced in the mixed outcomes of the control and combined treatments. Some of the reasons for this phenomenon are discussed later.

One final point deserves mention here. Ben-Ari and Amir (1981) reported that no overall differential gains were evident for the evaluation of Middle Eastern as compared to Western pupils within the experimental group. This means that the gains obtained by the two groups were more or less equal. Ideal outcomes of interventions in the desegregated classroom should provide benefits for all pupils, but the advantages to minority children should be greater than those acquired by majority pupils. This is not meant to negate the significance of the outcomes of the present study, but rather to highlight the difficulties that need be overcome in desegregation research.

Discussion

At first glance, not all the experiments reported here investigated clearly defined educational methods, theoretically or practically. It would seem that activity classrooms, open classrooms, or small-group learning classrooms do not share a given set of procedures relevant to achieving the goals of ethnic integration. Hence, it is not reasonable to anticipate that they would yield a coherent, consistent body of findings that might provide guidelines to educators for future instructional practice. On closer examination, however, it becomes evident that all three methods share certain basic assumptions critical for evolving instructional practices. These assumptions deal with the roles of the pupil and the teacher and with the nature of the social interactions that ought to take place in school as part of the learning process.

The underlying value base of the methods examined here is an educational orientation that views the child in a social context, rather than merely as an information processor. Indeed, this is the only appropriate way to tackle the integration of children from diverse cultural backgrounds within the same classroom. Also, this approach espouses a theory of human motivation consistent with its value orientation, namely, that motivation to learn is significantly increased when pupils are seen as a source of initiative and decisions, rather than being merely the recipients of decisions and information transmitted by the teacher. The active pursuit of knowledge, though guided by teachers, takes place within a process of interaction with peers. School learning can structure and regulate this experience to improve interpersonal relationships and the investment of pupils' energies in the pursuit of worthwhile topics. Proponents of activity-centered learning, the open classroom, and the small-group classroom claim that, if such principles are an integral part of educational practice, both learning and social experience will be enhanced, and along with them the relationships between children of different cultural backgrounds. The traditional classroom, emphasizing cognitive information processing and minimizing social interaction, highlighting competitive achievement and limiting cooperative relationships, isolating the individual and making the pupil the recipient of information in quantities and rates determined solely by others, is simply unable, structurally and dynamically, to foster the processes needed for social integration.

Not only are changes in the pupil's role required by the orientation examined here, but so are equally dramatic and perhaps more difficult changes in the teacher's role. The teacher in Israel—and in other countries—clings steadfastly to the primary role of subject-matter transmitter. This characterizes not only the secondary school teacher, but frequently those in the upper grades of primary school too. Little attention is paid to the child's personal and social development or to the quality of social relations in the classroom. Such attention is not planned by the administration, nor do teachers initiate it, because they feel they cannot afford to "steal" time from subject matter, so little is done to encourage the development of positive relationships in the classroom. Whole-class, lecture-discussion remains the instructional norm (Rich, Amir, & Ben-Ari, 1981). Yet, even proponents of this method agree that small-group work is preferable when concentrating on the achievement of social goals in the classroom (Good, 1979). Clearly, then, problems of social and interethnic relationships cannot be solved solely by the teacher's transmission of information; they need a broader range of skills. Because teachers frequently do not consider these skills to be in their domain, it follows that profound changes in teachers' role definition and professional skills must occur before the conditions for successful ethnic integration are met.

The basic premises of educational methods studied in most of the experiments reviewed here were not fully realized in practice. Consequently, it is not possible to make realistic predictions about the outcome of studies in which these principles would be fully applied. This is not unusual in educational field experimentation, where the gap between theory and practice makes the evaluation of educational outcomes very difficult. Often the independent variable is vague and poorly defined, and real events in the classroom either remain undocumented and outcomes are measured irrespective of prior events, or implementation bears little resemblance to the initial plan because the conditions necessary to proper implementation were lacking. At best, there is a mutual adaptation between planned strategies and the limitations of the actual classroom conditions (McLaughlin & Marsh, 1978). Thus we may be led to false conclusions about the relationship between the independent and dependent variables. Or, worse still, investigators may find themselves assessing the effects of "nonevents" on subjects who are tested for changes resulting from educational innovations, which, in fact, they never experienced.

However, the gap between theory and practice gives us little comfort for, if the orientation suggested here is to be put into practice, we must understand why the teaching methods studied in this research were implemented only partially, even perfunctorally. Why were the results so meagre when, theoretically, the interaction in open and small-group classrooms should effectively foster positive relationships among children of diverse backgrounds? We suggest—albeit tentatively—that one primary reason for the lack of full implementation, and the consequent mixed results, is that investigators did not cope with the school organization as a social system and its effects on instructional changes aimed at improving social relations among pupils.

Examination of the school environment in which these studies were conducted conveys the impression that these projects were indeed carried out in different organizational environments. A simple continuum between a supportive and nonsupportive school environment cannot adequately describe the variety of conditions in schools, but because this analysis is exclusively ex-post-facto and based on the occasional observations about the school environment included in the various research reports, such a scheme must suffice. By supportive or nonsupportive, we mean not only a moral stature in regard to ethnic integration, but also the school's use of its resources to exploit the opportunities provided by desegregation, by ensuring that the means needed to accomplish the goals of integration are being applied consistently.

We suggest, for example, that the Nachlaot project enjoyed relatively high success in academic achievement, because the implementation of the activity-oriented classroom was conceived as a central project of the school and supported by the entire staff. Changing teacher behavior in the classroom was not merely sanctioned by the school authorities but became a goal to which the school was publically committed and, hence, eager to implement as well as possible. Moreover, the moral support offered by the teachers was expressed as mutual assistance among them, as they were almost entirely dependent on their own initiative. Such system support for educational change appears to be critical for achieving some success in implementing innovations of this kind (McLaughlin & Marsh, 1978).

By contrast with the Nachlaot project, the Small-Group study involving Expectation Training suffered from the negative influence of the school environment, where behavioral norms were markedly competitive. In the latter case there seems to have been considerable scepticism, even antagonism, among the school staff, many of whom claimed that the cooperative, small-group treatment was unrealistic in an achievement-oriented society such as Israel. Furthermore, the treatment was administered in extracurricular clubs, a relatively minor component of the school experience as a whole. Accordingly, effective implementation of small-group techniques was limited to only some of the clubs, and results were therefore mostly negative.

Intermediate positions on this continuum are occupied by the Open-Education project and the Interpersonal Need–Satisfaction project. Although the initiative for educational change in the former case came from the school staff, who began the project enthusiastically, one gains the impression from the report that the institutional support and commitment necessary for implementing such change were not always forthcoming. Thus, when difficulties in implementing the new system were encountered in the classrooms, some teachers regressed to more familiar, conventional methods, thereby removing the opportunity for quality integrated education. A different set of contingencies was operating in the Interpersonal Need–Satisfaction project, which was initiated and implemented by persons who were not members of the school staff. Though principals were fairly supportive of the project, the fact that outsiders were responsible for implementation and that treatment was only 2 hours per week meant that, however well the treatment was thought out and implemented, its effects would be limited to events within the classroom. The institutional support available here was for a localized intervention, which did not make great demands on the school's resources. No true support or commitment was apparent among the school administration to broaden the positive effects of the project to other schooling situations. Thus, research results for both of these projects were mixed.

The important role that school-wide programs can play is consistent with the emphasis on the system properties of the school for promoting integration, but these programs have not as yet been studied systematically. This is all the more regrettable, because the authors know of several schools where programs of the kind we are about to suggest have been tried, in one form or another, but without any systematic evaluation, so no data are available about their effectiveness. We refer to programs involving supervised social activities encompassing the entire student body in a desegregated school, which require students to cooperate with each other in carrying out the activity, such as planning and supervising a trip, a picnic, or a large school party. Israel's schools have few if any school-wide events occurring *within* the school, perhaps because few schools have the physical facilities necessary for conducting such activities. Many schools do carry out school-wide activities *outside* the school, such as hikes to national sites of interest, but school-wide roles for pupils, serious cultivation of student government and committees, and similar activities, seem to be relatively neglected or treated only perfunctorily. Yet, such activities can be effective vehicles for fostering closer relationships among pupils of different ethnic backgrounds, and for enhancing the social status of pupils generally seen as being of low status because of their ethnic or academic background. Programs of this kind demand a commitment to the serious cultivation of social relations among pupils at the school-wide level, not only at classroom level (Schmuck, 1980).

These comments point to the necessity for change in the implementation of programs of ethnic integration at the classroom level if they are to be successful. It appears that the school should be approached as an organizational unit if changes in classroom teaching behavior are to have the desired impact. Although the ultimate target for change is the interpersonal relationship, either between teachers and pupils or among the pupils themselves, the approach to change is best initiated at the level of the principal and the teaching staff, who determine the prevailing behavioral norms for classroom behavior. This suggests a change in the scope of the educational treatments aimed at improving ethnic relations, from the individual classroom as the unit of operations and research to the entire set of classrooms and teachers.

This does not mean that instructional-change projects instituted at the classroom level without support from the entire school system are doomed to failure. Some of these efforts, particularly those fostering cooperative small-group learning, including the Hertz-Lazarowitz et al. (1981) and Sharan (1984) studies discussed here, and the work of Slavin (1979) in the United States, have reported positive and impressive results even without significant school-wide support. Yet we feel that these positive findings will be short lived unless there is some continuity in the application of these treatments over a broader period of time in the child's schooling experience. This continuity can best be assured over the long term when the entire school and not only a few teachers is committed to achieving the goals of integration. If we continue to act as if genuine progress in ethnic integration in school can be made without paying serious attention to the organizational condition of the school and its teaching staff, we may fail to identify some of the variables most crucial for determining the extent to which substantial innovations can be implemented at the classroom level.

Focusing on the school as an organizational unit should have especially positive effects on the training of teachers for integrated schooling. This is probably the most overlooked area in the desegregation literature, as virtually no systematic investigations of the effects of teacher training have been conducted, though some projects seem promising (Amir, Rich, Ben Ari, & Agmon, 1980; Beckum & Dasho, 1980). The lack of attention to this field is particularly unfortunate in light of the centrality of the teacher for the successful implementation of these programs (Forehand & Ragosta, 1976; Gerard & Miller, 1975). Undoubtedly, one of the major reasons why many instructional innovations lose their original character in the process of implementation is that teachers are not adequately retrained to master all aspects of the new method. Furthermore, the kinds of alternative methods discussed in this chapter require dramatic changes in teachers' behavioral repertoire as well as in their attitudes and values. The prolonged effort required to make these personal changes and to perfect new methods of instruction is more likely to be successful if the entire school is involved in the project. Accordingly, it is advisable that in-service teacher training projects not only enjoy moral support from the school administration, but that they should be conducted with the entire school staff, administrators as well as teachers, so that the implications are understood by all who may affect its ultimate success.

Although this discussion has focused on the impediments to change in the classroom, we are convinced that efforts to realize Miller's (1980) call for quality integrated education and the implementation of optimum conditions can be and indeed are being carried out in Israeli schools, albeit on a small scale. Clearly, the projects described here did not result in any breakthrough, but the general direction of the effort is defensible and potentially significant. Many teachers in Israeli desegregated schools are dissatisfied with the conventional teaching methods and are willing to invest the effort necessary to learn alternative methods. We believe that, if appropriate institutional support and effective training programs are provided, the opportunities offered by desegregation will be more fully exploited, and future research in the integrated classroom will produce more positive outcomes for pupils.

REFERENCES

Allport, G. *The nature of prejudice.* Reading, Mass.: Addison–Wesley, 1954.

Amir, Y., Rich, Y., Ben–Ari, R., & Agmon, T. *Social integration in the junior high school: An in-*

service staff training program. Center for Applied Manpower, Bar–Ilan University, Israel, 1980. (Hebrew)

Aronson, E., Blaney, N., Stephan, C., Sikes, J., & Snapp, M. *The jigsaw classroom.* Beverly Hills, Calif.: Sage, 1978.

Aronson, E., Bridgeman, D., & Geffner, R. Interdependent interactions and prosocial behavior. *Journal of Research and Development in Education,* 1978, *12,* 16–27.

Beckum, L., & Dasho, S. *Confronting adversity: A multi-disciplinary study of teacher training needs in newly desegregated schools.* San Francisco: The Far–West Laboratory for Educational Research and Development, 1980.

Ben–Ari, R., & Amir, Y. *Interpersonal need-fulfillment in interethnic contact as a means of improving interethnic relations in the junior high school.* Unpublished manuscript, Bar–Ilan University, Israel, 1981. (Hebrew)

Ben–Yitschak, Y., Lotan, M., & Sharan, S. *Developing equal-status interaction in groups of mixed-status Israeli youth.* Report submitted to the Israel Ministry of Education, Jerusalem, 1980. (Hebrew)

Berger, J., Fisek, M., Norman, R., & Zelditch, M. *Status characteristics and social interaction.* New York: Elsevier, 1977.

Brophy, J., & Good, T. *Teacher–student relationships.* New York: Holt, Rinehart, & Winston, 1974.

Chen, M., Levy, A., & Adler, C. *The junior high school research project: Process and outcome.* Unpublished manuscript, Tel–Aviv University, 1978. (Hebrew)

Cohen, E. Interracial interaction disability. *Human Relations,* 1972, *25,* 9–24.

Cohen, E. & Roper, S. Modification of interracial interaction disability: An application of status characteristic theory. *American Sociological Review,* 1972, *37,* 643–657.

Cohen, E., & Sharan, S. Modifying status relations in Israeli youth: An application of expectation states theory. *Journal of Cross-Cultural Psychology,* 1980, *11,* 364–384.

Crain, R., & Mahard, R. Desegregation and black achievement: A review of the research. *Law and Contemporary Problems,* 1978, *42,* 17–56.

Evans, J. *Characteristics of open education: Results from a classroom rating scale and a teacher questionnaire.* Newton, Mass.: Educational Development Corporation, 1971.

Forehand, G., & Ragosta, M. *A handbook for integrated schooling.* Washington, D. C.: U. S. Department of Health, Education, and Welfare, 1976.

Gerard, H., & Miller, N. *School desegregation.* New York: Plenum Press, 1975.

Good, T. Teacher effectiveness in the elementary school. *Journal of Teacher Education,* 1979, *30,* 52–64.

Harrison, J., Glaubman, R. & Strauss, H. Who benefits from the open classroom. *Journal of Educational Research,* in press.

Harrison, J., Strauss, H., & Glaubman, R. *Formative evaluation of activity classes.* Report to the Israel Ministry of Education and Culture, 1980. (Hebrew)

Harrison, J. Strauss, H. & Glaubman, R. The impact of open and traditional classrooms on achievement and creativity: The Israeli case. *The Elementary School Journal,* 1981, *82,* 27–36.

Hertz–Lazarowitz, R., Sapir, C., & Sharan, S. *The effects of two cooperative learning methods and traditional teaching on the achievement and social relations of pupils in mixed ethnic junior high school classes.* Manuscript submitted for publication, 1981.

Hertz–Lazarowitz, R., & Sharan, S. Self-esteem, locus of control and children's perception of classroom social climate: A developmental perspective. *Contemporary Educational Psychology,* 1979, *4,* 154–161.

Itskowitz, R., & Strauss, H. *The Bar–Ilan self-concept test.* Unpublished manuscript, Bar–Ilan University, Israel, 1979. (Hebrew)

Klein, Z., & Eshel, Y. *Integrating Jerusalem Schools.* New York: Academic Press, 1981.

McLaughlin, N., & Marsh, D. Staff development and school change. *Teachers College Record,* 1978, *80,* 69–94.

Megamot—Behavioural Sciences Quarterly. Jerusalem: The Henrietta Szold Institute, 1977, *23*, Nos. 3–4. (Hebrew)

Miller, N. Making school desegregation work. In W. Stephan & J. Feagin (Eds.), *School desegregation: Past, present and future.* New York: Plenum Press, 1980.

Minkovich, A., Davis, D., & Bashi, Y. *Evaluation of educational achievement in the Israeli elementary school.* Jerusalem: School of Education of the Hebrew University and the Ministry of Education and Culture, 1977. (Hebrew)

Rich, Y., Amir, Y., & Ben–Ari, R. Social and emotional problems associated with integration in Israeli junior high schools. *International Journal of Intercultural Relations,* 1981, *5,* 259–275.

Rich, Y., & Darom, E. Pupils' perceptions of the quality of life in advantaged and disadvantaged schools. In J. Epstein (Eds.), *The quality of school life.* Boston: Lexington Books, 1981.

Rich, Y. & Plato, R. Primary and secondary school teachers' interactions with advantaged and disadvantaged pupils in mixed-ability junior high school classrooms. Paper presented at the Annual Meeting of the American Educational Research Association, 1982.

Schmuck, R. Students as organizational coparticipants. In S. Sharan, A. Paul Hare, C. Webb, & R. Hertz–Lazarowitz (Eds.), *Cooperation in education.* Provo, Utah: Brigham Young University Press, 1980.

Schofield, J. School desegregation and intergroup relations. In D. Bar–Tal & L. Saxe (Eds.), *Social psychology of education: Theory and research.* Washington, D. C.: Hemisphere, 1978.

Schutz, W. *The interpersonal underworld.* Palo Alto, Calif.: Science and Behavioral Books, 1966.

Sharan, S. Cooperative learning in small groups: Recent methods and effects on achievement, attitudes, and ethnic relations. *Review of Educational Research,* 1980, *50,* 241–271.

Sharan, S. *Cooperative learning in the classroom: Research in desegregated schools.* Hillsdale, N. J.: Lawrence Erlbaum Associates, 1984.

Sharan, S., Hare, P., Webb, C., & Hertz-Lazarowitz, R. (Eds.) *Cooperation in education.* Provo, Utah: Brigham Young University Press, 1980.

Sharan, S., & Hertz-Lazarowitz, R. A group-investigation method of cooperative learning in the classroom. In S. Sharan et al. (Eds.), *Cooperation in education.* Provo, Utah: Brigham Young University Press, 1980.

Sharan, S., & Sharan, Y. *Small-group teaching.* Englewood Cliffs, N. J.: Educational Technology Publications, 1976.

Slavin, R. Student teams and achievement divisions. *Journal of Research and Development in Education,* 1978, *12,* 39–49.

Slavin, R. Effects of biracial learning teams on cross-racial friendship and interaction. *Journal of Educational Psychology,* 1979, *71,* 381–387.

Slavin, R. Cooperative learning. *Review of Educational Research,* 1980, *50,* 315–342.

Slavin, R. Cooperative learning and desegregation In W. Hawley (Ed.) *Effective Desegregated Schools.* Beverly Hills, Calif.: Sage, 1981.

Slavin, R., & Madden, N. School practices that improve race relations. *American Educational Research Journal,* 1979, *16,* 169–180.

10 School Desegregation: Some Challenges Ahead

Shlomo Sharan
Yehuda Amir
Rachel Ben–Ari

In several chapters in this book, the authors have pointed to various problems that had to be resolved, or to needs that had to be met, if desegregation policy in Israel was to be implemented effectively. In this chapter we consider some of the more salient challenges confronting educators in their attempt to achieve the goals of school desegregation. This presentation aims at providing a selective but focused view of critical topics or problems that, if treated systematically, could, in our estimation, make a major contribution toward ethnic integration in Israel's desegregated schools, and, perhaps, in Israel society at large. We also raise several issues that went unnoticed elsewhere in this volume. A thorough discussion of these issues cannot be presented here, but we preferred to mention them in the hope of stimulating further inquiry, rather than passing over them in silence.

The discussion of desegregation offered in the various chapters of this book ranges over all seven levels of the social and educational system, namely: Nation, Community, School, Principal, School Staff, Classroom, and Pupils. As in the book as a whole, we have divided our discussion in this chapter into those challenges to integration faced at the macrosocial level, and those relevant to the microsocial level of school and classroom. We also look at some of the necessary interrelationships between these two levels in respect to solving problems of desegregation.

THE MACROSOCIAL LEVEL

All the authors concerned with the effects of desegregation on the macrosocial level shared the view that Jews of Middle Eastern and Western ethnic background in Israel should have equal opportunity to participate in and benefit from the various resources of society. The concept of societal participation encompasses, in the work appearing in this volume, economic opportunity expressed in ethnic representation in the various occupations (an index of social status), representation in institutions of higher learning (which is both a means and an end of desegregation), and positive cross-ethnic relations to foster social cohesion as well as to prevent ethnic cleavage that could seriously disrupt society. Taken together, these goals constitute what was called "nation building." Although school desegregation is not the only vehicle for promoting social cohesion and equal societal participation in Israel for all ethnic groups, the consensus is that desegregation is viewed by members of both groups as a major device available for that purpose. Indeed, achieving the goals subsumed under the title of "nation building" may be well nigh impossible without desegregation. Carrying out desegregation policy of ethnic mix in the schools wherever possible thus satisfies the formal requirements of equal access to public resources, at the level of national policy.

Macro–micro Linkage

Perusal of the chapters of this book leaves us with the distinct sense of a gap between policy made at the macrosocial level, and the problems of implementation faced at the microsocial level. The people responsible for school desegregation policy did not explore or clarify the social, organizational, or instructional problems and processes that were to transpire in schools that became desegregated. Amazingly enough, the lack of attention to microlevel issues by groups concerned with policy characterized the work of the educational bureaucracy, not only of groups of parents or politicians who one would not expect to be concerned with such matters. It seems that professional educators as well as laymen were preoccupied exclusively with the mechanics of ethnic mixing. The discussions and debates that went on in all the government agencies about desegregation (Chapter 4) rarely revealed any attention to the complex problems that would confront the schools as a result of the new policy. The documents about the history of the government's and Education Ministry's treatment of school desegregation deal with ideology, with the disposition of persons (who goes where), and with political considerations, such as the projected reactions of parents to one or the other move of the Ministry. Social-educational technology, the procedures to be implemented, are left to "the troops" who are close to or on the "line of battle." Such topics apparently are simply not discussed at the level of policy making. That seems to be at least one important reason why desegregation is "more easily said than done," in the sense that political–bureaucratic decisions are verbal/written decrees that dictate only the administrative steps schools must take to bring about the formal fact of desegregation, but which do not even offer schools guidelines about *how* the new situation is to be managed once it is created.

One is tempted to ask why school organizational problems or classroom instructional strategies are not considered essential topics for clarification by educational governing bodies, particularly when the same groups initiated a radical change in the social composition of the student population of some schools? Are such topics not part of educational policy, only a matter of praxis?

Recent theorizing about the nature of educational organizations, particularly that body of theory and research known as "loose-coupling theory," would assert that, indeed, the instructional behavior of teachers, or the style of staff organization in particular schools, would not be treated by educational governing bodies. A loosely coupled organization is one whose subunits function in a relatively uncoordinated fashion with limited interunit linkages. These subunits are also supervised or monitored to a limited degree only by a central authority, so that each one operates with a large degree of independent discretion. For schools this means, inter alia, that there is only circumscribed linkage between policy makers and those who implement policy at the classroom level (Weick, 1976). The behavior of the groups in Israel who determined desegregation policy is, therefore, quite predictable on the basis of this approach to school-organizational theory. The *manner* in which services in schools are delivered to the clients does not regularly concern the higher echelons of school systems, only the allocation of resources needed for making those services possible. Often, school governing bodies may not even know if in fact the specific services are indeed delivered as mandated, only that those services are potentially available. This fact has far-reaching implications for the implementation of desegregation policy at the microsocial level, as we explore later in this chapter.

Of course, the loosely coupled nature of schools and school systems typical of conditions in the United States need not have been characteristic of conditions in Israel. Israel's miniature size compared to most other countries (not to speak of the United States), as well as its commitment to ethnic integration as a national priority, might have created closer ties between policy-making bodies and the educators at various ranks concerned with implementation. Moreover, the central office of the Ministry of Education is directly responsible for the design, production, and evaluation of curricular materials for the nation's school system. To this extent, as well, Israel's school system is not decentralized as are the centers of decision making about schools in the United States. With this apparently intimate involvement of the central educational bureaucracy in Israel in the practical workings of the schools, one could have anticipated sufficient attention at the policy-making level to the problems of implementation that principals and teachers would encounter, with the explicit goal of precluding makeshift solutions to these problems that could undermine the intentions of the nation's desegregation policy!

The expectation for central-office awareness of microlevel needs was all the more realistic in light of the fact that research efforts in Israel on various levels of desegregated schools had provided information about the nature of the problems that ordinarily arise (see Chapters 7 and 8). But, despite all these factors that might have, or even should have, led to a more tightly knit relationship between the macro and microlevels of the school system, Israel's schools, like those in other countries, are loosely coupled. This is true from the point of view of the limited extent to which the Ministry of Education actually monitors implementation procedures at the school level, and to which it supplies schools with technologies for problem solving in order to facilitate the realization of national policy.

Is this state of affairs an inevitable condition of hierarchical school system organization, as loose-coupling theory suggests? Available information conveys the message that individual schools do not have the human or material resources, including the necessary pool of skills and work time of personnel, to implement successfully complex programs of multiethnic instruction and social integration (Chapters 7 and 9; Sharan, 1984). Unless the Ministry of Education undertakes centrally supported integration programs, thereby making a concerted effort to close somewhat the gap between policy and implementation, the progress of ethnic integration at the microlevel will be distinctly hampered. Thus, the success of school desegregation at the macrosocial level may be independent of its success at the microlevel, at least in the short run (see Chapter 1). However, the reverse is patently not the case: Successful implementation at the microlevel of the schools and classrooms remains dependent on measures taken at the level of the central agencies of the Ministry of Education. If this gap cannot be overcome, the success of implementation will be determined exclusively by the initiative and hard work of each individual school, as some authors depict conditions existing in the United States (Crain, Mahard, & Narot, 1982).

Desegregation in Elementary and in Senior High Schools

The primary responsibility for carrying out ethnic desegregation and integration in Israel's schools has been borne hitherto by the junior high school system. In practice, therefore, desegregation constitutes a transitional episode in the children's school career, squeezed into the 3-year sequence of the junior high school, without extending into the earlier or later years of schooling (i.e., into the 11th and 12th grades in particular).

There appears to be widespread support among theorists, investigators, officials of the Ministry of Education, and even among parents that the extension of desegregation into elementary school is desirable and acceptable. However, on the practical level, neither parents nor government is inclined to engage in busing young children to school outside their neighborhood. Also, busing is not within fiscal reality, in terms of resources available to parents or to the Israel school system. Consequently, desegregation at the elementary school level will, it seems, remain confined to schools where a mixed-ethnic population lives within walking distance of a given school (although there are a few isolated instances of busing in Israel). Some school districts can be redrawn by local authorities to encompass a more ethnically heterogeneous population within a given school, but this solution cannot possibly counteract the fact that many neighborhoods tend to have large concentrations of people with a common cultural and socioeconomic background.

Obstacles to desegregation in the upper grades of high school, and in particular in the upper grades of academic as distinct from vocational schools, are very different from those affecting elementary schools. Thus far the government has not adopted a law or policy requiring Israel's academic high schools to desegregate, nor is such an eventuality likely in the foreseeable future. Academic and elite technical high schools practice selection policies whose effect is to severely limit the number of students of Middle Eastern background who qualify for entrance into these college–preparatory schools. Consequently, the Middle Eastern group is disproportionately represented in the several kinds of lower prestige vocational schools whose students are largely ineligible for college entrance. True, the number, and percentage, of students of Middle Eastern background who enter academic high schools has increased considerably over the last decade. Nevertheless, it cannot be gainsaid that the perpetuation of strict selection policies by the academic high schools, with procedures based almost exclusively on various test scores, has many negative implications for the "nation-building" goals of Israel's desegregation policy and for the promotion of ethnic integration in the schools.

One of the more obviously negative consequences of the fact that school children are resegregated when they reach the 10th grade, as an outcome of high school selection practices, is that the entire integration program remains largely restricted to, or even comes to an abrupt end at the conclusion of, junior high school (through 9th grade). The process of ethnic integration loses its continuity during the students' later years in high school. Even where large comprehensive high schools have been established with the express purpose of increasing the degree of ethnic mix in the higher grades of high school, much resegregation occurs when students are tracked into different programs of study within a given school on the basis of their past academic record. Clearly, the organizational and instructional problems, not to mention the complex issues of teacher training, which would arise in the wake of desegregating the academic high schools, are even more difficult to solve than those encountered at the junior high school level. However, it is not our purpose here to treat the school/classroom-level problems that will surface when extending desegregation to high schools. Rather, our purpose is to draw attention to the fact that Israel's academic high schools have not yet been brought into the service of ethnic integration, and whose academic selection practices appear to contradict the spirit of the "nation-building" goals inherent in the school desegregation policy now being implemented at the junior high school level. It appears that only some form of government intervention can change the prevailing conditions in order to bring about continuity in the nation's pursuit of ethnic integration throughout the years of public education.

What bears recognition is the considerable influence university admissions practices exert on the selection policies, and even on the instructional processes, of Israel's academic high schools, and the consequences of these practices and processes for ethnic integration in high schools. Universities in Israel[1] maintain highly competitive admission practices that serve as a criterion for the high schools to measure their own academic standards and to set their admission criteria. Moreover, because the academic high schools perceive themselves as college–preparatory schools, their instructional methods are geared to meet the entrance requirements of the universities. In this fashion, the influence of university admission policies extends downward into the public school system, and beginning with the upper grades of elementary school, or, at the latest, with junior high school, teachers and principals evaluate their educational effectiveness in terms of their pupils' upward mobility through high school and into the university. Thus, the competitive admissions policies of the universities, maintained without regard for ethnic or socioeconomic background (Israel's universities have no affirmative action policy regarding admissions), serve to perpetuate the selective orientation of the high schools and thereby have a negative effect on the progress of ethnic desegregation in the upper grades of high school. To this extent, the Universities play a nonintegrative role in terms of their effect on ethnic desegregation in the high schools. Only if the link between University and high school admissions criteria can be severed will ethnic desegregation in the high schools become possible, and only then can the junior high school cease being the sole bearer of Israel's prointegration policy for the nation's schools.

Beyond the issue of school desegregation at all levels of the school system intended to promote cohesiveness and equal opportunity at the macrosocial level is the task of ensuring ethnic integration in the other main settings of society at large, namely, in the work place, the army, the University, and housing. The ultimate criterion of success for the desegregation policy at the macrosocial level is if integration occurs in the adult world. It is then that the social conditions must prevail that embody in practice the fundamental principle upon which Israel society is built, namely the fact that Israel Jewry is indeed one People, without distinction due to the ethnic-cultural background of the various ethnic subgroups. If the larger society fails to implement ethnic integration in its major institutions and settings, in addition to the schools, the contribution to integration made by interethnic experiences during the school years is in danger of being erased. We cannot expect the schools to save society from itself. That expectation is not merely naive, but it threatens to turn schools into a scapegoat for a burden that they cannot sustain (Sarason, 1983).

---

[1]Readers should be informed that in Israel there are seven institutions of higher learning: five universities and two scientific/technological institutes. Some colleges are in the process of emerging to the point where they can grant a B.A. degree, but to date only the seven institutions mentioned are empowered to grant degrees in Israel.

THE MICROSOCIAL LEVEL

All the authors in this volume who wrote about the effects and problems of desegregation at the microsocial level concurred that a variety of changes are needed in the existing structure of and processes in desegregated schools if social integration is to be achieved. The reasons why these changes are needed were discussed in the relevant chapters (see Chapters 5 through 9) and are not repeated here. Nor is it our purpose to compile a list of specific changes to be carried out in desegregated schools. Again, we focus on some of the major domains where change appears to be critical for future progress, and on the direction that we think the change should take in order to be most productive.

Three central areas of school functioning are considered to be in need of substantive changes in order to realize significant gains in ethnic integration in Israel's schools. These are changes in: (1) school organizational processes; (2) classroom instruction and social relations; (3) structure of the learning task and curricular contents. Schools in Israel and in other countries have developed and implemented a variety of strategies in these three areas for coping with the problems of desegregation. Unfortunately, many of these splendid efforts have gone undocumented. More important, most innovations of these kinds remain to be implemented systematically and under controlled conditions so their effectiveness can be determined and made public.

We examine each of these three domains in some detail.

Organizational Processes

Recent theorizing and research strongly support the view that schools, like other organizations, display consistent and distinctive sets of norms about policies, procedures, relationships and goals. These variables have been collectively conceived as constituting the theoretical construct of 'school climate'. Israeli research on school variables and on school climate as they affect the progress and outcome of ethnic desegregation was reviewed in this book (Chapter 6). The authors' conclusions are consistent with findings from studies in the United States that there are differential effects of school variables on desegregation (Little, 1981) and of various school climates on pupils' academic learning and social relations (Brookover, Beady, Flood, Schweitzer and Wisenbaker, 1979; Lezotte, Hathaway, Miller, Passalacqua & Brookover, 1980; Schmuck & Schmuck, 1974). There is also widespread agreement between Israel and U.S. research findings about the decisive role of the school principal for setting in motion and maintaining those policies and procedures which support academic achievement and positive social relations among all groups of students, which constitute the critical ingredients of a positive school climate (compare Chapter 6 with Crain, Mahard & Narot, 1982).

The conflicts and obstacles principals are likely to encounter when they undertake to create a school climate which is supportive of ethnic integration were described in Inbar et al. (Chapter 6). One of the most salient obstacles, which should attract the attention of teacher trainers and of those who train and supervise school administrators, is the professional orientation, skills and attitudes of the administrative and teaching staff in Israel's secondary schools. Teacher training in the universities concentrates heavily on the study of subject matter. Secondary school teachers have limited competence for employing alternative (i.e., nonlecture type) instructional strategies that accommodate a range of pupil skills and interests. Teacher training in institutions of higher learning, as opposed to the Teacher Colleges in Israel that train elementary school teachers, apparently do not equip future secondary school teachers with skills in remedial teaching needed for assiting slow learners. Nor is any emphasis placed on preparing teachers to manage classroom social relations and to promote group cooperation so necessary for use in mixed-ethnic classrooms. As a result of this kind of professional preparation of teachers, principals dedicated to the goals of ethnic integration must assume a strong leadership role in staff development and the use of alternative pedagogical strategies, if social integration policy is to be realized in actual classroom behavior (Crain, Mahard, & Narot, 1982; Little, 1981).

The main implication of these comments is that secondary school principals and teachers who work in desegregated schools are called upon to make major accommodations in role definition and performance that differ from the role models they learned during their professional training. They must acquire a variety of new competencies needed to meet successfully the needs of an ethnically mixed student body. Lacking these competencies, teachers seek various organizational arrangements for coping with problems, some of which may sidetrack or actually undermine the goals of ethnic integration. Thus, for example, Inbar et al. (Chapter 6) point out that teachers in desegregated schools constantly referred "problem" pupils to school guidance counselors whose role gradually become redefined as the schools' expert on social relations, learning problems, etc. Shunting pupils onto the guidance teacher helped the teaching staff to avoid coping with interpersonal or intergroup relationships, and to continue to function in their traditional role as information transmitters. Teachers were not prepared to employ instructional strategies in the classroom that could meet the needs of an academically and culturally diverse group of students.

Referring "problem" children to the guidance counselor also served to emphasize the status hierarchy among students along ethnic and academic lines and undermined the creation of a school climate supporting academic achievement and positive ethnic attitudes among all groups of students (Chapter 6). Principals must be able to grasp the social implications of such organizational arrangements, identify their positive and negative features, and propose policies that will be more consistent with the goals of ethnic integration. When this does not occur, one finds organizational procedures in schools that appear to be operating at cross purposes. That is only one example of how the principal's organizational leadership is crucial for keeping the school "on course" if it is to realize its goals of promoting ethnic integration. Principals unaccustomed to being directly involved in the nature of classroom practices and in problems of intergroup relations will have to undergo a distinct change in their style of functioning.

Classroom Instruction and Social Relations

Ethnic resegregation at the classroom level through ability grouping is still practiced as a prominent strategy in desegregated junior high schools for coping with the complexities of the multiability classroom. Educators in Israel are often unaware of the ethnic consequences of the tracking practices. In any case, separation of the two ethnic groups is not the reason or purpose of tracking, only its by-product. Nevertheless, its consequences for ethnic integration are generally negative. The one major asset of ability grouping is in the realm of teacher satisfaction because they perceive the more academically homogeneous class as easier to teach. Beginning with the upper grades of elementary school, Israeli teachers feel they must—or are required by the official curriculum—to "teach" (i.e., to verbally present and explain) as much curricular material as possible. "To run with the material" is a well-known phrase among teachers for whom the pace of instruction is a central criterion for measuring their own success and the ability of the students. To teach less is tantamount to depriving "the stronger" students of their due to the benefit of "the weaker" ones. Teachers feel that they are able to maintain a pace of instruction commensurate with the ability of the pupils to "absorb" the material when pupils display a relatively uniform level of ability. If not, teachers feel "held back" by the "weaker" students and may even feel that they are forced to be unfair to the "stronger" students.

In our experience, the preceding orientation toward classroom teaching is widely subscribed to by secondary school teachers in Israel. This set of assumptions and goals presents formidable obstacles to implementing instructional strategies that are more supportive of ethnic integration and that are based on values and assumptions diametrically opposed to those underlying the prevailing orientation. The obstacles to be overcome in order to implement classroom teaching strategies that support social integration in the multiethnic classroom are singularly evident from a close inspection of the experiments that have been performed thus far in Israeli schools (see Chapter 9). Various social technologies emphasizing mutual acceptance, cooperative interaction, and a division of learning tasks that allow for multidimensional contributions to a collective group effort by pupils, appear to create a learning environment conducive to social integration and supportive of pupils' learning efforts on a range of academic levels. These cooperative learning methods have been described in detail and extensively studied in controled field experiments (Aronson, Blaney, Stephen, Sikes, & Snapp, 1978; De Vries, Slavin, Fennessey, Edwards, & Lombardo,

1980; Johnson & Johnson, 1975; Sharan, 1980; Sharan & Sharan, 1976; Sharan, 1984; Slavin, 1980a, b).

Clearly, the obstacle to integrative classrooms confronting the schools is no longer simply *what to do* in the classroom, despite all the questions that still remain unanswered. Rather, the prime obstacle is one of *implementation,* whose major component is developing the professional competence and skills of school personnel. Only then can they change existing organizational and teaching practices and adopt policies, procedures, and practices that are more socially oriented and more responsive to the needs of the students. A new focus of school improvement efforts and research on the implementation process and its obstacles is gaining increasing attention from investigators concerned with planned change in schools (Berman, 1981). Social scientists and educators interested in ethnic integration in the schools have begun to realize more and more that they too must place the topic of planned change in social institutions, with all its complexities, high on their list of professional priorities if substantial progress is to be made in promoting ethnic integration and studying its outcomes (Sharan, 1984). Continuing to place research efforts almost exclusively on the evaluation of treatment effects on school children without investigating how to mobilize organizational and instructional change by schools and teachers will leave the educational enterprise with much data about effects that cannot be utilized or duplicated in real life. Outcome data about children only document the effectiveness of given methods but say little as to what is required in order to have schools implement these methods (Fullan, 1981; Sieber, 1981). The net result will be that schools will not be able to utilize accumulated knowledge to foster ethnic integration.

Examination of the experimental studies on ethnic integration reviewed in this book (Chapter 9) reveals that, in most cases, the results were often equivocal because the instructional innovation being studied was at best only partially implemented and sometimes was carried out in name only. Indeed, evaluation efforts on occasion were invested in "nonevents"! This fact is *as* important as are the *results* of the studies, namely: Teachers require extensive training, and sometimes basic resocialization into new professional roles and skills, before they are able to change old habits and practices and successfully carry out new, often relatively more complex, teaching procedures. Evaluating the effects of teaching methods, such as the open classroom or various forms of cooperative learning, when teachers received little or perfunctory preparation, obviously can be very misleading. Researchers and educators alike often underestimate the time and effort needed to train teachers, to allow them the opportunity to practice new skills gradually, and to assimilate a teaching method completely foreign to them, conceptually and in terms of practical procedures. Even under relatively optimal conditions, such as when the entire staff of a given school decides to learn a new approach to teaching, some of the teachers in the school will find the new approach, such as cooperative learning techniques, unacceptable to them for various reasons (Sharan & Hertz–Lazarowitz, 1982). Again, with the proper administrative and educational leadership on the part of principals, in-service teacher training aimed at introducing more socially oriented learning into many classes in a school can be sustained long enough to provide teachers with the necessary competence.

An extensive study of desegregated schools in the United States demonstrated that schools adopting a human-relations program for pupils were perceived by students as far more supportive of ethnic/racial integration than schools without such a program (Crain et al., 1982). Noteworthy is the fact that this program consisted of face-to-face experiences in mixed-ethnic groups. One of the salient features of cooperative learning is precisely the positive social relations between members of small groups, who are of different ethnic backgrounds, while engaged in collaborating on the study of academic tasks. In this fashion, a human-relations "program" is built into the normative learning process, rather than being appendaged onto the regular course of study. Cooperative interaction with one's peers, of different sex or ethnic groups, is experienced simultaneously with the pursuit of knowledge and is accorded an equally important place alongside learning, so that it not be perceived as occupying lesser significance in the eyes of the teacher and the school (Sharan, 1980; Sharan & Hertz-Lazarowitz, 1980). Of course, the incorporation of human-relations methods into instructional processes through cooperative learning in no way forecloses any of the schools' options for introducing a specific human relations program directed *explicitly* at ethnic relations issues. Simultaneous use of both approaches would appear to be mutually reinforcing.

Structure of the Learning Task and Curricular Content

Even if teachers acquire high-level competence in the use of alternative teaching strategies, it is not reasonable to anticipate that they can supply all their curricular needs in the format required by cooperative learning methods, or remedial teaching, for example, in the multiethnic classroom. Moreover, the subject matter itself must be revised to include material about the historical-cultural background and identity of children from all the ethnic groups represented in the school. Thus, our discussion of the challenge to desegregation posed by curricular needs focuses on two aspects of this problem: the structure or format of the learning tasks (cooperative groups tasks, multiability tasks, etc.) and the need for historical-cultural topics relevant to the life of each ethnic group. Apropos of this latter topic we also touch upon the issue of teaching for cultural similarity or cultural pluralism in desegregated Israeli schools.

Structure of the Learning Task.   Learning tasks are typically designed for solitary study conducted by individuals surrounded by classmates with whom they have little direct contact. Rarely are standard curriculum materials designed for cooperative pursuit of learning goals where pupils interact directly, assist each other, and ultimately synthesize their contributions into a collective group product. In the multiethnic and multiability classroom, the persistent use of single-ability learning tasks does not allow pupils with different kinds of talents, interests, and cultural backgrounds to function as active members of a learning group and to achieve status in their own eyes and in those of their peers by virtue of their unique contribution to the group's progress (Cohen, 1980). Proper implementation of cooperative learning in small groups depends on a combination of social-management techniques employed by the teacher and pupils, with the use of learning tasks specifically designed for group work. Not infrequently teachers assign standard individual tasks to a group. When cooperative interaction becomes blocked or breaks down because the task did not invite or permit a multifaceted approach to this topic, with various kinds of learning activities, skills, and abilities, teachers may erroneously conclude that the pupils are incapable of collaborating constructively or that the entire method doesn't work.

Many subject areas lend themselves easily to the multifaceted, multiability approach. Teachers of Biology, Social Studies, or Humanities appear to experience relatively little difficulty in adopting standard curriculum materials to the needs of multiethnic learning groups, if they acquired an "inquiry-learning" orientation. On the other hand, teachers of foreign languages, mathematics, and some of the sciences (particularly chemistry and physics) express considerable resistance to cooperative learning, in large part due to the complexities of designing learning tasks appropriate for the new social conditions in the classroom. It seems clear that if the burden for designing and preparing cooperative, multiability learning tasks will fall solely on classroom teachers, resistance to the adoption of alternative teaching methods will remain high. If so, minority-group pupils will continue to be locked into their status positions in the desegregated classroom. Desegregation entails a radical change in the social composition of the classroom group. Such a change in one feature of the classroom social system must be accompanied by appropriate changes in other aspects of that system. Learning-task structure must fit the specifications of the cooperative learning methods that were implemented as part of the effort to foster cooperative interaction among peers from different ethnic and ability groups. Social and task structures have to be coordinated in order to have the classroom system function effectively (Cohen, 1980; Sharan & Hertz–Lazarowtiz, 1980). In our experience responsibility for such relatively complex coordination and for such investment in time and effort cannot be placed realistically on teachers. These efforts must come from agencies primarily devoted to curriculum development.

Curricular Content. Effects of students studying curricular materials about the history and culture of Israel's ethnic subgroups (on any dependent variables of relevance, such as ethnic self-concept) have not been evaluated as yet. In the United States, reanalysis of data from a large number of studies about ethnic integration did not yield any effect on cross-ethnic relations (Slavin & Madden,

1979). A more recent study in the United States found that a multicultural curriculum in desegregated schools was associated with higher academic achievement and more positive school adjustment for minority-group children, with the higher achievement probably mediated by improved ethnic self-concept and/or improved social status of the minority group in the school by virtue of their historical background becoming part of the official school curriculum (Crain et al., 1982). A positive approach to a culturally pluralistic curriculum is widely accepted in U.S. schools, because the United States is such a multinational nation (a "nation of nations").

In Israel the problem of introducing a multiethnic curriculum has aroused some debate among social scientists. Interestingly, the study of Middle Eastern Jewish culture in the schools appears to be gaining popularity despite the fact that there has been only minimal investment of resources and effort thus far, on the part of educational officialdom, in the preparation of texts and other curricular materials for schools on these subjects.

The objection some social scientists in Israel have expressed to a serious effort at teaching historical-cultural contents about Middle Eastern Jewry stems, in part, from the claim that such instruction would tend to highlight the Middle Easterners' distinctiveness and differences from Israelis of Western background rather than stressing their similarities. Because people are generally more attracted to others who are similar to themselves and are more likely to want to maintain relations with people of similar background, teaching children about the unique background of the two groups prior to their arrival in Israel might maintain, or even widen, the gap between them, not cultivate the sense of unity that is one of the primary goals of ethnic integration in the schools. According to this view, schools are best advised to teach all children about their common heritage and about the Israeli culture they all share. Unlike the United States, Israel is a very small country, settled by Jews from all over the world who are greatly in need of strengthening their social cohesiveness. Israel is not a "nation-of-nations." Its very existence is predicated on the fact that Jews everywhere, regardless of whatever host cultures they have adopted, belong to one nation, which, after 2000 years of exile, is reasserting its sovereignty in its own land. Israeli education must cultivate that sense of unity among all its children as their most salient social reality. A pluralistic approach to education in Israel potentially bears the seeds of ethnic divisiveness inimical to the goals of "nation building." In this view, the cultivation of ethnic identity through the teaching of the history and culture of the various ethnic groups is seen as reinforcing sectarian subidentities that could detract from these groups' identification with the broad, supraethnic goals of Israel as a nation. That is one view of social process in Israel with profound implications for curriculum development and curricular policy in general, and in desegregated schools in particular.

An opposing view exists as well, one that is not expressed often in public, but that—as noted—appears to be put into practice by a large number of educators in elementary and in junior high schools in Israel. This argument is as follows: Israel as a whole, and the Middle Eastern Jews themselves in particular, would be all the more impoverished culturally for having submerged and failed to keep alive an ancient heritage rich in a wide variety of cultural creations unique to the Middle Eastern Jews. A serious claim can be made for the notion that *only* a genuine awareness of Jewry's part in the Exile—be it in Western or in Middle Eastern countries—can provide a rationale for Jewry's return to Israel. Without knowledge of their Exile, Jews lack an understanding of why they came to Israel. The severance or severe attenuation of ties to one's cultural, ethnic, and familial roots can undermine a group's sense of identity, confidence, creativity, and self-esteem.

Furthermore, one may ask on what grounds it is asserted that the building of social cohesiveness in Israel must be accompanied by a loss of ethnic subgroup identity? In the United States, social scientists question the assumption that ethnic solidarity must decrease as a function of social integration (Schofield, 1981). Indeed, this dichotomous way of viewing the problem may be explained, in part, as the erroneous conclusion reached from the use of various measures on questionnaires (Schofield, 1981) that are: "structured so that improvement in black/white relations can occur only if students begin to choose outgroup members rather than ingroup members [p. 107]." Clearly the dichotomous approach does not reflect psychosocial reality. People can retain strong roots in their own tradition and yet participate fully in a multiethnic society. Israel, for all its being a country settled by Jews from the four corners of the earth, is still less ethnically variegated than the United States. There is no basis for the fear that ethnic subgroups from Middle Eastern countries or elsewhere will feel less of an obligation to serve the goals of Israel as a nation if we educate children to appreciate their own group's history and tradition. Quite the contrary, there is a basis for the suspicion that because many Western groups who came to Israel failed to educate their children in their pre-Israel history (except for stressing its negative features) many Israeli youth today appear alienated from their Jewish heritage. Whatever will be the nature of Israel's culture several generations from now, it best emerges from the contributions of groups deeply aware of their heritage and historical experience, rather than being the products of people who were torn loose from their cultural moorings and were left with only the most superficial and external manifestations of their millenia-old tradition. To allow this to occur in Israel would be tantamount to repeating the pattern of cultural assimilation that overtook much of Diaspora Jewry during the past 2 centuries. It is far more constructive, socially and historically, to recognize and teach the history and culture of Israel's subgroups as well as their common background and condition and not ignore them. Berlin (1982) states: "Ignored differences assert themselves, and in the end rise against efforts to ride over them in favor of an assumed, or desired, uniformity [p. 353]."

This debate is one of the important challenges facing curriculum developers in Israel. Whereas it transcends the subject of school desegregation, these curricular decisions are particularly important for the educational process in multiethnic schools. The course taken in the future may decide much about Israel's social and cultural development.

Another kind of criticism leveled against a multicultural curriculum in the United States claims that such a curriculum espouses a form of cultural relativism that leaves minority students stranded outside the mainstream of society. In their desire to have minority students identify with their own ethnic culture, which is largely quasirural and pretechnological, schools employing a multicultural curriculum fail to require students to master basic skills and to learn how to live in the prevailing capitalist society. Or, some observers claimed that teachers substitute the multicultural curriculum for coping with pupils' cross-ethnic relationships in desegregated schools, which often erupted into various forms of abuse or aggressive behavior (Hanna, 1982).

In our estimation, the argument that a multicultural curriculum would cause a neglect of cultivating basic learning skills and a broad cultural education is not relevant to Israel. Firstly, Israel does not need or employ bilingual education so that all children are taught the same linguistic skills. Secondly, the prevailing use of a multicultural curriculum in Israel requires pupils to learn about the other ethnic group's heritage as well as about their own in order to broaden their cultural perspective, rather than studying exclusively about their own culture, which would result in excluding them from the larger society. The goal of multicultural education in Israel would be to provide appropriate representation to the history and culture of all ethnic groups in pupils' school learning, in order to avoid the impression that one group only comprises, nourishes, and controls Israel society.

Finally, we suggested in this chapter that desegregated schools employ various versions of cooperative learning methods for managing classroom social process, which would serve as the social substructure for the implementation of a multicultural curriculum serving as the substantive superstructure of classroom learning. Theorists of classroom instruction would not substitute content for social process, an error of omission one sees frequently in desegregated schools. The social interactive dimension must be treated together with the cognitive-cultural aspects of pupils' educational experience.

CONCLUSION

We have tried to portray a coherent program geared to promoting ethnic integration in the schools in the realm of instructional policy, teaching methods, and some aspects of curriculum. Clearly this program concentrated on one, albeit central, set of topics concerning desegregated schools, whereas we disregarded here other realms of concern, such as the entire domain of political and/or school–community relations. What we are suggesting is that the leadership needed to create a school climate that supports mutual acceptance among pupils from different groups, as well as full participation of all students in learning experiences, must be persistent and vigorous. It must pursue the implementation of a prointegrative policy at all levels of school functioning, including staff involvement in development and training, classroom organization and instructional procedures, and curriculum contents. In order to conceive of and pursue such a policy, school administrators must have a perspective broad enough to grasp the interrelationships of systemic properties of all the components, even if principals cannot be expert in all these fields.

Given this decisive role of principals in determining the progress of desegregation policy in schools, and in light of the importance of teacher training, both pre and inservice training, for the ultimate implementation of the policy, our conception of the challenges ahead for the success of desegregation places great emphasis on the professional preparation of school personnel. Of course, curriculum development to provide schools with a wide variety of multiability learning tasks and accompanying resources must progress apace with professional training. But, ultimately, curricula cannot substitute for teachers and their abilities. Intergroup relations, classroom organization, peer cooperation, and the management of the learning process itself will not be supplanted, only facilitated, by the multiability curriculum.

In our view, therefore, policy makers would be well advised to focus their attention on the training programs intended to provide schools with professional leadership in the realm of ethnic integration. These programs must be designed to provide trainees with the knowledge and skills needed to implement the social-educational processes that promote integration, or else policies made at governmental or central-office levels will never become social reality.

REFERENCES

Aronson, E., Blaney, N., Stephen, C., Sikes, J., & Snapp, M. *The jigsaw classroom.* Beverly Hills, Calif.: Sage, 1978.

Berlin, I. *Against the current. Essays in the history of ideas.* New York: Penguin, 1982.

Berman, P. Educational change: An implementation paradigm. In R. Lehming & M. Kane (Eds.), *Improving schools: Using what we know.* Beverly Hills, Calif.: Sage, 1981.

Brookover, W., Beady, C., Flood, P., Schweitzer, J., & Wisenbaker, J. *School social systems and student achievement.* New York: Praeger, 1979.

Cohen, E. Design and redesign of the desegregated school: Problems of status, power and conflict. In W. Stephen & J. Feagin (Eds.), *Desegregation: Past, present and future.* New York: Plenum, 1980.

Crain, R., Mahard, R., & Narot, R. *Making desegregation work.* Cambridge, Mass.: Ballinger, 1982.

DeVries, D., Slavin, R., Fennessey, G., Edwards, K., & Lombardo, M. *Teams–games–tournaments: The team learning approach.* Englewood Cliffs, N.J.: Educational Technology Publications, 1980.

Fullan, M. School district and school personnel in knowledge utilization. In R. Lehming & M. Kane (Eds.), *Improving schools: Using what we know.* Beverly Hills, Calif.: Sage, 1981.

Hanna, J. Public social policy and the children's world: Implications of ethnographic research for desegregated schooling. In G. Spindler (Ed.), *Doing the ethnography of schooling.* New York: Holt, Rinehart, & Winston, 1982.

Johnson, D., & Johnson, R. *Learning together and alone.* Englewood Cliffs, N.J.: Prentice–Hall, 1975.

Lezotte, L., Hathaway, D., Miller, S., Passalacqua, J., & Brookover, W. *School learning climate and student achievement.* Tallahassee: Florida State University, 1980.

Little, J. *School success and staff development: The role of staff development in urban desegregated schools.* Boulder, Colo.: Center for Action Research, 1981.

Sarason, S. *Schooling in America: Scapegoat and salvation.* New York: The Free Press, 1983.

Schmuck, R., & Schmuck, P. *A humanistic psychology of education.* Pal Alto, Calif.: National Press Books, 1974.

Schofield, J. Desegregation school practices and student race relations outcomes. In C. Rossell (Ed.), *Assessment of current knowledge about the effectiveness of school desegregation strategies* (Vol. V). Institute for Public Policy Studies, Vanderbilt University, 1981.

Sharan, S. Cooperative learning in small groups: Recent methods and effects on achievement, attitudes and ethnic relations. *Review of Educational Research,* 1980, *50,* 241–271.

Sharan, S. *Cooperative learning in the classroom: Research in desegregated schools.* Hillsdale, N.J.: Lawrence Erlbaum Associates, 1984.

Sharan, S., & Hertz–Lazarowitz, R. A group investigation method of cooperative learning in the classroom. In S. Sharan, P. Hare, C. Webb, & R. Hertz–Lazarowitz (Eds.), *Cooperation in education.* Provo, Utah: Brighham Young University Press, 1980.

Sharan, S., & Hertz–Lazarowitz, R. Effects of an instructional change program on teachers' behavior, attitudes and perceptions. *The Journal of Applied Behavioral Science,* 1982, *18,* 185–201.

Sharan, S., & Sharan, S. *Small-group teaching.* Englewood Cliffs, N.J.: Educational Technology Publications, 1976.

Sieber, S. Knowledge utilization in public education. Incentives and disincentives. In R. Lehming & M. Kane (Eds.), *Improving schools: Using what we know.* Beverly Hills, Calif.: Sage, 1981.

Slavin, R. Student team learning: A manual for teachers. In S. Sharan, P. Hare, C. Webb, & R. Hertz–Lazarowitz (Eds.), *Cooperation in education.* Provo, Utah: Brigham Young University Press, 1980. (a)

Slavin, R. Cooperative learning. *Review of Educational Research,* 1980, *50,* 315–342. (b)

Slavin, R., & Madden, N. School practices that improve race relations. *American Educational Research Journal,* 1979, *16,* 169–180.

Weick, K. Educational organizations as loosely coupled systems. *Administrative Science Quarterly,* 1976, *21,* 1–19.

11 Israel and the United States: Comparisons and Commonalities in School Desegregation

Norman Miller

The preceding chapters present a comprehensive picture of the educational system in Israel and its attempt to deal with ethnic and social class divergence among Jews. This chapter discusses some of the findings and ideas presented in the preceding chapters and relates them to school desegregation outcomes in the United States. As is often true when one seeks to compare individual cases, similarities and disparities emerge. Given the many objective differences between Israel and the United States in history, geography, populations, racial ethnic composition, and international politics, however, the parallels that characterize the ways in which the two countries have approached the fact of ethnic divergence in their schools are the more striking. Before beginning my discussion I trace briefly these broad similarities in approach to the issues and problems over the course of time.

In the United States, following a period during which the Government channeled substantial money and effort into compensatory educational programs, a national assessment of schools and their comparative effects on blacks and whites was undertaken (Coleman, Campbell Hobson, McPartland, Mood, Weinfeld, & York, 1966). Following publication of this report, efforts toward school desegregation were intensified. Although Foster (1973) argues that the largest school districts in the United States, those with 15% or more blacks, were in various stages of the desegregation process at the beginning of the 1970s, today this optimistic view bears some tempering. In the current political climate, whatever momentum had gathered in the past seems to have waned as minority enrollments in large cities increasingly dominate those of whites, as courts steer clear of interdistrict solutions, as some sectors of our ethnic subgroups express increasing disenchantment with the promise of school desegregation as a social reform, and as the National Institute of Education diverts research support away from issues related to it.

In Israel the sequence, at least in its initial stages, appears to be similar: the introduction of compensatory education programs; disappointment in their results; national educational assessment, revealing substantial disparity in the academic performance of Middle Eastern and Western Jews (Minkovitch, Davis, & Bashi, 1977); and a vigorous initiation of efforts to desegregate (see Chapter 7). Moreover, as was true in the United States, desegregation, like compensatory education, has failed to fulfill the expectations of many of its advocates.

Macro and Microgoals of Desegregation

Chapter 7 draws attention to the distinction between desegregation "as an end in itself" as opposed to desegregation "as a means" to the achievement of other goals. In court litigation in the United States the former position dominates, perhaps largely because the U.S. Supreme Court viewed segregated schooling as stigmatizing blacks. Implicit in the historic *Brown* decision to desegregate the nation's schools was the notion that desegregation will reduce stigmatization. The critical issue, however, is whether or not desegregation per se will reduce it without additional specific steps to change children's attitudes, social categorization processes, and intergroup behavior. This question raises legitimate concern with the viability of viewing desegregation as an "end in itself."

In a sense, a somewhat similar distinction can be made between macro and microsocial goals, in that, presumably, success at one level may be independent of that obtained on the other. In Chapter 1, Amir and Sharan make the point that desegregation of the nation's schools will help to implement and, indeed, may be essential to the macrolevel goal of creating and maintaining national solidarity. They further note that macrolevel goals such as "nation building" may not necessarily require success in achieving microlevel goals such as, for instance, reducing the academic achievement gap between Middle Eastern and Western Jews. Making this point may reflect in part the fact that educators in Israel as well as in the United States have found it so difficult to take steps that effectively narrow the gap. In the United States, too, commentators have tended to downplay the relevance of achievement gains to the promulgation of desegregation as a social policy. Stuart Cook, who was one of the authors of the Social Science Statement appended to the plaintiff's case in the U.S. Supreme Court's historic *Brown* decision, stated recently (Cook, 1979) that it did not specifically predict that desegregation would improve the scholastic achievement of black children.

In testimony before the U.S. Congress (Miller, 1982) I took a position very similar to that of Amir, Sharan, and Ben–Ari (Chapter 1) and argued that "abandoning attempts to enable minority children to break out of the poverty-incompetence-welfare cycle seems likely to further demoralize such groups and thereby further increase their social cost to . . . society" (p. 393). Obviously, I agree with the view that desegregation conveys an important symbolic message to minority groups. I think it is important to note, however, an artificiality in the distinction between macro and microgoals that parallels the distinction between desegregation as a means and desegregation as an end. Implicit in the positive symbolic meaning of desegregation—that the society cares about its ethnic minorities and is willing to take steps to integrate them into full participation in the culture—is the fulfillment of the microlevel goal of increased intergroup acceptance. When, instead, increased contact confirms existing stereotypes, intensifies social categorization processes, and increases interethnic conflict, the symbolic promise that constitutes the macrolevel goal has evaporated. Thus, when viewed from this perspective the goals at the two levels are intimately related.

Academic Achievement

Although scholars readily acknowledge the important role that desegregation can play in promoting intergroup acceptance and social integration, it seems to be the case that minority groups, both in the United States and in Israel (see Chapter 8) have primarily viewed it as a means of access to better schools. For them, its promise lies in the academic dimension—better education. In the United States the extent to which this promise has been fulfilled has been hotly debated (Armor, 1972; Crain & Mahard, 1983; Pettigrew, Useem, Normand, & Smith, 1973; Stephan, 1978; St. John, 1975).

In an attempt to provide some resolution to this issue, the United States National Institute of Education recently convened a panel of seven experts to evaluate the effect of desegregated schooling on black academic achievement. A common set of criteria for including and excluding studies was developed and basically adhered to by the four of the seven researchers who individually performed meta-analyses of this literature.

Most of the studies examined were of relatively short duration (1 year), and in most cases the desegregation involved children in the elementary school years. Though their results show effect sizes that vary from + .07 to + .159 and, thus, are of small to moderate magnitude, these summaries show a consistent positive effect. At the upper end, they approach the effect size of + .20, which Walberg (1983) cites as average for educational interventions.

Should this outcome be viewed as indicating that minority-group expectations for improved schooling will be fulfilled by desegregation? When multiplied by some factor reflecting the facts that schooling persists over more than a decade and that most of these studies examined a 1-year effect, it might be argued that very substantial gains can be expected.

Several considerations, however, suggest otherwise. First, a satisfactory theoretical account at the social psychological level of how a change in the ratio of black and white children within a class might produce academic benefit to blacks continues to elude researchers. The lateral transmission of high-achievement values from whites (who more typically are middle class in family origin), to blacks (who are typically of lower class origin), though frequently invoked in the past as an explanatory mechanism, fails to find any noteworthy empirical support (Maruyama & Miller, 1979, 1983). Second, the NIE reviews find historical effects—greater achievement gains for black children in the 1960s than in the 70s (Miller, 1983; Stephan, 1983), content area effects—more positive effects on verbal than on math test scores (Armor, 1983; Miller, 1983; Stephan, 1983; Wortman, 1983), sample size effects—more positive effects in studies of smaller size (Miller, 1983), and greater verbal gains for black children when they comprised a smaller proportion of the class (Miller, 1983), all of which suggest that factors other than a change in the ratio per se of black and white children play an important role in the outcome. Were the ratio per se critical in implementing an important within-classroom social psychological process, these other variables should not substantially affect the outcome. Finally, white students' gains exceed substantially those of blacks, suggesting that the benefits to blacks were the effect of a school or district-wide change rather than being attributable specifically to the change in racial-ethnic ratios (Miller, 1983).

Thus, my own reading of the situation in the United States concurs with that presented by Klein and Eshel (Chapter 7) and Amir, Sharan, and Ben–Ari (Chapter 1). Little progress toward closing the academic achievement gap can be expected from desegregation per se. If it is to be successful as a social reform that will close the achievement gap, additional investments in teaching resources and program interventions are necessary.

Although scholars seem to have frequently focused on closing the achievement gap, minority parents appear more concerned with seeing their youngsters in a school that they believe to be a good one. This appears true in Israel as well (see Halper, Shokeid, & Weingrod, Chapter 3). In the United States, with some notable exceptions (e.g., San Diego, Calif.), the schools in the inner cities contain the heaviest concentrations of ethnic minorities, are characteristically more dilapidated, and offer poorer facilities than those attended by whites. Though many have interpreted the Coleman report as arguing that monetary and other "hard" inputs do not affect students' outcomes, such a view is obviously misleading. In an ambitious randomized experimental evaluation of a U.S. government funding program, one of each of 50 pairs of high schools judged as similar by the local school officials was randomly chosen as ineligible for funding that year (due to insufficient funds). Funding contributed achievement gains to black males in this (Crain & York, 1975) and in a similar but larger second study (Coulson, Hanes, Ozenne, Bradford, Doherty, Duck, & Hemenway, 1977).

Amir, Sharan, and Ben Ari (Chapter 1), in accord with my earlier point that macro and microgoals are inextricably linked, argue that it is a mistake to focus only on macrolevel goals. They believe that eventually desegregated schools must deliver the promises implicit in desegregation. If not, progress toward national social integration will show an "about face." The point that I wish to make here is that, although for the scholar "success in closing the educational achievement gap" may depend on characteristics of the schools that minority children attend, the closing of the achievement gap may not be part of the "promise" of school desegregation from the eye-view of the ethnic minority parent; the opportunity for one's children to attend a "good school," however, may indeed be a critical part of that promise.

The notion of "good" and "bad" schools finds increasing confirmation in data from the United States. In the past, researchers have argued that school variance is relatively small, particularly when considered in comparison to that produced by family background. More recently, researchers suggest that these findings are misleading. Crain, Mahard, and Narot (1982) go to considerable lengths to argue that had Coleman et al. presented their data in a different form the interpretation of their outcome would have been considerably different, and more like that of Rutter, Maughan, Mortimore, and Ouston (1979) in England, which suggests that schools do differ. Others (Entwisle & Hayduk, 1982) suggest that virtually all the large-scale sociological studies, which are those from which the conclusion of little school variance derives, rely on high school data and that such data give a misleading picture. Failure to find differences among schools has also been attributed to the use of cross-sectional rather than longitudinal designs. Although the precise manner in which these factors operate to generate small school effects may be somewhat obscure, other studies have in fact found dramatic differences in the effectiveness of elementary schools that serve ethnic minority children of similarly low-social-class background (Brookover, Beady, Flood, Schweitzer, & Wisenbaker, 1979; Entwisle & Hayduk, 1982).

Personality

Many researchers have expected personality changes to accompany desegregated schooling. In particular, they have focused on self-esteem, perceptions of personal control over life outcomes, and academic motivation and aspirations. In the Social Science Statement appended to *Brown,* a poor self-concept among minority children was seen as an inevitable consequence of their segregated schooling. In the interpretive emphasis prevalent at that time, this poor self-concept was seen as undermining academic aspirations and achievement and contributing to intergroup hostility and conflict. Perceptions of little control over life outcomes were also interpreted, probably mistakenly, as causal antecedents of poor academic performance (Coleman et al., 1966; Crain & Weisman, 1972).

Current Israeli data concurs with recent data in the United States which suggest that the relation between academic achievement and personality is rarely strong, and that personality appears to be a consequence of school outcomes rather than a causal antecedent (Gottfredson, 1980; Rubin, Maruyama, & Kingsbury, 1981). Rosenberg (1983) has recently summarized the literature on the self-esteem of blacks in the United States. He notes the discrepancy between the outcomes of the doll choice and other projective studies, which were interpreted as showing that black children had poor self-concepts, and the survey and questionnaire data, which, if they show any direction of difference, suggest that black self-esteem exceeds that of whites.

His overall conclusions concur with those of other recent reviews, which find no general impairment of the self-esteem of blacks (Epps, 1979; Porter & Washington, 1979; Wylie, 1979). More importantly, he provides some theoretical insight into why minority children in segregated settings are likely to have higher self-esteem than their counterparts who experience desegregated schooling, and why the self-esteem of minority children in segregated settings generally fails to be lower than that of whites. His discussion points to important differences in the concrete experiences of segregated living as opposed to its symbolic meaning. Drawing out the implications of an array of theoretical principles such as social comparison, reflected appraisals, self-attribution, and within- and between-group perspectives, he shows how the obtained outcomes of no impairment of self-concept make sense from the minority-child's eye-view. Parenthetically, although social scientists have recently provided a number of reinterpretations of the meaning of the early doll studies (Banks, 1976; Brand, Ruiz, & Padilla, 1974; Stephan & Rosenfield, 1978), Rosenberg, again emphasizing the importance of a phenomenological approach, argues that from the eye-view of many "black" children the lighter doll was objectively more similar to their own skin color. In the original study of Clark and Clark (1939) among light-skinned (almost "white") children, 20% gave the black doll when asked to "give me the doll who looks like you." For medium (light brown to dark brown) and for dark brown to black, the percentages who gave the black doll were 73 and 81%, respectively.

Interethnic Attitudes

As noted earlier, many of the preceding chapters view the goal of "nation building" as the most important among the several goals of desegregation. In both Israel and the United States, residential and occupational differences provide boundaries that act to maintain ethnic segregation. The magnitude of the problem, however, appears to differ dramatically in the two countries, no doubt for a variety of reasons. Commonalities in the political goals of Middle Eastern and Western Jews, for instance, make a positive contribution to mutual acceptance. A shared religious identification and commitment to the goals of reunification of Jewry and national survival form a foundation for interethnic acceptance. These positive features obviously are not available to the same degree in the United States as a basis for intergroup acceptance among the various ethnic subgroups. Additionally, although Western Jews obtain better life outcomes and more social power than their counterparts of Middle Eastern origin (Adler, Chapter 2), the embarrassing history and institutionalization of social mistreatment of blacks in the United States is not paralleled in the relations of Middle Eastern and Western Jews within Israel.

As the experimental literature on group formation and intergroup relations shows, however, such historical factors are not necessary antecedents of ingroup bias. On the basis of the most meager and arbitrary pretexts, people will quickly develop loyalties and patterns of favoritism toward others with whom they are arbitrarily grouped, readily exhibiting preferential reward allocation to ingroup members (Billig & Tajfel, 1973; Tajfel & Billig, 1974), heightened attraction toward ingroup members (Rabbie & Horowitz, 1969; Rabbie & Wilkins, 1971), and perceptions of ingroup similarity (Allen & Wilder, 1979). These effects are found when the basis for group membership is as trivial and meaningless as an arbitrary assignment by an experimenter based on persons' alleged tendencies to overestimate or underestimate the number of dots on a briefly presented slide. Even in the face of explicit statements that such over and underestimation is unrelated to any other known differences in human capacity or preference, ingroup loyalties and bias emerge to promote psychological distance between these arbitrary groups. Such tendencies are undoubtedly likely to be stronger when real differences such as religion, skin color, occupation, or language distinguish groups from one another.

It can be argued that the real differences between whites and Hispanics or blacks within the United States substantially exceed those between Middle Eastern and Western Jews in Israel. Furthermore, intermarriage rates and social mobility suggest that the objective differences between Middle Eastern and Western Jews are declining (Adler, Chapter 2). Nevertheless, they are of sufficient magnitude to form a substantial basis for the social categorization processes that underlie ingroup–outgroup relations, and thereby, to interfere with the goal of national integration. Consequently, as argued cogently by Sharan and Amir (Chapter 10), it makes sense to avoid adopting a passive stance that assumes that natural events can be counted on to decrease intergroup friction. An active stance will minimize the chance that differences will become institutionalized.

In the research on intergroup attitudes, one striking difference emerges between the U.S. research and that in Israel. Several chapters (e.g., Chapter 4) note that in the Israeli research the relative frequency of children of Middle Eastern and Western background has not been an important factor in moderating intergroup acceptance within schools. In contrast, in the United States a different picture seems to emerge. For instance, Rogers, Hennigan, Bowman, and Miller (1983) compare two schools, one of which was a multiethnic school in which white children form the plurality, whereas the other was a black receiving school with a black majority. Being a member of the group that was numerically less frequent went hand-in-hand with higher levels of hostility and perceived dissimilarity to outgroup members.

Cohen (1984) reports on desegregated schools that varied in their ethnic composition but were exemplary in that they exhibited many practices currently recommended for successful integration. Nevertheless, the proportion of minority students in the school was important. In School A, which contained the highest percentage of blacks (52%), white choices of blacks on a social-power index were highest (51%). School B, with a white plurality of 39%, Hispanics and Asians 16 and 17%, respectively, and blacks 25%, 39% of white choices went to blacks. In School C, with the largest ratio of whites to blacks (50 to 26%, respectively), the fewest white choices (27%) went to blacks. Thus, as might be expected, numerical strength translates into attributions of power and such power seems to reduce the tendency to reject a group socially. Cohen further argues that, when minority groups lack power, are numerically infrequent, and are of relatively lower as opposed to equivalent social-class backgrounds, the stage is set for academic performance differences to generalize and result in white domination in social interaction, as well as to produce deleterious effects on the academic performance of the minority children.

Crain et al. (1982) also report substantial data on the effects of the respective percentages of blacks and whites in the school. They show that being in the numerical minority increases pressure from peers against cross-racial contact. This effect appears to operate somewhat differently for the two racial-ethnic groups. Among blacks, pressure against cross-racial contact is highest when they are in a small minority (less than 20%), whereas among whites it operates most powerfully when their numerical preponderance is ambiguous (i.e., not a clear minority or majority). Though, the sources of this asymmetry remain somewhat unclear, such results are not theoreticaly meaningless. The black data fit with recent theorizing on the effects of numerical ratios on salience or focus of attention (Duval & Duval, 1983; Taylor & Fiske, 1978). That which is infrequent is more noticed and salient, and consequently it makes sense that blacks feel more threatened in such settings.

Such effects do not merely remain perceptions; they are translated into actions. Being in a numerical minority enhances ingroup acceptance and outgroup rejection (Edwards, Miller, McCormack, Mitchell, & Robinson, 1983). Though the data for whites appears less straightforward, it too makes sense. Whereas blacks are accustomed to being in the minority in white settings, whites are accustomed to being in the majority. Consequently, they may feel most threatened and most inclined to engage in behavior designed to strengthen group identity when their numerical dominance is threatened, namely, in settings where whites constitute 40–65% (see Rogers et al. 1983).

In other analyses, Crain et al. (as well as Patchen, 1982, p. 337) report that racial tension is greater when groups are more nearly equal in number. These data are more difficult to interpret. Do they reflect actual incidents of intergroup aggression? If so, a correction factor should be applied to such data in order to adjust for "opportunity"; as one group decreases in percentage there are fewer persons available to provide or participate in such "instances," and, consequently, observed rates of aggresion between groups of unequal size require an upward adjustment if they are to be compared with situations in which the two groups are equal in size. Alternatively, such data may reflect the consequences of the greater pressure against contact when blacks are infrequent. If such pressure is a consequence of rejection of and hostility toward outgroup members, however, corrected rates of overt conflict might be expected to be higher when one group is clearly in a numerical minority. Finally, it is possible that when ratios are drastically unequal, power and control are a fait accompli, whereas when equal, a real struggle for dominance ensues and thereby generates more tension.

At any rate, both theory and empirical outcomes suggest that variation in the ratio of black and white children affects their interracial behavior in a number of important ways. The absence of such effects in the Israeli setting is thus noteworthy and warrants further examination.

School Interventions

Researchers both in the United States and Israel seem to be increasingly aware that the contact provided by desegregated schooling will not consistently produce intergroup acceptance. As a consequence, they have sought interventions that promote increased intergroup acceptance. Sharan and Rich (Chapter 9) discuss some recent explorations in Israel. In several instances, programs apparently failed to fulfill expectations because they were not implemented effectively. They astutely note, however, that such failures of implementation are often attributable to system effects that operate within schools. As indicated previously, the importance of school climates and normative systems have been increasingly recognized by researchers in the United States (Brookover et al., 1979; Cohen, 1983; Davidson, Hoffman, & Brown, 1978; Metz, 1978) as well as those in Israel (Inbar et al., Chapter 6). Thus, Sharan and Rich are correct, I believe, in emphasizing the importance of school organizational variables. The operation of reciprocal influence systems between the principal and teachers and among principal, teachers, and students has not been well studied, undoubtedly because it is so unamenable to experimental manipulation. It seems reasonable, however, that interventions can be ordered on a continuum of imperviousness to the debilitating effects of systemic sabotage. Interventions like those of DeVries and Edwards (1974), which can be implemented with self-contained curriculum materials for almost every academic component of the curriculum, may be least likely to be susceptible to such undermining. Those in which teachers play a more critical role, in which they must develop by themselves new classroom procedures and new teaching materials, are likely to be more problematic. Displaying an even broader perspective, however, Amir et al. (Chapter 10) wisely recognize that system-wide preparation for integration not only requires preparation of the teachers and administrators, and a reconsideration of curricula and teaching materials, but requires preparation of the parents, as well. As dramatically illustrated by case-study material, motivated parents can undermine reasonable desegregation plans (e.g., Chapter 8).

The interventions that Sharan and Rich (Chapter 9) reviewed are interesting, however, because they emphasize the importance of attempts to actively develop within the classroom an integral relation between the child's cognitive mastery and the social context of the learning situation. Interventions that promote academic mastery in the context of small cooperative groups in which the children themselves take substantial responsibility for the teaching and assimilation of information have not only been shown to promote better academic mastery, (Johnson, Maruyama, Johnson, Nelson, & Skon, 1981; Sharan, 1980) but also to enhance intergroup acceptance (Johnson, Johnson, & Maruyama, 1984; Sharan 1984).

Generalization of Intergroup Acceptance

Debate about whether social status must be generally equal if intergroup contact is to produce positive effects continues. Although some have argued that it need only be equal in the contact setting and need not be generally equal in the society at large, this view is misleading when applied to the school setting. Whereas soldiers in infantry divisions bring equivalent skills to the task at hand (aiming and firing a gun; or defeating an enemy), school children do not. In schools the relevant skills are cognitive abilities and resources; children who differ in their social-class background (and ethnicity) also differ in the extent to which they possess these relevant resources. Riordan (1978) argues that, in many of the studies that examine the role of contact in increasing intergroup acceptance, equal status is mistakenly implicated as the critical factor. Amir and Bizman (Chapter 8) show that in school settings social-status differences do indeed have important consequences for intergroup relations.

Added to these complexities, however, is the fact that relatively little is known about the extent to which intergroup acceptance that is established in classroom settings generalizes to situations where the children are together in nonclassroom settings; to other outgroup members in classes other than the one in which the intergroup contact occurred; or to new outgroup members in non-school settings. The paucity of well-articulated theory that speaks on this issue undoubtedly contributes to the failure of researchers to address it. In noting the lack of evidence on the generalization of intergroup acceptance, Cook's research (Cook, 1983) emphasizes the importance of social norms against discrimination, a position that builds on Pettigrew's (1964) observation several decades ago that much of the prejudice found toward blacks in the southern United States represents conformity to prevailing community social norms. Brewer and Miller (1983) argue that generalization requires a two-stage process: First, there must be a substantial decrease in the extent to which a person's membership in a social category provides the basis for responding to him or her; second, one's social interaction with outgroup members must be structured to allow mutual exchange of personal information that is self-relevant.

Although the qualifications commonly amended to the contact hypothesis include the points made by both of these positions, substantially more incisive, theoretically oriented research can clarify the circumstances that are critical for generalization. For instance, Rogers (1982) has shown that competitive inter-team activity, in which one's own team is comprised of both ingroup and out-group persons, is likely to generate the greatest acceptance of outgroup members, provided that they are members of one's own team. At the same time, however, this competitive goal structure is least likely to lead to generalization of outgroup acceptance.

Despite gaps in our knowledge, social engineers concerned with school set-tings can make better use of well-established social-psychological principles in their design and implementation of school interventions. For instance, in many interventions, the teacher explicitly uses race, ethnicity, or gender as a basis for assigning children to teams or small work groups. In doing so, the children observe that a high-status model, the teacher, uses social-category membership as a basis for his or her decision making, thereby increasing rather than decreas-ing its salience and importance to children. Similar reinforcement of the use of social-category labels as a basis for responding to minority-group members is likely to result from compensatory educational programs and from programs that use tracking.

Teachers

Although a number of distinct factors contribute to a school's climate, the behav-ior of the teacher is probably the most salient feature in the day-to-day experience of the child. In Chapter 6, Inbar et al. distinguish between two attitudinal ap-proaches taken by teachers—the conservative-achievement-oriented set—and the progressive-integration-oriented set. Curiously, and paradoxically, the achieve-ment-orientation set is more pervasive in low-achieving schools and in those with higher percentages of Middle Eastern Jews. In contrast, teachers with the pro-gressive-integration set are more inclined to approach students as individuals, as well as to acknowledge the relevance of social concerns to education goals. Thus, it seems likely that teachers with this latter orientation are much less likely to promulgate use of social-category membership as a cue for guiding social interaction.

Although direct data is not available, teachers with an achievement orienta-tion seem to overlap with those identified as prejudiced in our Riverside, Califor-nia study (Gerard, Miller, 1975) both in their approach to education and in their attitudes and behavior toward students. Unprejudiced teachers in desegregated classrooms provide more opportunities for positive interaction between Anglo and minority children by making greater use of aspects of minority culture in the classroom; giving minority students more specific duties; structuring more contact with Anglo students (e.g., via seating plans); using class discussion to foster cross-racial interaction; and providing a positive example of interaction with minority children with their own behavior.

The two types of teachers also differ in their attitudes and beliefs. Those low in discrimination tend not to believe in a single performance standard for all children, thus providing more opportunity for success experiences in learning for all children regardless of their racial-ethnic background. In many ways, unprejudiced teachers seem to correspond to the type of teacher that Brophy (1979) identifies as effective in low-socioeconomic settings, namely: "determined to get the most out of students . . . by being warm and encouraging rather than more businesslike and demanding [p. 738]." In contrast, the prejudiced teachers run a fairly rigid classroom and indicate having undertaken very little change in order to accommodate to desegregation. Their classrooms have a more rigorous, business-like atmosphere focused on academic rather than social or emotional objectives. It is teacher dominated and higher structured, with fewer opportunities for student interactions, cross-racial or otherwise (Fraser, 1981).

It seems likely that the differences between these two types of teachers produce effects not only on the academic performance of the minority children in their classes, but also on the amount and quality of cross-racial interaction among students. The classroom behaviors of the unprejudiced teacher appear to correspond to the warm, accepting, and supportive environment that has been identified as a meaningful predictor of cross-racial association (Lewis & St. John, 1975; Serow & Solomon, 1979) and positive relations between Anglo students and their minority classmates (Patchen, Davidson, Hoffman, & Brown, 1977).

As noted previously, researchers and policy advisors in the United States adopted the view that peer values and influence patterns exerted the critical force in the desegregated classroom. This view implicitly argued for a numerical preponderance of middle-class children within each classroom. Katz's (1968) influential review was apparently the source of this view, despite the fact that the major data he presented spoke on social threat from high-status adults as the inhibitor of black cognitive functioning. Whereas one interpretive extrapolation might have focused the removal of such threat and the substitution of a supportive and reinforcing role by high-status authorities (teachers), he chose instead to depart from the direct implications of his own data to draw upon other social-psychological principles that emphasize instead the effects of normative influence processes among peers. The widespread acceptance of this view is difficult to account for in that not a single study ever provided strong support for it. Moreover, without denying that middle-class children are more prone to espouse academic achievement values than are their lower class counterparts, ordinary observation of children's behavioral preferences suggest that normative pressures in regard to sports (for boys) and physical attractiveness (for girls) create stronger impact during early and middle school years. The one study (Lewis & St. John, 1975) that seemed to provide some acceptable support for this lateral transmission of academic achievement values appeared well after widespread acceptance of the hypothesis had infused policy pronouncements.

The preceding data on teacher attitudes and practices suggests that if the notion of normative influence possesses any merit, it is with respect to teacher, rather than peer influence. Moreover, it seems likely that the teacher behavior directly experienced by children is the most telling influence on their behavior in the classroom. From this standpoint, points made in Chapters 6 (Inbar et al.) and 5 (Schwartzwald) highlight a key problem in Israel. Ironically, the schools that primarily service Middle Eastern Jews (and frequently are also religious rather than secular schools) are the ones in which one finds a preponderance of teachers who exhibit an academic orientation that exacerbates the negative effect of the existing academic performance disparities and probably come closer to creating the debilitating threat that Katz's research emphasized.

Conclusion

In his conclusion to a chapter concerned with developing a model for racial contact in schools, Blalock (1983) discusses the prospects for intergroup relations in the United States and the role of schools in shaping them:

> it seems very unlikely that the American public will place a sufficiently high priority on increasing pressure on school administrators and teachers to make the needed effort. . . . While lip service may be given to such things as learning to cooperate with others, appreciating cultural differences, and understanding the problems faced by others who may be less fortunate than themselves, it may be too much to expect that an educational system embedded in a society which merely gives lip service to such goals, will itself be able to induce students to behave very differently from their elders.

Does this pessimistic view apply equally to the situation in Israel too? Perhaps, but several factors argue for a more optimistic view. First, as seen from the preceding chapters, educational leadership in Israel exhibits an insightful awareness of the gap between the promises of school desegregation and that which can be realistically expected when it is implemented as a social reform unaccompanied by adequate preparation, ancillary programs, strong leadership, etc. Second, the Israeli government appears to be able to implement social and educational reforms more effectively than is the case in the United States. Third, it seems likely that Israeli education faces less parental resistance and political opposition than does desegregation of blacks and Hispanics in the United States. In part, this may reflect the fact that physical appearance cues that differentiate Middle Eastern and Western Jews are not as great as those that differentiate the relevant racial ethnic groups in the United States. Consequently, divisive social categorization habits may not be as entrenched in Israel. Fourth, Israel is a younger society; the prejudices of Middle Eastern and Western Jews toward one another, although perhaps traceable well back in the historical past, are not linked to the national history of the State, as are black–white relations in the United States. Finally, Israel appears to be a more integrated society than that of the United States. It is smaller and possesses a commonality in national aspiration. Furthermore, constant external threat must for the most part function to promote national solidarity.

Perhaps these differences between Israel and the United States portend educational and social outcomes that match the generally enthusiastic tone of the chapters that comprise this book.

REFERENCES

Allen, U. L., & Wilder, D. A. Group categorization and attribution of belief similarity. *Small Group Behavior*, 1979, *110*, 73–80.

Armor, D. J. The evidence on busing. *The Public Interest*, 1972, *28*, 90–126.

Armor, D. J. *The evidence on desegregation and black achievement*. Paper commissioned by the National Institute of Education. Washington, D. C., 1983.

Banks, W. C. White preference in blacks: A paradigm in search of a phenomenon. *Psychological Bulletin*, 1976, *83*, 1179–1186.

Billig, M. C., & Tajfel, H. Social categorization and similarity in intergroup behavior. *European Journal of Social Psychology*, 1973, *3*, 27–52.

Blalock, H. A model for racial contact in schools. In *Advancing the art of inquiry in school desegregation research*. Santa Monica, Calif., System Development Corporation (TM–7081/001/01), April, 1983.

Brand, E. S., Ruiz, R. A., & Padilla, A. M. Ethnic identification and preference. *Psychological Bulletin*, 1974, *81*, 860–890.

Brewer, M., & Miller, N. Theoretical perspectives on desegregation. In N. Miller & M. Brewer (Eds.), *Groups in contact: The psychology of desegregation*. New York: Academic Press, 1984.

Brookover, W., Beady, C., Flood, P., Schweitzer, J., & Wisenbaker, J. *School social systems and student achievement: Schools can make a difference*. New York: Praeger, 1979.

Brophy, J. E. Teacher behavior and its effects. *Journal of Educational Psychology*, 1979, *71*, 733–750.

Clark, N. & Clark, N. Development of consciousness of self and the emergence of racial identification in Negro preschool children. *Journal of Social Psychology*, 1939, *10*, 591–599.

Cohen, E. G. The desegregated school: Problems in status, power, and interethnic climate. In N. Miller & M. Brewer (Eds.), *Groups in contact: The psychology of desegregation*. New York: Academic Press, 1984.

Coleman, J. S., Campbell, E. Q., Hobson, C. J., McPartland, J. M., Mood, A. M., Weinfeld, F. D., & York, R. L. *Equality of educational opportunity*. Washington, D. C.: U. S. Government Printing Office, 1966.

Cook, S. W. Social science and school desegregation: Did we mislead the supreme court? *Personality and Psychology Bulletin*, 1979, *5*, 420–437.

Cook, S. W. Cooperative interaction in multiethnic contexts. In N. Miller & M. B. Brewer (Eds.), *Groups in contact: The psychology of desegregation*. New York: Academic Press, 1984.

Coulson, J. E., Hanes, S. D., Ozenne, D. G., Bradford, C., Doherty, W. J., Duck, G. A., & Hemenway, J. A. *The Third Year of Emergency School Aid Act (ESAA) Implementation.* Santa Monica, Calif.: System Development Corporation, 1977.

Crain, R. L., & Mahard, R. E. The effect of research methodology on desegregation-achievement studies: A meta-analysis. *American Journal of Sociology,* 1983, *88,* 839–854.

Crain, R. L., Mahard, R. E., & Narot, R. E. *Making desegregation work: How schools create social climates.* Cambridge, Mass.: Ballinger, 1982.

Crain, R. L., & Weisman, C. S. *Discrimination, personality, and achievement: A survey of Northern Blacks.* New York: Seminar Press, 1972.

Crain, R. L., & York, R. L. Evaluating a successful program: Experimental method and academic bias. *School Review,* 1975, *84,* 233–254.

Davidson, J. D., Hofmann, G., & Brown, W. R. Measuring and explaining high school interracial climates. *Social Problems,* 1978, *26,* 50–70.

De Vries, D. L., & Edwards, K. Student teams and learning games: Their effects on cross-race and cross-sex interaction. *Journal of Educational Psychology,* 1974, *66,* 741–749.

Duval, S., & Duval, V. H. *Consistency and cognition: A theory of causal attribution.* Hillsdale, N.J.: Lawrence Erlbaum Associates, 1983.

Edwards, K., Miller, N., McCormack, M., Mitchell, C., & Robinson, C. *Effects of individuation, status, and threat on in-group bias.* Paper presented at American Psychological Association Meetings, Anaheim, California, 1983.

Entwisle, D. R., & Hayduk, L. A. *Early schooling: Cognitive and affective outcomes.* Baltimore: Johns Hopkins University Press, 1982.

Epps, E. G. The impact of school desegregation on the self-evaluation and achievement orientation of minority children. *Law and Contemporary Problems,* 1979, *43,* 57–76.

Foster, G. Desegregating urban schools. *Harvard Educational Review,* 1973, *43,* 5–36.

Fraser, R. W. *Behavioral and attitudinal differences between teachers in desegregated classrooms.* Unpublished doctoral dissertation, University of Southern California, 1981.

Gerard, H. B., & Miller, N. *School desegregation,* New York: Plenum, 1975.

Gottfredson, D. C. Personality and persistence in education: A longitudinal study. Paper presented at the Annual Meeting of the American Psychological Association, Montreal, Canada, 1980.

Johnson, D. W., Johnson, R. T., & Maruyama, G. Effects of cooperative learning: A meta-analysis. In N. Miller & M. B. Brewer (Eds.), *Groups in contact: The psychology of desegregation.* New York: Academic Press, 1984.

Johnson, D. W., Maruyama, G., Johnson, R., Nelson, D., & Skon, L. The effects of cooperative, competitive, and individualistic goal structures on achievement: A meta-analysis. *Psychological Bulletin,* 1981, *89,* 47–62.

Katz, I. Factors influencing Negro performance in the desegrated school. In M. Deutsch, I. Katz, & A. R. Jensen (Eds.), *Social class, race, and psychological development.* New York: Holt, Rinehart, & Winston, 1968.

Lewis, R., & St. John, N. Race and the social structure of the elementary classroom. *Sociology of Education,* 1975, *48,* 346–368.

Maruyama, G., & Miller, N. Reexamination of normative influence processes in desegregated classrooms. *American Educational Research Journal,* 1979, *16,* 273–284.

Maruyama, G., & Miller, N. *The relation between popularity and achievement: A longitudinal test of the lateral transmission of value hypothesis.* Unpublished paper, 1983.

Metz, M. H. *Classrooms and corridors: The crisis of authority in desegregated schools.* Berkeley: University of California Press, 1978.

Miller, N. *The effects of school desegregation on academic performance.* Hearings before the Subcommittee on Civil and Constitutional Rights of the Committee of the Judiciary, House of Representatives, 97th Congress (Serial No. 26, pp. 389–96), U. S. Government Printing Office, 1982.

Miller, N. The effect of school desegregation on black academic achievement: A meta analysis. Paper, Commissioned by the *National Institute of Education*, 1983.

Minkovitch, A., Davis, D., & Bashi, J. *An evaluation study of Israeli elementary schools*. Hebrew University School of Education, Jerusalem, 1977.

Patchen, M. *Black–White contact in schools*. West Lafayette, Ind.: Purdue University Press, 1982.

Patchen, M., Davidson, J., Hoffman, G., & Brown, W. Determinants of interracial behavior and opinion change. *Sociology of Education*, 1977, *50*, 55–75.

Pettigrew, T. F. *A profile of the Negro American*. Princeton, N. J.: Van Nostrand, 1964.

Pettigrew, T. F., Useem, E. L., Normand, C., & Smith, M. Busing: A review of the evidence. *Public Interest*, 1973, *30*, 88–118.

Porter, J. R., & Washington, R. E. Black identity and self-esteem: A review of studies of Black self-concept 1968–1978, *Annual Review of Sociology*, 1979, *5*, 53–74.

Rabbie, J. M., & Horowitz, M. Arousal of ingroup–outgroup bias by a chance win or loss. *Journal of Personality and Social Psychology*, 1969, *13*, 269–277.

Rabbie, J. M., & Wilkins, G. Intergroup competition and its effect on intragroup relations. *European Journal of Social Psychology*, 1971, *1*, 215–234.

Riordan, C. Equal-status interracial contact: A review and revision of the concept. *International Journal of Intercultural Relations* (Summer), 1978, 161–185.

Rogers, M. *The effect of interteam reward structure on intragroup and intergroup perceptions and evaluative attitudes*. Unpublished dissertation. University of Southern California, December, 1982.

Rogers, M., Hennigan, K., Bowman, C., & Miller, N. Promoting voluntary interethnic interaction on the playground. In N. Miller & M. Brewer (Eds.), *Groups in contact: The psychology of desegregation*. New York: Academic Press, 1984.

Rosenberg, M. Self-esteem research: A phenomenogical corrective. In *Advancing the art of inquiry in school desegregation research*. Santa Monica, Calif.; System Development Corporation (TM-7081/001/01), April, 1983.

Rubin, R. A., Maruyama, G., & Kingsbury, G. G. *Self-esteem and educational achievement: A causal model analysis*. Paper presented at the Annual Meeting of the American Psychological Association, New York, 1979.

Rutter, M., Maughan, B., Mortimore, P., & Ouston, J. *Fifteen thousand hours: Secondary schools and their effect on children*. Cambridge, Mass.: Harvard University Press, 1979.

Serow, R. C., & Solomon, D. Classroom climate and students intergroup behavior. *Journal of Educational Psychology*, 1979, *71*, 669–676.

Sharan, S. Cooperative learning in small groups: Recent methods and effects on achievement, attitudes, and ethnic relations. *Review of Educational Research*, 1980, *50*, 241–271.

Sharan, S. *Cooperative learning in the classroom: Research in desegregated schools*. Hillsdale N. J.: Lawrence Erlbaum Associates, 1984.

Stephan, W. G. School desegregation: An evaluation of predictions made in Brown vs. Board of Education. *Psychological Bulletin*, 1978, *85*, 217–238.

Stephan, W. G. Blacks and *Brown: The effects of school desegregation on black students*. Paper commissioned by the National Institute of Education. Washington, D. C., 1983.

Stephan, W. G., & Rosenfield, D. The effects of desegregation on race relations and self-esteem. *Journal of Educational Psychology*, 1978, *70*, 670–679.

St. John, N. H. *School desegregation outcomes for children*. New York: Wiley, 1975.

Tajfel, H., & Billig, M. G. Familarity and categorization in intergroup behavior. *Journal of Experimental Social Psychology*, 1974, *10*, 159–170.

Taylor, S. E., & Fiske, S. T. Salience, attention, and attribution: Top of the head phenomena. In L. Berkowitz (Ed.), *Advances in experimental social psychology* (Vol. II). New York: Academic Press, 1978.

Walberg, H. *Desegregation and educational productivity.* Paper commissioned by the National Institute of Education. Washington, D. C. 1983.

Wortman, P. M. *School desegregation and black achievement: A meta-analysis.* Paper, commissioned by the National Institute of Education, Washington D. C., 1983.

Wylie, R. C. *The self-concept: Theory and research on selected topics (Vol. 2).* Lincoln: University of Nebraska Press, 1979.

Author Index

Subject Index

and teachers' background, 120–122
of schools, 119, 190
religious affiliation, 121–122
Students, advantaged and disadvantaged, 33,
    Table 34, 100–104
and intergroup acceptance, 246
first vs. second generation in Israel, 35–37
geographical dispersion, 104
percentage by sector, Table 105
religious observance, Table 107
self-concept, 109
Subject factors in integration, 173–175
first vs. second generation in Israel, 35–37
personality variables, 176–178
slow learners, 175
Western vs. Middle-Eastern, 174

T

Teachers:
and pedagogical methods, 92
and school climate, 247–249
as a structural variable, 120–126
as a subject-matter transmitter, 211–212
behavior and attitudes, 9
conservative-achievement-oriented set vs.
    progressive-integration-oriented set, 127–
    128, 247–249

effects of expectations on pupils, 8
importance of curricula, 234
in integrated schooling, 215
ratio of teachers of Middle-Eastern to West-
    ern background, 121–122
subject matter vs. homeroom teacher, 123
variables, affective, 124–125

U

United States, desegregation in, 229, 231–
    233, 237–241, 245, 248–250
and contact in summer camps, 165
and small group learning, 144
Brown decision, 138, 238, 241
Coleman report, 237, 240, 241
comparison to Israel, 231, 237, 243, 245,
    250
differences between Israel and England, 94
effects of desegregation, 179
evaluations of desegregation, 189–190
"good" vs. "bad" schools, 241
National Institute of Education, 238–240

V

Variables, affective:
of teachers, 124–125